W9-AAX-902

Privatizing the Economy

Privatizing the Economy

Telecommunications Policy in
Comparative Perspective

Raymond M. Duch

Ann Arbor
THE UNIVERSITY OF MICHIGAN PRESS

Copyright © by the University of Michigan 1991
All rights reserved
Published in the United States of America by
The University of Michigan Press
Manufactured in the United States of America

1994   1993   1992   1991   4   3   2   1

Library of Congress Cataloging-in-Publication Data

Duch, Raymond M., 1953–
    Privatizing the economy : telecommunications policy in comparative
perspective / Raymond M. Duch.
      p.   cm.
    Includes bibliographical references and index.
    ISBN 0-472-10191-9 (cloth : alk.)
    1. Telecommunication policy.   2. Telecommunication—Deregulation.
3. Telecommunication policy—Germany—History.   4. Telecommunication
policy—France—History.   5. Telecommunication policy—Great
Britain—History.   I. Title.
HE7645.D83   1991
384'.068—dc20   91-7880
                                          CIP

British Library Cataloguing in Publication Data
Duch, Raymond M.
    Privatising the Economy : telecommunications policy.
    1. Public sector. Privatisation
    I. Title
    351.0072

    ISBN 0-472-10191-9

Distributed in the United Kingdom and Europe by
Manchester University Press, Oxford Road,
Manchester M13 9PL, UK

*This book is dedicated to
my grandmother, Nora Duch*

Preface

When I initially set out to write this book, the advanced economies of the world were in an early stage of experimentation with liberal economic policies. The reforms advocated by the Thatcher and Reagan governments were just beginning to have an impact throughout both developed and developing capitalist nations. As a result, many countries have undertaken extensive privatization of state-owned industry and dismantled government-enforced entry barriers. This book addresses two important questions raised by this sweep of economic reform: Does government ownership actually affect economic performance and, if so, how? Second, how do political institutions shape the liberalization initiative that we have witnessed in the advanced capitalist economies?

The analysis and conclusions are based on an extensive study of the telecommunications industries of the advanced economies of the world. Telecommunications proved to be the ideal focus for two reasons. First, telecommunications service is an industry sector that has been almost universally state-owned and therefore proved an excellent subject for the study of economic performance under government ownership.

Second, telecommunications is one of the industries most significantly affected by this recent wave of economic liberalism—an economic sector universally subject to strict government regulation and, in most countries, under government ownership. Technological developments such as satellite communications, fiber optics, and dramatic advances in microelectronics have been the catalyst for changes in industry structure, but, ultimately, political institutions have determined the policy responses of different nations. In an attempt to understand how political institutions shape the liberalization process, this book exploits the considerable variation in how nations responded to pressures for liberalization of the telecommunications industry.

The notion that government ownership of firms per se has a significant impact on their performance is challenged by the findings presented in this book. A much better explanation for economic performance is the degree to which management is subject to political constraints. As I point out, the two are quite distinctive: for example, there are many firms that are government-owned, yet subject to little political oversight. In an industry so heavily dominated by government ownership, the only way to account for cross-national variations in the performance of telecommunications service is with reference to the degree of political oversight exercised over the management of these entities.

Having come to this conclusion, I was naturally led to the second question: Why do nations vary so much in terms of their enthusiasm for liberal economic policies that either reduce government oversight of the telecommunications service providers or promote competition in the industry? Because these liberal changes represent a significant challenge to the status quo—labor, industry, and the bureaucracy—I hypothesized that certain political institutions would be more conducive to such initiatives than would others. This, in fact, proved to be the case: pluralist regimes, such as the United Kingdom and the United States, were most receptive to such liberal changes, statist political systems, somewhat less so, and corporatist ones were the least open to liberal policy initiatives.

As I complete this book, world attention has shifted from the liberal reforms inspired by Reagan and Thatcher to the political and economic revolutions occurring in the Soviet Union and Eastern Europe. The insights on the relationship between political institutions and liberal reform and economic performance have been based on a century of experience within the advanced capitalist nations. I would hope that my conclusions will make some small contribution to the efforts of these newly forming liberal democracies to shape appropriate political institutions and to identify suitable new economic structures for formerly state-owned firms.

This book has been made possible by the cooperation and generosity of a number of people. Certainly the most significant contribution has come from Wolfgang Hirczy, who has worked as a research assistant for four years on this project, providing translation assistance with the German material, insightful editorial comments, and data analysis support. I am truly indebted to him for his considerable effort on this project. I was also assisted by Lynette Brimble, who did an excellent job typing the manuscript.

Alan Stone, Douglas Pitt, Malcolm Goggin, and Patti Hardy very generously read various versions of this book and provided constructive and useful criticism. For their assistance in data collection I would like to thank Jean-Yves Burgot, the very competent staff of the AT&T Information Resources Center, and Robert R. Bruce. I also benefited from the encouragement and industry insights that I received while working as an advisor with AT&T—I am particularly indebted to George Malone for facilitating this unique opportunity. This book was made possible by the generous financial assistance of AT&T General Business Systems, and the University of Houston Center for Public Policy.

My old friends Rick Kronick, Bing and Lynda Powell, and Peter

Lemieux were a great inspiration for the initiation and completion of this project. Finally, I would like to acknowledge the encouragement and support of Donna Kline, who so graciously tolerated numerous evenings of grumbling over the incomplete manuscript.

Finally, I thank Mr. Colin Day, the Director of the University of Michigan Press, for his encouragement.

Contents

CHAPTER 1

Introduction

The last quarter of the twentieth century will be remembered as a period in which government's role in the economy came under increasing criticism. Governments throughout the world have, with increasing enthusiasm, embraced policies calling for the privatization of public enterprises and the liberalization of entry barriers to industry.[1] This tendency has not been confined to the developed market economies, reaching virtually all of the world economies. These policies have been adopted by many of the newly industrializing countries (NICs) of Asia that see privatization and competition as means of maintaining their impressive growth rates.[2] The Eastern European countries are rapidly moving in this direction, with Hungary and Poland taking the lead.[3] China has experimented with private ownership and competition.[4] Even third world countries, with the encouragement of the World Bank and IMF, are dismantling entry barriers and privatizing government-owned firms.[5] And this trend extends beyond national governments; similar initiatives can be seen at both the local and state government levels in a number of countries.[6]

---

1. Public enterprises refer to commercial entities in which government has a controlling interest.

2. Pauley has a discussion of the various reasons that Asian nations have warmed to the notion of privatization in Robin Pauley, "A Universal Desire to Reduce the Role of the State," *Financial Times*, 16 September 1987, 8.

3. See "The Soviet Economy: Russian Roulette (survey)," *Economist*, 9 April 1988; Dariusz Filar, "Poland on a Rough Road Toward Economic Pluralism," *Wall Street Journal*, 13 March 1989; Jacqueline Henard, "Ungarn im Fegefeuer," (Wirtschaftsreform im Kommunismus [4]) *Frankfurter Allgemeine Zeitung*, 8 March 1989; Jeffery Sachs, "What is to be done," *Economist*, 13 January 1990.

4. See "China (survey)," *Financial Post*, 14 December 1988; Nathan Gardels, "The Rise of Atari Communists," *New York Times*, 2 April 1989.

5. Don Babai, "The World Bank and the IMF: Rolling Back the State or Backing its Role," in *The Promise of Privatization: A Challenge for American Foreign Policy*, ed. Raymond Vernon (New York: Council on Foreign Relations, 1988). See also Allan H. Meltzer, "Debt Crisis: A Familiar Fall Guy," *Wall Street Journal*, 27 March 1989; Jonathan Aylen, "Privatization in Developing Countries," in *Lloyds Bank Annual Review: Privatization and Ownership*, vol. 1, ed. Christopher Johnson (London: Pinter Publishers, 1988).

6. See Barbara J. Stevens, "Comparing Public and Private Sector Productive Efficiency: An Analysis of Eight Activities," *National Productivity Review* 3 (Autumn 1984): 395–406; Louis

These profound policy changes raise two important political questions that are the central theme of this book: First, does government ownership actually affect the performance of firms, and if so, how? Second, how do we explain the considerable cross-national variation in the extent to which privatization and liberalization policies have been adopted? In both cases, the explanations proposed are decidedly political. They illustrate the extent to which differences in political institutions and processes can affect policy outcomes: depending upon how government ownership is institutionalized, it can either have a negative or positive effect. Similarly, the likelihood that pressures for liberalization and privatization will succeed in a country depends upon the nature of its political institutions.

Does Ownership Matter?

Underlying much of the recent enthusiasm for privatization is the rather simplistic notion that government ownership results in economic inefficiency. Political actors are assumed to have certain goals that are fundamentally inconsistent with economic efficiency and government ownership allows these goals to be imposed on the management of nationalized firms. Because the formulation of this explanation is decidedly economic, it ignores, for the most part, political institutions that mediate this effect. In other words, the extent to which economic performance is sacrificed to short-term political priorities depends to a large extent on institutional factors that regulate the relationship between publicly owned entities and their governmental shareholders.[7]

Looking to political variables to explain variations in the performance of government-owned firms only makes sense where an economic explanation is clearly insufficient. There would be little unexplained variance if most government-owned firms performed poorly and most private entities performed well. This is not the case; a considerable amount of variation in the performance of firms cannot be accounted for by the ownership variable.

How, for example, do we explain the dismal performance of such large French companies as Thompson and Rhone-Poulenc under private ownership and their dramatic turnaround after nationalization?[8] Why do the French banks continue to perform well under nationalization? How do we account for

Uchitelle, "Public Services Found Better if Private Agencies Compete," *New York Times*, 26 April 1988.

7. For an excellent discussion of this, see John Freeman, *Democracy and Markets: The Politics of Mixed Economies* (Ithaca, N.Y.: Cornell University Press, 1989).

8. Roger Ricklefs, "Socialism Inc.: Concerns Nationalized by France Put Profits Ahead of Social Goals," *Wall Street Journal*, 18 April 1985, 1; Eric Le Boucher, "Nationalisations: la fin du dogme," *Le Monde*, 21 April 1985, 1; Steven Greenhouse, "State Companies Thrive in France," *New York Times*, 9 May 1989.

the significant improvement in the performance of the British nationalized sector in the late 1970s and 1980s—British Steel being one of the prime examples? Why have some Italian nationalized firms—such as Italtel—done so well while others have foundered? Finally, what explains the strong historical performance of public telephone companies such as the Swedish Televerket, compared to the dismal track record of the French and British PTTs? The point here, of course, is that we need to look beyond economic explanations that focus simply on ownership.

Political Control

State-owned firms are not a homogeneous group. They are subject to varying degrees of political control, making it more or less difficult for government officials to impose their preferences on the management of public enterprise. For example, the management of a government-owned entity like Rhone-Poulenc in France is more independent of political oversight than its counterparts at France Telecom. The evidence presented in this book indicates that the economic performance of state-owned firms declines as political control increases. Once we take into account the impact of political control, ownership has little effect on economic performance.

There are two different models of how political actors influence public enterprise management. One suggests that political actors will champion the interests of groups for whom public enterprises can deliver very concentrated benefits (their employees and suppliers, for example) while spreading the costs over a very diffuse taxpaying public. Pressures on management to serve these powerful and concentrated constituencies tend to detract from the entity's economic performance. Another model suggests that political officials will champion the interests of the diffuse taxpaying public and therefore will constrain management to perform efficiently and to minimize economic losses. This should enhance the economic performance of public enterprises. The evidence from the developed economies supports the former model.

Market Structure

Some argue that privatization simply creates a private monopoly and that there is virtually no difference in the performance of private versus public monopolists. Market structure, they argue, is the variable that primarily drives performance. While the evidence presented here suggests that market structure is important, the notion that it overrides the effect of political constraints entirely is without much merit. Nonetheless, dismantling government-enforced entry barriers is a policy response that has gained widespread popularity in the 1970s and 1980s.

Why Do Policy Responses Vary?

The developed nations have responded very differently to the debate over privatization and liberalization. Governments in some countries, such as Canada, the United Kingdom, the United States, Spain, Argentina, and New Zealand, have been quite enthusiastic. Those in others, such as Germany, Italy, and Belgium, have been more circumspect.[9] How do we explain the adoption of these liberal policies in some countries and their failure in others?

A number of explanations have been proposed. Particularly in light of the aggressive liberal policies pursued by Margaret Thatcher, there is some evidence to suggest that policy differences are shaped by the ideological predispositions of the party in government.[10] But the "party-in-government" explanation is clearly inadequate because there are too many anomalies. How, for example, do we explain the reluctance of conservative governments in Italy and Germany to implement liberalization and privatization policies? Similarly, how do we explain the enthusiasm shown for privatization and liberalization by the socialist governments of Spain and New Zealand, not to mention the former Eastern bloc countries of Hungary, Poland, and even the Soviet Union?[11]

Clearly, pressures for changing established policies (government ownership and government-enforced entry barriers) originate from outside the ruling party. A simple economic explanation might attribute policy change to a shift in the costs and benefits for interested groups of maintaining public ownership or entry barriers.[12] But this explanation in itself seems inadequate because most of the developed economies have similar configurations of interests likely to benefit or suffer from liberalization or privatization.

Countries vary in their receptiveness to demands for liberalization and privatization because of differences in their political institutions and processes. European nations have gone through a number of different stages of economic policy since the end of World War II. Throughout this period,

---

9. For a review of different national policies regarding privatization, see Raymond Vernon, ed., *The Promise of Privatization: A Challenge for American Foreign Policy* (New York: Council on Foreign Relations, 1988).

10. This is in the tradition of Richard Rose, *Do Parties Make a Difference?*, 2nd ed. (Chatham: Chatham House, 1984); and Douglas Hibbs, "Political Parties and Macroeconomic Policy," *American Political Science Review* 71 (December 1977): 1467–87.

11. For a discussion of the enthusiasm of the Spanish Socialist government for privatization initiatives, see David White, "The Socialist Sell-Off," *Financial Times*, 16 September 1987; and Gary S. Becker, "When the Going Gets Tough, Ideology Gets Flexible," *Business Week*, 22 January 1990, 18.

12. See Barry Mitnick, *The Political Economy of Regulation: Creating, Designing, and Removing Regulatory Forms* (New York: Columbia University Press, 1980), chap. 3.

decision makers in different countries have faced similar economic challenges. Where their responses have varied, observers have tended to look for institutional explanations. Shonfield set the stage with his seminal work, *Modern Capitalism*, arguing that Britain, Germany, and France had varying degrees of success in implementing economic planning because of their very different political institutions.[13] Similarly, Freeman suggests that corporatist and mixed economies are well suited to promoting long-term capital investment and efficient management of state-owned resources.[14] Focusing on the period of economic crisis that confronted European governments in the 1970s, Mancur Olson pointed out how consensual, as opposed to pluralist, political institutions facilitated necessary economic readjustments.[15] Addressing a similar issue—different national responses to economic challenges—Zysman also stressed the importance of institutional factors, noting that different styles of organizing financial institutions can affect the ability of nations to adjust to economic challenges.[16] More recently Hall has made a strong case for the notion that institutions are an important variable for understanding the policy choices of European governments, specifically that the organization of capital, labor, and the state plays an important role in the determination of policy.[17]

I propose an explanation for differences in liberalization and privatization that takes into account both the demands by interested parties for liberal policies and the political institutions through which these demands are processed.

Demands for Liberalization

The costs to society of maintaining government-enforced entry barriers and state ownership of enterprises can vary as a function of such factors as technological advances, changes in consumer demand, and the costs of producing certain goods and services. As these costs rise, the demand for policy changes (dismantling entry barriers or privatization) mount, and the incentives for groups to resist these changes decline. This relationship is evident in the fact that pressures to liberalize or privatize vary by industry sector. For example,

---

13. Andrew Shonfield, *Modern Capitalism: The Changing Balance of Public and Private Power* (London: Oxford University Press, 1965).

14. Freeman, *Democracy and Markets*.

15. Mancur Olson, *The Rise and Decline of Nations: Economic Growth, Stagflation, and Social Rigidities* (New Haven, Conn.: Yale University Press, 1982).

16. John Zysman, *Governments, Markets and Growth* (Ithaca: Cornell University Press, 1983), chap. 2.

17. Peter Hall, *Governing the Economy: The Politics of State Intervention in Britain and France* (New York: Oxford University Press, 1986), 21.

the demands for liberalization and privatization seem to be higher in sectors such as telecommunications as opposed to the Post Office; airlines as opposed to railways; and electronics firms as opposed to the steel industry.

Demands for liberalization or privatization are a necessary, but not a sufficient, condition for such policy initiatives to occur.

Political Institutions

Political institutions set the rules of the game by which conflicting interests in society are mediated. Since these rules vary, the outcomes of these conflicts will also differ on a country-by-country basis. This, I would argue, is one of the major reasons that policies promoting liberalization and privatization have been implemented in some countries but not in others. The research challenge is to determine whether there are any general patterns in how "rules of the game" or institutions vary, and then to demonstrate that this variation is clearly associated with policy differences.

Recent theoretical and empirical developments in political economy suggest three ideal-type characterizations of institutions: pluralist, statist, and corporatist. No country perfectly fits the criteria for any of these categories. Nevertheless, it can be demonstrated that political institutions and systems are more characteristic of one ideal-type category than the others. Second, there is evidence that variations in these institutional characterizations help explain cross-national differences in variations in public policy initiatives, their implementation, and their outcomes.[18]

Demands for reductions in entry barriers and the privatization of government enterprise will be processed quite differently depending on which of the three institutional structures they confront. These structures vary on two critical dimensions:

1. the ease with which challenges to established public policy can be mounted, and
2. the institutional resources available to threatened interests that resist any changes in the policy status quo.

Pluralist institutions are the most conducive to liberalization and privatization because they pose fewer barriers to new and unconventional interests that advocate policy change, while at the same time vested interests have less institutionalized protection against these challenges. Statist institutions are a mixed type: on the one hand, ease of access to the political process is difficult

---

18. See Frank Wilson, "Interest Groups and Politics in Western Europe: The Neo-Corporatist Approach," *Comparative Politics* 10 (October 1983): 105–23.

TABLE 1.1.   Typology of Political Institutions

Political Institutional Type	Access to Political Process	Protection of Entrenched Interests	Example
Pluralist	High	Moderate	United Kingdom
Statist	Low	Low	France
Corporatist	Low	High	Germany

for interests demanding liberalization; on the other hand, there is less institutionalized protection for established interests. Once the state decides to act, few barriers hinder implementation of liberalization or privatization policies.[19] Finally, corporatist institutions provide the least promising environment for interests demanding privatization or liberalization: access to the political process for new and unconventional interests is restricted while established groups enjoy advantages.

With the caveats noted above, the three countries in this study are representative of these institutional types. In the United Kingdom, more so than in Europe, pluralist characteristics prevail. France falls in the statist category, while Germany represents the corporatist grouping. Table 1.1 summarizes the characteristics of the three different categories and the nations that fall within them.

Testing the Hypotheses

Two questions are evaluated here: Does ownership affect the performance of firms and, if so, why? Second, how do we account for cross-national variation in the implementation of liberalization and privatization policies? The explanations I propose are tested with data from the telecommunications sectors of the developed economies. I present two sets of analyses. First, I construct and estimate a statistical model of the performance of telecommunications service providers (telcos) in the developed market economies. Second, three case studies—the United Kingdom, France, and Germany—are presented.

Why Telecommunications?

The telecommunications sector was selected because it met the criteria necessary to test the two central arguments of the book. First, it satisfied the

---

19. Witness the relative ease with which the Socialists nationalized (and then the Conservatives privatized) industries in France during the 1980s.

requirement of adequate variation on both the dependent and independent variables. The performance of national telcos has varied dramatically both cross-nationally and over time. Moreover, the industry has existed for more than 100 years, providing an extended time-series. The two most important independent variables, political constraints and market structure, also evidence considerable variation.

A second reason for choosing the telecommunications sector is the recent dramatic changes in the industry's technology and consumer demand. My intent here is not simply to link political variables with economic performance, but also to explain why governments are more or less likely to embark on privatization or liberalization of industry sectors. The telecommunications sector satisfies two important criteria:

1. the period from the late 1960s to the 1980s has been one of dramatic change in technology and consumer demand, generating pressures for change in government policies; and
2. the industry is populated by a variety of interested parties, both those who stand to benefit from change and those with significant investments in maintaining the status quo.

Selecting a Sample of Countries

Theory and data constraints shaped the selection of countries included in the analysis. Because of the overriding interest in the impact of political variables on performance and change, the sample was restricted to democratic countries with market economies. The arguments developed here apply primarily to the political process associated with democratic institutions. While the generalizations might be expanded to cover nondemocratic and nonmarket economies where there is a keen interest in the economic consequences of privatization and liberalization, such an undertaking is beyond the scope of this book.

Statistical analyses are based on all of the OECD countries for which data on telecommunications penetration was available. Three detailed case studies are also incorporated into the research: France, the United Kingdom, and Germany. They were selected primarily because of the variation in their institutional arrangements for mediating conflicting political interests—an important independent variable in the argument developed above.

Why Case Studies?

The case studies serve a number of functions. First, they provide an explication of the argument linking styles of interest mediation and liberalization policies. The fairly detailed discussion of interest mediation in the three countries demonstrates the validity of the pluralist, statist, and corporatist trichotomy. It also affords the reader a greater understanding of the very different interaction between interest groups and policymakers in these three varied institutional settings. Finally, the in-depth study adds weight to the hypothesized link between institutional differences and the implementation of privatization and liberalization policies.

The case studies illustrate the nuances of the interrelationship between political constraints and economic performance. Although I am hardly the first to suggest a link between political control of firms and their performance, the case studies afford a unique opportunity to delineate those aspects of the firms' decision making that are either negatively or positively affected by its political masters.

While the following analysis is restricted to three cases, the link between the independent and dependent variables is suggestive and provides grounds for further inquiry. In fact, policy outputs and the performance levels of the three national telcos correspond to the predictions of the theoretical arguments. Each of the three cases document the extent to which political constraints inhibited the performance of their government-owned telcos for much of the twentieth century. Secondly, pressures to change government policies had the predicted responses: they were rapidly accommodated in the United Kingdom, resisted in Germany, and played little role in the liberalization process in France.

Organization of the Book

Chapters 2 and 3 address the issue of public ownership and its impact on economic performance. Chapter 2 discusses the costs and benefits to society of having state-owned enterprises and includes a review of recent empirical studies of the impact of public ownership on economic performance. It is followed by a chapter that makes the case that political control, as opposed to ownership, is the relevant explanatory variable. Chapter 4 tests this hypothesis with data from over twenty developed nations.

Market structure is a second factor typically associated with economic performance. A political explanation for the liberalization of entry barriers is presented in chapter 5. It is argued that styles of interest accommodation help explain why some countries reduced these barriers to competition, while others have not. Chapters 6 through 8 present three detailed case studies of the development of telephony in the United Kingdom, France, and Germany. A concluding chapter summarizes the findings and suggests their implications for future public policy.

CHAPTER 2

Government Enterprise: Public Goods and Economic Efficiency?

Adam Smith's comment that "No two characters seem more inconsistent than those of trader and sovereign," captures the antipathy many have toward public ownership.[1] Even in the case of monopoly industries, many critics argue against state ownership, preferring government regulation of private monopoly.[2] The recent wave of privatization in countries such as the United Kingdom, Canada, France, and Mexico is, at least ostensibly, justified by the inefficiencies of state ownership.

Why then have capitalist economies spawned such a diverse and significant number of publicly owned enterprises?[3] The justification for public ownership rests on the economic and political shortcomings associated with the market economy. When the market fails, as it may in the case of a natural monopoly, governments have assumed ownership of firms in order to minimize the economic inefficiencies that might otherwise result. Similarly, public goods, such as the equitable distribution of income, public transportation, or wildlife preserves, which are often undersupplied by the market, become the responsibility of state-owned enterprises.

These institutions gained particular importance during the twentieth century.[4] Shonfield has documented their popularity during the post–World War II era as a tool for managing national economies and, in particular, for promoting economic growth.[5] More recently, scholars have suggested that public enterprises play a key role in promoting the international competitiveness of national industries.[6] Even Adam Smith argued that there were certain areas of

---

1. Adam Smith, *An Inquiry into the Nature and Causes of The Wealth of Nations* (Chicago: University of Chicago Press, 1976), 343.

2. Smith, *Wealth of Nations*, 249; Friedrich A. Hayek, *The Road to Serfdom* (Chicago: University of Chicago Press, 1944), 197–98.

3. See Jean-Pierre Anastassopoulos, Georges Blanc, and Pierre Dussauge, *Les Multinationales Publiques* (Geneva: Presse Universitaires de France, 1985), 32.

4. Anastassopoulos, Blanc, and Dussauge, *Multinationales Publiques*, 61.

5. Andrew Shonfield, *Modern Capitalism: The Changing Balance of Public and Private Power* (London: Oxford University Press, 1965), 66.

6. See C. Stoffaes, *La grande menace industrielle* (Paris: Calmann Levy, 1978); and Jeanne Kirk Laux and Maureen Appel Molot, *State Capitalism: Public Enterprise in Canada* (New York: Cornell University Press, 1988).

commerce where public ownership might be appropriate—in particular, education and mail service.[7]

Critics of public ownership, such as Smith, Hayek, and Friedman, recognized that markets sometimes fail to supply certain public goods.[8] But they contended that the costs associated with public ownership are too high and recommended other strategies, such as government regulation, for rectifying these market shortcomings. This chapter assesses the advantages and drawbacks of public ownership.

Benefits of Government Ownership

From a purely economic perspective, government ownership of industry is prompted by market failures that can be broadly categorized as (1) increasing returns to scale (or natural monopoly) and (2) externalities of social benefit not valued in unregulated transactions (or "neighborhood effects" as they are sometimes labeled). Public ownership provides officials with a direct means for correcting these market failures. Government ownership also generates political benefits. For the elected official, public enterprises can be an effective vehicle for serving important constituencies.

Natural Monopoly

Natural monopolies have been the most popular candidates for nationalization. Because of declining economies of scale, these are industries where it is economically inefficient to have more than one firm.[9] Competition leads to inefficiency in these industries because each firm is required to duplicate very high capital investments, yet no firm benefits fully from the significant scale economies offered by the industry. The outcome is ruinous competition and a waste of scarce economic resources. Few scholars deny its existence, but there is considerable disagreement on the extent to which industries can be considered natural monopolies.[10]

7. Smith, *Wealth of Nations*, 342.

8. Smith, *Wealth of Nations*, 342. Also see Hayek, *Road to Serfdom*; and Milton Friedman, *Capitalism and Freedom* (Chicago: University of Chicago Press, 1962).

9. For a discussion of the economic nature and implications of natural monopoly see William W. Sharkey, *The Theory of Natural Monopoly* (Cambridge: Cambridge University Press, 1982); George Stigler, *The Organization of Industry* (Homewood, Ill.: R.D. Irwin, 1968); Harold Demsetz, "Why Regulate Utilities?" *Journal of Law and Economics* 11 (April 1968): 55–65; Richard Posner, "Natural Monopoly and Its Regulation," *Stanford Law Review* 21 (February 1969): 548–643; Elizabeth Bailey and William Baumol, "Deregulation and the Theory of Contestable Markets," *Yale Journal on Regulation* 1 (1984): 111–37.

10. Friedman, *Capitalism and Freedom*, 28.

Telephone service, particularly local service, has traditionally been considered a natural monopoly.[11] During the late nineteenth and early twentieth centuries, when the technology was in its infancy, the capital costs associated with establishing telephone service were so high and scale economies so significant it was generally felt that competition was untenable. This led to widespread nationalization of the industry.[12]

More recently, technological developments have raised questions as to whether there is any basis for treating the industry as a natural monopoly.[13] Such reservations have led the United States, Japan, and the United Kingdom to introduce widespread competition in the industry. Examples are long-distance telephone service, certain value-added services, and the provision of customer premises equipment. And while no government has seriously questioned the telco's monopoly over the delivery of local telephone service, there are increasing signs that even this sector of the industry might face competition from alternative delivery media such as local PBX switches, mobile telephony, and Personal Communications Networks (PCNs).[14]

Even if some aspects of telephone service are natural monopolies, public ownership is not the only, nor necessarily the most appropriate, government policy option. As Milton Friedman points out, "When technical conditions make a monopoly the natural outcome of competitive market forces, there are only three alternatives that seem available: private monopoly, public monopoly, or public regulation. All three are bad so we must choose among evils."[15] Friedman advocates private monopoly on the assumption that the costs associated with unfettered monopoly are smaller than government ownership or public regulation.

To the extent that the problem is simply one of natural monopoly where the regulatory challenge for government officials is to ensure that pricing conforms to certain rules (such as approximating marginal cost), a regulated private monopoly might be just as acceptable as a public monopoly. This option has been adopted with some success in the United States and parts of

---

11. See Sharkey, *The Theory of Monopoly*; J. Warren Stehman, *The Financial History of the American Telephone and Telegraph Company* (Boston: Houghton Mifflin, 1925), 234; Alfred Kahn, *The Economics of Regulation: Principles and Institutions*, 2 vols. (New York: Wiley, 1976), 2:123.

12. See Arthur N. Holcombe, *Public Ownership of Telephones on the Continent of Europe* (Boston: Houghton Mifflin Company, 1911).

13. See Bailey and Baumol, "Deregulation"; David S. Evans and James J. Heckman, "Natural Monopoly" in *Breaking Up Bell: Essays on Industrial Organization and Regulation*, ed. David S. Evans (New York: North-Holland, 1983), 127–56; John T. Wenders, "Natural Monopoly and the Deregulation of Local Telephone Service," *Telecommunications Policy* 14 (April 1990): 127.

14. Edward Carr, "A Survey of Telecommunications: Netting the Future," *Economist*, 10 March 1990.

15. Friedman, *Capitalism and Freedom*, 28.

Canada. But historically, for most countries, neither private monopoly nor public regulation have been acceptable policy options because governments have entertained more complex political and economic goals than simply minimizing the inefficiencies associated with natural monopoly.

Externalities

The presence of externalities is a stronger justification for public ownership than is increasing returns to scale.[16] Externalities are benefits (or costs) resulting from the provision of private goods that accrue to society but are not adequately reflected in their price. These benefits are social goods consumed collectively and, therefore, very difficult to price efficiently. Unlike strictly private goods, demand for collective goods is expressed through democratic institutions such as elections and lobbying activities. Consumers express their satisfaction or dissatisfaction by rewarding or punishing political incumbents (through elections, campaign contributions, direct contact with elected representatives, etc.).

Through its provision of private goods, the telcos can promote a wide range of social goals. Six positive externalities are commonly associated with the public ownership of telcos: universal service, risk acceptance, infrastructural development, defense and security, protectionism, and macroeconomic adjustments.

Universal Service

Because telephone service is considered by many to be an essential public utility—as are electricity and water service—it has assumed the status of a universal good to which all citizens should have access.[17] This is a political goal, one that commands considerable support among national electorates. For example, a Harris poll commissioned by AT&T indicated that a large majority of consumers, 76 percent, think that it is important for AT&T to maintain its commitment to universal service.[18] As a result of strong public

---

16. Externalities and public goods are discussed in Anthony B. Atkinson and Joseph E. Stiglitz, *Lectures on Public Economics* (New York: McGraw-Hill, 1980), 482–518; Paul A. Samuelson, "Pure Theory of Public Expenditures and Taxation," in *Public Economics*, ed. J. Margolis and H. Guitton (London: Macmillan, 1969); Richard A. Musgrave, "Provision for Social Goods in the Market System," *Public Finance* 26 (1971): 304–20; and in a review essay by J. C. Milleron, "A Theory of Value with Public Goods: A Survey Article," *Journal of Economic Literature* 5 (1972).

17. See Robert A. Meyer, Robert Wilson, M. Baughcum, Ellen Burton, and Louis Caouette, *The Economics of Competition in the Telecommunications Industry* (Cambridge: Oelgeschlager, Gunn and Hain, 1980), 75.

18. "AT&T's Harris Poll Backs Price Caps," *Communications Week*, 15 February 1988.

support, most governments promote universal telephone service through regulation or ownership of the industry.

Government action is deemed necessary because of the concern that firms would otherwise avoid serving less profitable consumer groups, thereby engaging in what is labeled "creamskimming."[19] Because some groups of consumers are more expensive to serve than others, there is a disincentive for telephone service providers to serve these consumers, especially those in less densely populated regions where the costs are highest. Without the ability to charge compensatory rates, competitive service providers would not serve these high-cost consumers.

Related to the universal service concept is the notion that service be priced similarly for all consumers. For example, basic telephone service in Amarillo, Texas, should be priced similarly to that in Houston. Moreover, long-distance calls from Amarillo should be priced similarly to long-distance calls of comparable distance originating in Houston. Without government-enforced entry barriers, this principle would certainly be violated. Because the average costs of servicing smaller communities are likely to be higher, private firms would either avoid them or charge higher tariffs.

Public ownership is a means to overcome creamskimming and inequitable pricing. A publicly owned entity is more likely to cross-subsidize less profitable consumers (rural/low density residential subscribers) with proceeds from more lucrative markets (higher density residential areas and business users). This issue provoked opposition to the liberalization of the telecommunications industries in the United Kingdom. Critics argued that, as a result of privatization, British Telecom (BT) would be less concerned with improving service to low-density residential subscribers and would favor high-density urban areas where potential profits are higher and competition is keener.

Risk

Society benefits from the introduction of new innovations in the communications industry. If the cost of communications falls, the nation becomes a more attractive site for industries, employment rises, the balance of trade improves, military security is enhanced, and the overall quality and pricing of telecommunications improve. These are all positive externalities. But the investment costs associated with innovative research and development are typically very high, and the risks of failure are substantial. Faced with such expensive and risky undertakings, some argue that private firms would be reluctant to invest, depriving society of these external benefits generated by innovation.

---

19. For an examination of creamskimming see: Kahn, *The Economics of Regulation*, 221–46; William Brock and David S. Evans, "Creamskimming," in *Breaking Up Bell*, ed. David S. Evans, 61–94.

Public corporations, on the other hand, can discount the risk factor and thereby increase the likelihood that society will benefit from innovation. Arrow and Lind demonstrate that since the costs of publicly borne risk are negligible, "public investment with an expected return which is less than that of a given private investment may nevertheless be superior to the private alternative."[20] There are numerous examples of public enterprises undertaking investments that private firms would consider too risky: the participation of European nationalized firms in the Ariane space program and in the Airbus venture, the Anglo-French cooperation in developing the Concorde, investments in advanced computer technologies by such nationalized firms as Inmos of the United Kingdom and Honeywell-Bull of France, the ambitious nuclear power program of Electricité de France, and the oil and gas exploration activities of such government oil firms as Elf-Aquitaine, ENI, Veba, and BNOC.[21]

It should also be noted, however, that publicly owned monopolies face certain economic disincentives to innovate. Having invested heavily in plant and equipment based on old technology, the public monopoly may be reluctant to entirely scrap their investment in favor of a new technology.

In the latter part of the twentieth century, telegraph administrations moved quickly to assume responsibility for telephone service because of its threat to the telco's investment in telegraph plant and equipment. Telephony was introduced slowly in Western Europe in part because the telegraph monopoly wanted to protect its capital investment for as long as possible.[22] Holcombe, who describes this process, concludes that one of the handicaps of a publicly owned monopoly is "a less rapid introduction of technical improvements than under a regime of free competition, but a more economical dispensation of the public resources."[23] This is the case because society's investment in old technology is not simply abandoned but is rather slowly phased out of use.

Paradoxically, the very threat of government policies raises the risk to private investment capital—a risk that can be eliminated by public ownership. Zeckhauser and Horn refer to this as the "problem of government opportunism."[24] The authors point out that public officials have difficulty resisting the

20. K. Arrow and R. Lind, "Uncertainty and the Evaluation of Public Investment Decisions," *American Economics Review* 60 (June 1970): 375.

21. Leslie E. Grayson, *National Oil Companies* (New York: Wiley, 1981), 17.

22. Gerald Brock, *The Telecommunications Industry* (Cambridge, Mass.: Harvard University Press, 1981), 146–47.

23. Holcombe, *Public Ownership of Telephones*, 463.

24. Richard Zeckhauser and Murray Horn, "The Control and Performance of State-Owned Enterprises," paper presented at the conference on Privatization in Britain and North America sponsored by the Bradley Policy Research Center, University of Rochester, Washington, D.C., 1987.

increased regulation or taxation of monopolists. Such actions are rarely un-popular with the public—in fact, they are likely to marshal a substantial amount of public support. As a result, they are a politically efficient strategy for raising revenues or forcing monopolists to provide certain public goods.

Regardless of government assurances, the threat of increased regulation or taxation is always a possibility because public officials cannot ignore the political opportunities associated with such initiatives.[25] Where the risk of these adverse government policies (such as expropriation, burdensome reg-ulations, or "windfall" taxation) are high, private investment is likely to be discouraged altogether.

The risk of such adverse government action varies with political and economic circumstances. Monopolies are the most likely targets for govern-ment regulation or expropriation. In addition, firms that realize significant returns to their investments—regardless of the level of initial risk—are also likely candidates for government regulation. Politically, they are popular tar-gets because high rates of return and monopoly profits have a very negative symbolic value with the electorate, whether or not these profits can be justi-fied by the risk investors assume.

Another factor is the degree of shareholder concentration. When the burden of regulation is widely dispersed among shareholders, government is more likely to take adverse actions because the firm's shareholders do not represent a very effective collective force.[26] The costs of organizing share-holders who each own a small fraction of the total outstanding shares in a publicly traded company are very high because of the free-rider problem. No single shareholder considers his or her participation essential in efforts to fight government actions, and as a result commitment is low in the expectation that other shareholders will participate. As Olson has elegantly demonstrated, collective action under these circumstances is very unlikely.[27] Government can therefore impose regulatory burdens on widely held private corporations with almost certain impunity. Firms with concentrated ownership can more effectively lobby against any adverse government initiatives because the costs of inaction by any one large shareholder are much more apparent.

Frequent turnover in a nation's ruling political party or coalition in-creases the probability of significant changes in government policies, which, in turn, raises the risk to private investors. These risks are accentuated when

25. Zeckhauser and Horn, "Control and Performance," 33.

26. See Harold Demsetz and Kenneth Lehn, "The Structure of Corporate Ownership: Causes and Consequences," *Journal of Political Economy* 96, no. 6 (1985): 171–73; and Mancur Olson, *The Logic of Collective Action* (Cambridge, Mass.: Harvard University Press, 1965).

27. Olson, *Logic of Collective Action*, 45.

the opposing political parties have significantly different platforms. For example, when the socialists assumed power in France in 1982, their positions regarding regulation and taxation of private industry were in marked contrast to the previous conservative government of Giscard d'Estaing. The socialists won power on a platform that called for extensive nationalization of French industry. Needless to say, this produced a certain anxiety in French business circles. Such wide shifts in policies regarding state ownership characterized much of the post–World War II period in the United Kingdom, where the two major political parties have maintained very different stances regarding government ownership. This has led to a series of nationalizations and denationalizations of the same industry (British coal and steel, for example).[28]

The threat of government opportunism may be high enough to discourage private investment altogether, leaving public ownership as the only viable alternative. The irony of this is that government creates the problem—high risk for private investors—and resolves it by forming government-owned enterprises.

Regardless of the source of risk (government actions, technology, or the size of initial capital expenditures, for example), public entities can discount its magnitude and thereby proceed with investments that private investors would avoid.

Infrastructural Development

Many of the nationalized industries in Europe are found in infrastructural sectors such as transport (air, highway, and rail), electrical utilities, oil, water service, and communications (broadcasting and telephone). Governments justify these investments on the basis of important externalities associated with the services they provide.[29] For example, the benefits of good airline service are not entirely reflected in the transactions between passenger and carrier. Quality airline service encourages tourism and facilitates international trade that helps promote exports. In the case of broadcasting, government ownership is justified on the grounds that the social benefits of quality television programming (a better educated public and protection of the national "cultural heritage," for example) would not be served by commercial television that generates its revenues from advertising and subscriptions.[30]

---

28. Richard Pryke, *The Nationalised Industries: Policies and Performance Since 1968* (Oxford: Martin Robertson, 1981), 183–85.

29. The public goods provided by nationalized infrastructural companies are reviewed by Grayson, *National Oil Companies*; and R. Kent Weaver, *The Politics of Industrial Change* (Washington, D.C.: Brookings Institution, 1985).

30. The creation of the Canadian Broadcasting Corporation is a case in point. See Jeanne Kirk Laux and Maureen Appel Molot, *State Capitalism: Public Enterprise in Canada* (Ithaca, N.Y.: Cornell University Press, 1988), 49.

Because it is difficult to charge all beneficiaries for the benefits they receive from these infrastructural services, many governments assume the responsibility themselves, subsidizing revenue shortfalls with general tax revenues.

Once again, there are alternative strategies for ensuring the provision of these public goods; governments could subsidize private entities in order to encourage the provision of these goods and services. In the case of airlines, for example, the U.S. government has subsidized air service through generous contracts for carrying airmail. Both the U.S. and Canadian governments granted generous land concessions in the nineteenth century to private firms as an incentive for the construction of transcontinental railways.

Defense and Security

There is a long tradition of governments owning strategically important industries. In the eighteenth and nineteenth centuries, the inland waterways were of considerable military significance for the French government. To ensure military access, the inland water canals were nationalized by the French Revolutionary government and have remained in government hands ever since.[31] Because of their strategic importance to the British navy, Cornwall brought the shipbuilders under government ownership. More recently, the military importance of space research and travel led to the creation of the U.S. government-controlled National Aeronautics and Space Agency.[32] One reason for the establishment of state-owned oil companies is governments' fear of losing access to vital oil and gas supplies in the event of war.[33]

Since its introduction, telecommunications have been considered important for defense and security reasons. The optical telegraph, for example, was introduced in France largely to improve communications during the Napoleonic wars.[34] Maintaining the integrity of the national telecommunications infrastructure, particularly during a time of national emergency or war, remains a top priority of all governments. Public ownership of telecommunication providers is frequently justified on the basis of the industry's strategic importance for national security. In the case of the United States, where the service provider was at one time a regulated monopolist, national defense was cited by many in opposition to divestiture of the Bell system.[35]

---

31. Yair Aharoni, *The Evolution and Management of State Owned Enterprises* (Cambridge, Mass.: Ballinger, 1986), 98.

32. Stuart M. Butler, *Privatizing Federal Spending: A Strategy to Eliminate the Deficit* (New York: Universe Books, 1985), 128.

33. Grayson, *National Oil Companies*, 10.

34. Holcombe, *Public Ownership of Telephones*, 4.

35. For a detailed discussion of this theme, see Ashton B. Carter, "Telecommunications Policy and U.S. National Security," in *Changing the Rules: Technological Change, International*

Protectionism

Public enterprises are a very effective instrument of government protectionist economic policies. Where they are in monopoly sectors, public enterprises can virtually exclude foreign companies from supplying goods and services. This is quite prevalent in industries such as telecommunications, electrical utilities, and railroads, where government monopolies are common. Because telcos make very substantial purchases of capital equipment, public owner-ship provides governments with a means to control their purchasing policies. Government can favor domestic equipment manufacturers, thereby protecting jobs and contributing to a positive balance of trade by discouraging imports.[36] For example, France's accelerated effort to modernize its telephone network was seen as a means to create a market for French-manufactured digital exchanges.

Because of the importance of the telecommunications industry, most governments have been reluctant to loosen their control over their telcos. They see their continued control as a means to shape the industry and ensure a market for locally produced telecommunications equipment. In France, for example, the government has erected significant protectionist barriers because it considers the industry of key importance in the nation's efforts to maintain technological sovereignty.[37] This protectionism may change somewhat in Europe as a result of recent efforts by the European Community to reduce internal European barriers to the trade in telecommunications equipment and services.[38]

Macroeconomy

The capital expenditures of public enterprises are subject to manipulation to promote the political and macroeconomic goals of government.[39] In an effort

---

Competition, and Regulation in Communications, ed. Robert W. Crandall and Kenneth Flamm (Washington, D.C.: Brookings Institution, 1989), 221–53.

36. Michael Tyler, "After the Telecom Earthquake: Were PTT Monopolies Cracked, Shaken, or Only Stirred?" *Communications Week*, 19 October 1987, 4.

37. See the government report that gave birth to many of these policies: Simon Nora and Alain Minc, *The Computerization of Society: Report to the President of France* (Cambridge, Mass.: MIT Press, 1980). Also see the discussion in Eli M. Noam, "International Telecom-munications in Transition," in Crandall and Flamm, *Changing the Rules*, 257–97.

38. European Economic Community, *Towards a Dynamic European Economy: Green Pa-per on the Development of the Common Market for Telecommunications Services and Equipment* (Brussels: Commission of the European Communities, 1987).

39. John Vickers and George Yarrow, *Privatization: An Economic Analysis* (Cambridge, Mass.: The MIT Press, 1988), 132.

to curb inflation during the 1970s, both the British and French authorities put pressure on public enterprises to restrain wage and price increases. There is some evidence that wage settlements and price increases in the nationalized sector were somewhat less inflationary during this period.[40] Other empirical studies of public enterprise yielded mixed results, with some suggesting a countercyclical effect[41] and others indicating either a neutral or procyclical effect.[42] On balance, the evidence points to a small countercyclical effect.

Because telco capital expenditures represent such a significant share of gross national capital formation, they have important consequences for national economic activity. As is the case with other nationalized industries, they may be subject to countercyclical manipulation by government officials. One of the major factors driving France's efforts to modernize its telecommunications infrastructure in the 1970s was the promise of increased manufacturing and consequent job creation—very important issues during a period of rising unemployment and a deteriorating trade balance. Elsewhere I have provided statistical evidence of the countercyclical patterns of telco investments.[43]

These six principal collective benefits—universal service, risk acceptance, infrastructural development, defense and security, protectionism, and macroeconomic adjustments—have played an important part in governments' decisions to assume and maintain ownership of telcos. But these cannot be the sole explanations, because public ownership is not the only strategy for dealing with natural monopoly and the provision of public goods. Governments can either choose to live with the costs of private monopoly—which a number of economists now believe to be minimal, assuming the markets are "contestable"—or they can impose regulations on private monopolists. Rather than entrusting state enterprises with the task of providing collective goods, governments can subsidize private entities in order to achieve the same ends. What then makes public ownership more attractive than these other alternatives? The other variable favoring public ownership is the political benefit it generates for incumbent officials.

---

40. Robert Millward, "Price Restraint, Anti-Inflation Policy and Public and Private Industry in the United Kingdom, 1949–1973," *Economic Journal* 86 (June 1976): 226–42.

41. Wayne W. Snyder, "Public Enterprise Investment and Economic Stability: A Six Country Comparison," *Annals of Public and Cooperative Economy* 42 (1971): 37–45; Ewald Nowotny, "Nationalized Industries as an Instrument of Stabilization Policy: The Case of Austria," *Annals of Public and Cooperative Economy* 53 (1982): 41–58; Fritz Knauss, "Federal Enterprise as a Boost to the Economy," *Annals of Public and Cooperative Economy* 48 (1977): 421–28.

42. John Zysman, *Governments, Markets and Growth* (Ithaca, N.Y.: Cornell University Press, 1983).

43. Raymond M. Duch, "The Politics of Investment by the Nationalized Sector," *Western Political Quarterly* 43 (June 1990).

Political Benefits

State-owned enterprises are a vehicle by which elected officials can generate political goodwill among the electorate. Not only can they provide tangible benefits to the consumer—low transportation costs, underpriced mail service, cheap medical care, etc.—but the true magnitude of these subsidies can be hidden. These costs can be easily disguised because the exact mandate of state enterprises is typically vague.[44] When government subsidizes these entities, it is not clear whether the subsidies compensate for inefficiencies or whether they underwrite the provision of collective goods. Moreover, in the latter case it is virtually impossible to determine which particular public goods are being underwritten. In the case of subsidies to British Rail or Air France, it is very difficult to measure the extent to which subsidies preserve uneconomical routes, protect jobs, or support regional development. There is no one-to-one correspondence between the public goods provided by these entities and the subsidies received from the government.[45]

These ambiguities could be significantly reduced if government were to compensate state enterprise directly for any public goods supplied.[46] Without such compensation, evaluation of public enterprise performance is difficult because management can attribute its poor record to their provision of certain collective goods. Management argues that if it were not under political pressure to supply these collective goods, its performance might be better. Office holders, on the other hand, downplay the cost to public enterprises of providing public goods and claim that subsidies are necessary, not to underwrite the provision of social goods, but in order to compensate for inefficient management.

The notion of compensation for the provision of collective goods has been proposed by a number of official commissions, including the British National Economic Development Office's *Study of UK Nationalised Industries*, the French *Rapport sur les Entreprises Publiques*, and the Canadian Privy Council Report, *Crown Corporations: Direction, Controls and Ac-*

---

44. Aharoni, *Evolution and Management*, chap. 4.

45. Grayson, *National Oil Companies*, 13; Michael Beesley and Tom Evans, "The British Experience: The Case of British Rail," in *State-owned Enterprise in the Western Economies*, ed. Raymond Vernon and Yair Aharoni, 117–32 (New York: St. Martin's Press, 1981); H.M. Treasury, *Nationalised Industry: A Review of Economic and Financial Objectives* (London: H.M. Treasury, 1967).

46. Alec Nove, *Efficiency Criteria for Nationalised Industries* (Toronto: University of Toronto Press, 1973); James R. Nelson, "Public Enterprise: Pricing and Investment Criteria," in *Public Enterprise: Economic Analysis of Theory and Practice*, ed. William Shepherd (Lexington, Mass.: Lexington Books, 1976); Richard A. Musgrave, "Provision for Social Goods in the Market System," *Public Finance* 26 (1971): 304–20.

countability.[47] In essence, this compensation would demand that all public enterprise activities be transparent—goods and services that were not strictly commercial in nature would be clearly identified and subsidized out of the government's general revenues.

These recommendations for transparency have never won the wholehearted support of governments because elected officials have little interest in distinguishing the public enterprise's commercial and political activities.[48] One of the political benefits of government ownership is the creation of an "invisible surplus" that can be used for redistributive purposes.[49] Sources of this surplus include government-enforced monopoly, relief from regulation, and concessions to use land and waterways.[50] In Canada, for example, the Canadian National Railway has been granted extensive land concessions in return for commitments to serve communities that it would not otherwise serve.[51] Elected officials often prefer that subsidies to particular groups, regions, or constituencies not be made public. The public enterprise with its invisible surplus is often an ideal vehicle for allocating such ex publicus subsidies. Rendering them transparent could be politically costly.[52]

On the other hand, establishing a public enterprise that is nominally independent of the government allows politicians to distance themselves from governmental activities that are unpopular with the electorate. Nationalized activities such as railway, postal, and airline service can create major problems for politicians if consumers become disgruntled. Tierney argues that this was the principal reason why the U.S. Congress divested itself of responsibility for the U.S. Post Office.[53] He noted, "The post office had been a colossal headache to members of Congress. Citizens disgruntled over the slightest ineptitude or inconvenience complained to their congressional representatives . . . . Apart from, say, the occasional chance to fight for keeping a small

---

47. British National Economic Development Office, *Study of UK Nationalised Industries* (London: HMSO, 1976); Simon Nora, *Rapport sur les Entreprises Publiques*, Groupe de Travail du Comité Interministeriel des Entreprises Publiques (Paris: La Documentation Française, 1967); Canadian Privy Council Report, *Crown Corporations: Direction, Controls and Accountability* (Ottawa: Information Canada, 1977).

48. Such a scheme also poses a number of practical problems associated with implementation (see Aharoni, *Evolution and Management*).

49. Aharoni, *Evolution and Management*, 124.

50. Zeckerhaus and Horn, "Control and Performance."

51. G. P. deT. Glazebrook, *A History of Transportation in Canada* (Toronto: McClelland and Stewart, 1964).

52. Richard A. Posner, "Taxation by Regulation," *Bell Journal of Economics and Management Science* 2, no.1 (Spring 1971): 22–50.

53. John T. Tierney, "Government Corporations and Managing the Public's Business," *Political Science Quarterly* 99 (1984): 73–92.

community post office, the postal system offered lawmakers little in the way of opportunities for enhancing their reelection chances."[54]

Needless to say, the task of public enterprise management is complicated by the need to respond to the various economic, social, and political priorities reviewed here. Compared to private firms, government-owned enterprises face a considerably more complex set of pressures. Even private monopolists regulated by the state face a much more limited and well-defined number of political and social expectations.

The Performance of Government-Owned Enterprises

The performance of the public enterprise is undermined by two primary factors: its lack of accountability and its sensitivity to political manipulation. In an environment of complex economic, social, and political priorities, management is subject to a variety of political pressures that undermine operational efficiency.[55] Complicating this factor is ineffective monitoring of public enterprise performance. The ultimate controllers of public enterprise performance, the electorate, are too numerous and diffuse to effectively monitor its behavior.

Agency Losses

All enterprises encounter agency costs resulting from the diverging interests of owners and managers.[56] Principal-agent theory characterizes the interaction between owners and managers as an agency relationship whereby the agent (usually, the manager) acts on behalf of the principal (typically, the owner). The principal seeks to control the agent by entering into a contractual relationship that induces the agent to act as if he or she were maximizing the welfare of the principal. These types of implicit contractual understandings are pervasive: between shareholders and managers in a firm, between the government and managers of public institutions, between investors and their brokers, etc. There are no circumstances in which the interests of the principal and of the agent exactly coincide. The principal, therefore, must bear certain costs to enforce compliance.

---

54. Zeckerhaus and Horn, "Control and Performance," 24.

55. For a description of how the complexity of goals can undermine the performance of public enterprise, see George W. Downs and Patrick D. Larkey, *The Search for Government Efficiency: From Hubris to Helplessness* (Philadelphia: Temple University Press, 1986).

56. This discussion is based on Aharoni, *Evolution and Management;* Eugene Fama, "Agency Problems and the Theory of the Firm," *Journal of Political Economy* 88 (1980): 288–307; and Eugene Fama and M. C. Jensen, "Separation of Ownership and Control," *Journal of Law and Economics* 26 (June 1983): 301–26.

Some of the agency costs are expressed in the contractual arrangement between the principal and the agent, that is, the cost of engaging the agent. But there are significant other costs, including the costs of monitoring the performance of agents and, most important, lost revenues resulting from unsanctioned divergences in the interests and risk preferences of the principal and his agent. Although both private and public enterprises face agency costs, they are considerably higher in the case of the latter.

Agency costs are magnified under public ownership for three primary reasons: the very diffuse nature of ownership, the absence of share prices, and the nontransferability of management.[57] The more diffuse the ownership base of a firm, the higher the costs of monitoring the performance of the shareholders' agents. As Olson pointed out, the costs of collective action (in this case, monitoring the performance of principals and forming a coalition to take action) rise with the number of interested individuals.[58] Agents in a firm controlled by a small number of shareholders can be much more effectively held accountable to the firm's owners than is the case when there are a large number of very dispersed shareholders. Where ownership is concentrated, the benefits of monitoring agent behavior are much higher for any single shareholder and, therefore, more salient to each individual owner. The consequences of inaction by any single shareholder are more serious and, therefore, less likely to occur. With diffuse ownership, there is a strong incentive for shareholders to act as free riders by not contributing to the monitoring costs but reaping all the benefits of others' efforts in this regard.

In effect, the ownership base of the typical public enterprise is the entire electorate that exercises ultimate control over the fate of management and its policies (in the case of enterprises owned by municipalities or provinces, the ownership base is smaller). The taxpayer-shareholder will suffer much greater agency costs than is the case with shareholders in publicly traded firms because the electorate is much more numerous and diffuse. The costs of poor management to any particular citizen are minimal; hence there is little incentive to monitor the activities of public corporations.

This is not to suggest that shareholders in publicly traded firms are not dispersed. They are, and this detracts from their effectiveness in monitoring management. Moreover, the interests of shareholders will not necessarily coincide, which also undermines any efforts to discipline management.[59] These are, of course, general problems in the theory of the firm. But these shortcomings do not render any less valid the argument regarding the relative effectiveness of shareholders of publicly traded firms versus the taxpayer-

---

57. The argument developed here is based on Zeckhauser and Horn, in "Control and Performance."

58. Olson, *Logic of Collective Action*.

59. Vickers and Yarrow, *Privatization*, 11.

shareholder. Taxpayer-shareholders are much more dispersed than share-holders in publicly traded firms and therefore monitor management less effectively.

Agency losses in private firms are reduced by public trading of their stock. Although shareholders in private firms rarely take an active role in the evaluation of management, they can signal their disapproval by selling the company's stock. This is eventually reflected in the value of the firm's shares. In the face of a steadily declining share value (relative to other traded firms), the tenure of senior management becomes tenuous. Management in public enterprises, on the other hand, are not disciplined by the financial markets, which contributes to the inflated agency losses of government-owned enterprises.

Finally, management in private firms is disciplined by the ever-present threat of a transfer of assets. Dissatisfied with the returns on their investments under current management, owners can opt to sell their assets to a new owner. Because transfers of this nature typically involve a shake-up in management and therefore threaten job security, they represent an incentive for management to maximize the internal efficiency of the firm, thereby upholding the market value of the firm's stock. The assets of government-owned enterprises are not transferable (except in the extreme case of privatization). Management, as a result, is not disciplined by the threat of a transfer to new ownership. Without the menace posed by the transfer of assets, agency losses for government enterprises are further inflated.

Many argue that the analogy between the shareholders of the publicly traded firm and the taxpayer-shareholders of the public enterprise is inappropriate because it ignores the political checks on public sector performance. The role of the political process as a check on public enterprise performance is examined in the next section.

Political Pressure

Intervening between the "taxpayer-shareholder" and public enterprise management are political agents who advocate the interests of individuals and groups affected by public enterprise policies. There are two quite different models of political actor behavior. On the one hand, economic models suggest that rational political actors respond to those constituents with the most intense preferences or for whom organizational costs are low.[60] According to this model, policies that generate very diffuse benefits or dispersed costs are not likely to have effective political advocates or critics.

---

60. George Stigler, "The Theory of Economic Regulation," *Bell Journal of Economics and Management Science* 2 (Spring 1971): 3–21; S. Peltzman, "Towards a More General Theory of Regulation," *Journal of Law and Economics* 14 (1976): 109–47.

A second perspective offered by Wilson counters that "political entrepreneurs can mobilize latent public sentiment" in favor of policies with very diffuse benefits and against those with dispersed costs.[61] The implications of these two models for the performance of public enterprises are very different: the economic model suggests that political influences will detract from performance while the Wilson model of the political entrepreneur holds up the possibility that political pressures will enhance performance.

Economic Models
The economic model suggests that narrow interests, which expect concentrated benefits or losses as a consequence of public enterprise actions, will mobilize the most effective pressure on political decision makers. As a result, public enterprise management can be expected to adopt policies favoring these concentrated interest groups. The interests of three major types of groups weigh heavily on public enterprise decision making: favored political constituents, consumers and suppliers, and public sector employees.

Governments often exploit public enterprises as vehicles for rewarding political constituents—this includes contracts, hiring priorities, favorable tariffs to select groups of customers, etc. In Canada, for example, the Crown corporations have been an important source of patronage to professionals (such as lawyers, advertising executives, and accountants) that have supported the incumbent political party.[62] Governments attach considerable political importance to the appointments of senior executives in public enterprises. It is well documented, for example, that senior positions in most of the major Italian public enterprises are allocated on the basis of political patronage considerations.[63] Recent changes in the French government in 1981, 1985, and 1988 have all prompted major shake-ups in the top personnel of government-owned enterprises. French politicians are very sensitive to the political advantages afforded those who exercise control over the public sector.[64]

Public enterprise management is also vulnerable to the lobbying efforts

61. James Q. Wilson, "The Politics of Regulation," in *The Politics of Regulation*, ed. James Q. Wilson, 370 (New York: Basic Books, 1980).

62. C. A. Ashley and R. G. H. Smails, *Canadian Crown Corporations: Some Aspects of Their Administration and Control* (Toronto: Macmillan Co. of Canada, 1965), 11; Freeman, *Democracy and Markets*, 207–8.

63. Franco A. Grassini, "The Italian Enterprises: The Political Constraints," in *State-Owned Enterprise*, 79–80.

64. Thomas Kamm, "France's New Socialist Finance Minister Hints at Changes for Privatized Firms," *Wall Street Journal*, 20 May 1988; Jacques Jublin, "Le Governement déclenche une rédistribution dans les affaires," *La Tribune de l'Expansion*, 27 July 1988; Harvey B. Feigenbaum, "Privatization and Interest Groups in France," paper presented for the SOG Conference on Government and Organized Interests, Zurich, Switzerland, 1989.

of specific groups of consumers and suppliers. The organizational and coalition-building costs for such entities are likely to be much lower than is the case for the taxpayer-shareholder because they are often a much more concentrated group of individuals or firms. As a result of these unequal organizational resources, public enterprises have higher input costs and generate lower revenues than is the case for private firms. The nationalized British Central Electricity Generating Board, for example, is forced, as a result of the lobbying efforts of British Coal (also a public enterprise) and its associated mining companies and employees, to purchase British coal at £45 when equivalent foreign coal costs £25.[65] Similarly, large users of nationalized transportation facilities can have an important say in the setting of tariffs. In Canada, the well-organized farming lobbies have kept railroad tariffs for grain at levels dramatically below market rates.[66]

Public enterprises are more sensitive to the political power of organized groups than are private firms because state enterprises are ultimately controlled by politicians and government can more easily compensate public enterprises for the costs of accommodating these powerful groups.

Finally, public enterprise employees exert considerable political influence. First, they are a concentrated interest group with very intense preferences regarding wages and employment policies. Second, no government is anxious to be viewed by the public as an unsympathetic employer or a union buster (particularly governments of the Left). Employees of public enterprises exploit this political advantage in order to exact concessions from management.[67] In Europe, for example, the employees of the government-owned telcos have exercised tremendous control over labor policies. The *Deutsche Postgewerkschaft* (German Post Workers' Union) has effectively blocked any attempts to reduce the Bundespost's labor force or cut back on rigid hiring and promotion practices protected by the *Bundesbeamtengesetz* (the federal civil servants law). As Pryke noted in his analysis of British Rail, the company was hopelessly overstaffed because of union intransigence, but the British governments have been reluctant to assume the political costs of forcing changes in employment practices.[68]

Governments have generally been unwilling to bear the political costs associated with cutbacks in public sector labor forces and reductions in their

---

65. "A Goal for Coal: Britain's Coal Mines Have Come a Long Way. Next Stop, the Real World," *The Economist*, 23 April 1988, 17.

66. Weaver, *Politics of Industrial Change*, 28. Tariffs resulting from this statutory decision are called the "Crow's Neck Pass" rates. Weaver notes that this legislation kept tariffs on grain shipments from the Pacific to the Great Lakes ports to levels prevailing in 1899. See also A. W. Currie, *Canadian Transportation Economics* (Toronto: University of Toronto Press, 1967), chap. 4.

67. Aharoni, *Evolution and Management*, 187; Freeman, *Democracy and Markets*.

68. Pryke, *The Nationalised Industries*, 85–88.

wages and benefits. Compared to private firms, this puts public enterprises at a distinct disadvantage in efforts to control labor costs.[69]

The economic model offers little hope that political pressures will promote the efficient operation of public enterprises. This model suggests exactly the opposite: most political pressures will inhibit the economic performance of these entities. The next section explores a somewhat more sanguine view of the political process and its impact on public enterprise management.

The Political Entrepreneur

Wilson convincingly argues that political entrepreneurs (elected politicians, public interest agents, the media, or industry lobbyists) can mobilize public support on issues for which there are no concentrated benefits or costs.[70] This raises the possibility that political entrepreneurs will monitor public enterprise management in order to ensure high levels of performance, even though the only constituency for such action is the very diffuse and poorly organized taxpayer-shareholder. For example, opposition politicians could use information regarding wasteful management practices and political favoritism to embarrass the government. Politicians have succeeded in stimulating debate over the management practices of such public enterprises as Air Canada, Amtrak in the United States, Renault in France, and British Steel. Pressure from consumer lobbyists could also mobilize political support for higher levels of efficiency and thereby lower consumer prices (although for the most part consumers are primarily concerned with price and have little interest in efficiency).

It is not the case, as Wilson has correctly noted, that initiatives conferring very general (although small) benefits—good management practices, for example—will always fail to generate political support.[71] If championed by entrepreneurial political actors, such initiatives could have a positive impact on public enterprise performance.

But *not* all initiatives that generate diffuse benefits enhance public enterprise performance. As noted above, the public enterprise is a vehicle by which government can subsidize the price and availability of private and public goods (such as transportation, mail, health care, etc.). Often these policies confer benefits on a very diffuse electorate, the costs are borne by a small segment of society, and they negatively affect the efficiency of the public enterprise. One example is the subsidization of residential telephone rates with revenues from business and long-distance telephone tariffs. The costs of

---

69. Freeman, *Democracy and Markets*.
70. Wilson, "Politics of Regulation," 370.
71. Wilson, "Politics of Regulation," 370.

subsidizing a very diffuse segment of society are borne by a more concentrated constituency. Although such pricing policies tend to command widespread political support, they are inefficient from a strictly economic perspective because the tariffs have little relation to the cost of providing the services.

Wilson is correct in that there are opportunities for political entrepreneurs to champion the interests of the taxpaying public. But to the extent that political entrepreneurs have advocated the interests of the general public, it has been to protect subsidized prices for consumers as opposed to promoting the interests of taxpayer-shareholders. A major reason for governments' reticence regarding liberalizing entry barriers is the impact it would have on local telephone rates (both U.S. and British subscribers experienced significant increases in their rates). While residential consumers have not been well organized in any of the European countries, they have had political advocates (for example, the Conservative backbenchers that championed the interests of rural British telephone subscribers). Moreover, even the threat of a political backlash has persuaded governments to avoid liberal initiatives that might raise the price of ordinary telephone service.

To briefly summarize, two competing models of public enterprise performance have been proposed. Economic models of the political process predict that the interests of a very diffuse taxpaying public would be sacrificed to the political demands of small, concentrated special interests (such as suppliers, employees, and important political constituents). Public enterprise performance would suffer because political priorities (serving these special interests) are often inconsistent with economic goals, such as minimizing costs and maximizing returns. Wilson has challenged this naive economic approach, raising the possibility that political entrepreneurs will champion the interests of the taxpayer-citizen.[72] To the extent that political entrepreneurs can mobilize latent public support for initiatives favoring efficient management of government corporations, the performance of these entities should improve.

Neither of these models, in fact, hold out much hope for efficiency in the state-owned enterprise. The economic models suggest that special interests (such as labor and suppliers) will have a political edge in their dealings with managers. But even the Wilson model is, at best, ambiguous as to the nature of political pressures that will be brought to bear: Will the political entrepreneur champion the interests of the taxpayer-shareholder or the taxpayer as consumer? Overall, political pressures are likely to undermine rather than promote the economic performance of public enterprises.[73]

---

72. Wilson, "Politics of Regulation."

73. Laux and Molot note that "The less 'visible' the corporation, the more likely it is that management will benefit, acquiring the relative autonomy to follow business logic in decision

The Public Enterprise Track Record

With few exceptions, research suggests that the *economic* performance of private firms is superior to that of publicly owned firms. The results of Monsen and Walters's comparisons of public and private firms in Western Europe are presented in tables 2.1 and 2.2. Their evaluation of various economic performance measures indicates that private firms outperform the nationalized sector. They found, as do most scholars, that profits are lower and losses higher in publicly owned firms. The returns on sales of the twenty-five largest industrial state-owned firms in Western Europe (table 2.1) are compared with those of the twenty-five largest industrial private sector firms (table 2.2) for the period 1972–81. In each year the average return for state-owned firms was negative (the average over the ten-year period was −0.04) and the average return for private firms was positive (the average over the ten-year period was 0.02).[74]

Quite reasonably, critics argue that profits are not an appropriate criterion for comparison because in many cases public enterprises are required to price services and products at levels lower than private enterprise would. This reduces profits but is not necessarily an indicator of relative efficiency.

To a large degree, the comparative data in table 2.3 avoid this problem: first, by measuring performance in terms of revenue per employee; and second, by comparing private and state-owned firms in the same industry and the same country. Where private and state-owned firms are competing in the same market, it is unlikely that the government could successfully force state-owned firms to keep prices significantly below their market level. The data are quite persuasive: sales per employee are mostly higher in the private as opposed to the public sector. Overall these findings hold up across different industries and different countries.

Pryke takes a closer look at British nationalized industries and comes to a similar conclusion. Most of the industries, with the exception of telecommunications and gas, have performed quite poorly since 1968. By examining *change* in output, employment, and productivity, Pryke avoided the problems associated with sales and profits figures. His results are summarized in table 2.4.

In the 1968–78 period he found that output in the British manufacturing sector as a whole grew 10 percent. Note, however, from column 1 in table 2.4

---

making." They also argue that the high public visibility that may characterize certain public enterprises erodes over time. Without this visibility, there is little payoff to political entrepreneurs seeking to mobilize public sympathies. See Laux and Molot, *State Capitalism*, 99.

74. R. Joseph Monsen and Kenneth D. Walters, *Nationalized Companies: A Threat to American Business* (New York: McGraw-Hill, 1984), 84–85.

TABLE 2.1. Profit and (Loss) of Twenty-five Largest Industrial State-Owned Firms in Western Europe, 1972–81

	1972	1973	1974	1975	1976	1977	1978	1979	1980	1981
Aérospatiale	363	(98,942)	(76,569)	(113,816)	(129,902)	(91,045)	(19,238)	1,956	28,092	29,343
Alfa Romeo	3,677	3,677	(89,423)	(178,632)	(102,632)	(169,839)	(149,506)	(109,920)	(88,218)	(103,685)
BL (British Leyland)			(56,318)	(283,359)	61,205	(90,562)	(72,329)	(306,632)	(1,245,316)	(1,007,315)
British Aerospace						51,364	54,786	86,844	266,272	126,920
British Shipbuilders								(124,573)	(332,102)	(75,460)
British Steel	7,369	120,831	170,455	171,867	(541,209)	(164,727)	(797,597)	(600,796)	(3,891,296)	115,483
Charbonnages de France	(52,048)	(8,789)	(2,573)	(138,769)	(158,132)	(46,907)	(40,957)	(18,249)	(50,182)	(49,318)
Cockerill							(227,625)	(122,423)	(269,582)	(464,989)
Italsider	(29,056)	34,038	50,413	(110,654)	(157,609)	(446,619)	(411,236)	(309,730)	(873,700)	(1,510,775)
National Coal Board	(205,338)	(205,338)	(315,777)	-0-	11,382	47,164	36,696	(37,671)	343,600	(135,239)
Renault	14,800	12,902	7,261	(128,702)	122,870	4,070	2,222	241,520	160,165	(124,916)
Rolls-Royce	926	2,323	28,650	65,970	(16,538)	25,503	13,746	(133,475)	(62,789)	(6,080)
Saarbergwerke	(17,217)	(36,234)	(10,157)	(2,555)	5,059	12,100	NA	NA	2,704	31,400
Sacilor							(249,096)	(358,452)	(469,984)	(531,887)
Salzgitter	0	11,009	20,503	6,567	(18,517)	(40,119)	(48,272)	(1,997)	(48,668)	(175,708)
SEAT	15,083	22,869	6,463	1,085	(6,834)	5,387	(135,488)	(224,855)	(287,005)	(219,439)
SEITA		9,359		109,278	(1,581)	(32,885)	(67,218)	(55,532)	(47,445)	(22,047)
SNECMA	3,792			10,578	22,419	19,333	15,195	15,527	15,240	(24,743)
Södra Skogsägarna				4,049	4,248	(8,732)	(10,450)	(5,960)	(1,537)	NA
Statsföretag	19,025	31,561	16,869	(25,555)	44,682	(145,827)	(113,638)	45,000	29,346	(169,011)
SWEDYARDS						(414,509)	541,485	98,724	(260,212)	(56,913)
Usinor									(296,963)	(777,271)
Valmet					7,782	1,444	2,898	5,509	18,792	(38,937)
VIAG	10,680	8,971	23,684	(17,170)	16,096	14,071	(9,606)	25,325	49,290	4,210
VÖEST-Alpine	2,615	019	9,901	086	17,000	(1,500)	(23,867)	(29,124)	(65,026)	(9,356)

Source: R. Joseph Monsen and Kenneth D. Walters, Nationalized Companies: A Threat to American Business (New York: McGraw-Hill, 1983).

Note: All figures in $000.

TABLE 2.2. Profit and (Loss) of Twenty-five Largest Industrial Private Firms in Western Europe, 1972–81

	1972	1973	1974	1975	1976	1977	1978	1979	1980	1981
BASF	128,106	194,144	205,196	152,831	241,176	167,444	210,170	338,040	197,641	162,890
BAT Industries	197,775	272,213	275,735	314,041	323,541	357,987	411,061	398,940	323,247	370,903
Bayer	118,297	164,866	189,388	128,229	181,364	136,169	203,857	239,376	356,342	224,634
Ciba-Geigy	26,745	35,803	159,426	73,953	128,045	175,405	202,716	195,504	182,100	273,152
Daimler-Benz	85,993	97,527	100,496	125,768	164,182	211,010	295,054	347,794	605,149	365,212
Dunlop	9,153	42,471	19,768	(198)	68,100	NA	22,500	NA	(35,900)	(83,098)
Fiat	27,147	450	56	164	80,412	71,225	88,062	49,100	44,400	81,500
Fried. Krupp	(239)	26,275	27,444	(19,223)	10,048	NA	(10,500)	37,200	33,547	(20,858)
Générale d'Electricité	31,125	35,832	25,654	25,451	46,723	53,785	56,848	73,255	96,407	74,607
Gutehoffnungshütte	8,730	14,198	26,213	22,295	31,241	38,755	41,856	47,453	48,243	44,478
Hoechst	99,423	176,330	205,196	100,972	188,010	92,969	107,559	141,684	251,605	132,167
Imperial Chemical	229,082	449,510	567,953	424,294	442,328	394,476	577,791	880,638	(46,510)	386,983
Mannesmann	30,144	38,237	87,182	238,833	109,372	92,940	119,317	79,820	95,932	115,483
Michelin	15,425	81,419	17,322	95,164	157,140	123,658	136,976	128,540	65,813	(66,628)
Nestlé	170,759	217,783	250,093	309,365	348,922	346,633	416,131	490,865	407,785	492,604
Pechiney Ugine Kuhlmann	54,202	82,256	154,589	(37,150)	31,994	76,781	57,981	233,124	143,935	NA
Peugeot-Citroën	65,383	72,782	33,262	65,817	287,426	238,700	300,200	254,318	(348,998)	(368,825)
Philips'	233,427	323,096	273,493	152,190	212,940	258,255	327,117	308,701	165,210	143,682
Saint-Gobain	87,386	138,084	146,386	28,025	98,775	130,766	91,783	154,350	215,310	83,180
Siemens	124,694	161,897	189,149	201,275	221,969	272,971	322,021	361,938	332,434	208,157
Schneider	5,957	7,128	24,967	NA	10,706	9,829	1,044	2,422	(30,517)	(63,346)
Thomson-Brandt	26,136	48,953	34,339	38,316	43,936	42,793	53,152	65,457	72,852	(13,625)
Thyssen	15,002	61,240	201,026	99,926	105,499	65,744	61,238	87,262	61,611	(32,341)
Unilever	331,869	423,284	362,807	322,108	517,614	456,789	531,337	920,320	658,820	800,379
Rhône-Poulenc	49,073	127,328	179,556	(205,246)	(76,265)	17,094	52,872	186,019	(461,303)	(61,995)

Source: Monsen and Walters, Nationalized Companies.
Note: All figures in $000.

TABLE 2.3.   Sales/Employees of Seven Pairs of State-Owned and Private Firms in Western Europe, 1972–81

	1972	1973	1974	1975	1976	1977	1978	1979	1980	1981	Avg.
Alfa Romeo	14.6	14.6	15.9	24.7	24.4	26.1	35.9	41.5	49.8	40.0	28.7
Fiat	19.2	20.3	23.1	32.0	32.5	32.3	42.8	50.8	73.4	62.3	38.9
BL	17.0	18.8	17.5	22.4	22.8	23.3	30.7	37.6	46.7	49.7	28.7
Ford (Brit.)	NA	NA	32.3	36.4	43.2	51.1	58.2	84.7	85.0	82.9	59.2
Renault	22.5	27.4	25.9	35.2	38.8	41.2	53.1	69.1	88.8	75.2	47.7
Peugeot	23.6	29.5	31.4	40.0	39.5	46.2	55.9	47.4	68.8	61.5	44.3
Salzgitter	22.6	32.9	49.7	49.9	47.7	52.4	64.1	69.5	85.2	74.6	54.8
Thyssen	33.2	46.0	57.4	62.0	57.0	62.0	70.7	87.5	100.4	87.5	66.4
Aerospatiale	16.9	21.5	26.9	47.0	53.7	57.1	63.8	79.1	90.6	86.4	55.3
Dassault	28.8	52.5	49.2	63.8	81.0	76.4	90.2	107.9	156.6	146.0	85.3
Volkswagen	26.1	29.8	32.2	43.4	46.5	54.3	64.4	69.9	71.1	68.1	50.9
Daimler-Benz	27.8	35.6	40.6	52.7	55.6	62.4	72.3	85.7	93.3	86.3	61.2
BP	73.5	112.5	268.7	222.5	244.9	258.5	251.5	342.0	406.4	340.6	252.1
Shell	68.8	111.1	201.4	199.4	235.9	256.0	278.8	333.8	479.0	495.7	266.0

Source: Monsen and Walters, *Nationalized Companies.*

that output actually dropped significantly in six of the nationalized industries; it increased well below average in the postal service and British Leyland. On the other hand, the output of the telecommunications sector, British Gas, and British Airlines grew at a rate much higher than the average 10 percent.

Column 3 of table 2.4 presents Pryke's measures of the percentage increase in labor productivity (real staff costs per unit produced). The average increase for manufacturing is 28 percent—four of the eleven public enterprises had rates substantially above that level while six had rates significantly lower. Conclusions based on this data must be tentative because Pryke does not control for secular trends in these industries. It may simply be the case that in other countries private firms in the same industries have performed just as poorly.[75]

Further evidence of the poor performance record of public enterprise is provided by a recent IMF analysis, the results of which are summarized in table 2.5. For each developed country in the sample, the aggregate return on investment made by public enterprises is either very low or negative. In addition, self-financing by these entities is nil.[76]

U.S. public enterprise has also come under critical scrutiny. Amtrak is a

---

75. Pryke, *Nationalised Industries.*
76. Aharoni, *Evolution and Management*, 180.

TABLE 2.4. Change in Output, Employment, and Productivity in Public Enterprise and Manufacturing

	Percentage Change in Output	Percentage Growth in Employment	Percentage Growth in Labor Productivity
Telecommunications	129	2	120
British Airways (airline activities)	129	22	86
British Gas	82	−18	126
British Electricity Board	−20	−26	68
Postal services	1	−1	−12
BL (vehicles UK)	3	−1	−17
British Rail	−7	−24	8
National Freight Corporation	−22	−39	31
BSC (iron and steel)	−26	−26	−2
National and Scottish Bus Groups	−33	−27	−5
NCB collieries	−36	−28	−7
Manufacturing, all industries	10	−12	28
Manufacturing, excluding BSC (1968–78) and BL (1973–78)	12	−12	30

Source: Richard Pryke, *The Nationalised Industries: Policies and Performance Since 1968* (Oxford: Martin Robertson, 1981), 238.

public enterprise created in 1970 in order to save the nation's rail passenger service by separating it from the U.S. rail freight companies.[77] This initiative has been an unqualified failure. Between 1970 and 1983, the federal government has provided a total of $11 billion in subsidies to Amtrak. The Congressional Budget Office estimates that in 1970 the federal subsidy per passenger mile on Amtrak was $.236, compared to $.002 for commercial aviation and $.001 each for buses and private automobiles.[78]

The U.S. Post Office, another public enterprise, has also come under attack for inefficiency. Low labor productivity is one of the chief criticisms. Many claim that because the costs are simply passed on to consumers, postal employees are too highly paid.[79] The U.S. Post Office also receives a plethora of government subsidies.

---

77. Stuart M. Butler, *Privatizing Federal Spending: A Strategy to Eliminate the Deficit* (New York: Universe Books, 1985), 75.

78. Butler, *Privatizing Federal Spending*, 78.

79. Butler, *Privatizing Federal Spending*, 123–25.

TABLE 2.5.   After Tax Profit/Loss of Public Enterprise

Industrialized Country	Before Depreciation	After Depreciation	Current Subsidies	Gross Margin (Surplus/Deficit) before Subsidies, Interest, and Depreciation
Australia (1974–77)	1.0	0.00	NA	2.2
Canada (1978–80)	1.1	0.40	NA	NA
France (1978–81)	1.2	NA	0.7	1.1
Italy (1978–80)	−0.3	−2.00	NA	NA
Japan (1978–80)	1.0	−0.01	NA	NA
Netherlands (1978)	2.3	0.60	NA	NA
Norway (1977–80)	0.8	NA	NA	NA

Source: R. Peter Short, "The Role of Public Enterprise: An International Statistical Comparison," in *Public Enterprises in Mixed Economies: Some Macroeconomic Aspects,* ed. Robert H. Floyd (Washington, D.C.: International Monetary Fund, 1984).

The evidence is not all negative regarding public ownership in the United States. A number of studies have compared the relative performance of private and public electrical utilities.

Although the results have been somewhat ambiguous, overall they suggest publicly owned utilities are somewhat more efficient than privately held firms. There is a tendency for profits in publicly owned firms to be lower than in the privately owned utility, but this is a function of lower prices.[80] Comparative evaluations of costs in the two groups of utilities suggest that when one controls for the effect of size and excludes hydroelectric generation, municipally owned utilities are more efficient than the privately owned ones.[81]

Conclusion

This chapter has outlined the economic, social, and political benefits that help account for state ownership of industry. It has also suggested why public enterprises are likely to underperform private firms. Finally, the chapter presents empirical data comparing the performance of public and private enterprise. With only a few exceptions, the evidence suggests that public enterprises, from a strictly economic perspective, perform less well than private

80. Robert A. Meyer, "Publicly Owned Versus Privately Owned Utilities: A Policy Choice," *Review of Economics and Statistics* 57 (1975): 391–99.

81. James A. Yunkers, "Economic Performance of Public and Private Enterprise: The Case of U.S. Electric Utilities," *Journal of Economics and Business* 28 (1975): 60–67; Leland G. Neuberg, "Two Issues in the Municipal Ownership of Electric Power Distribution Systems," *Bell Journal of Economics* 8 (1977): 303–23.

firms: their costs are higher, their prices are lower, and their profits are slimmer. Yet, the issue of public ownership is somewhat more complex than these sweeping conclusions might lead us to believe. There are a number of cases in which public ownership appears to equal, if not exceed, the performance of the private sector. In the case of telephony, there are some publicly owned telcos, such as Televerket in Sweden, that perform just as well, on a number of measures, as private telcos in the United States, and certainly much better than many of the other publicly owned telcos in Europe. These exceptions suggest that not all public enterprises perform similarly and that we are premature in treating all government ownership as a second best alternative to the private sector. They raise the possibility that something other than ownership influences the performance levels of public and private enterprises. The next chapter develops the argument that, in addition to ownership, political control is an important explanation for variation in the performance levels of private and state-owned firms.

CHAPTER 3

Political Control and Public Enterprise Performance

Typically, the impact of ownership on performance has been cast in simple dichotomous terms: private entities perform better than publicly owned firms.[1] This explanation is not very useful because it ignores the considerable variation in the performance of public enterprises. Political control is proposed as an alternative explanation. To some extent it is equivalent to ownership, in that state-owned firms are more likely to face political pressures. But, as this chapter points out, there is a continuum of political control anchored on one end by private entities that face limited political constraints and certain state-owned firms on the other that are heavily influenced by political pressures. Between these extremes fall a number of different public and private entities that are subject to varying degrees of political constraints.

This chapter explores the operationalization of political control and its hypothesized impact on economic performance. First, a scheme is developed for measuring variations in political control. I then demonstrate that political control over public enterprises varies from case to case and suggest how this variation affects economic performance. The chapter concludes by suggesting that the relationship between political control and performance may vary depending upon levels of economic development or on industry type (i.e., certain industries are more sensitive to political control than others).

There are two distinct perspectives on the question of political control. On the one hand, some argue that subjecting corporate management to increasing levels of political control inhibits economic performance. Firms subject to strict governmental control are more responsive to political pressures from special interest groups, consumers, suppliers, employees, political patronage seekers, etc. The more autonomous the entity, the less important are these political pressures in corporate decision making. Aharoni notes that

. . . the more financially independent these firms are, the more their operations are inconspicuous or incomprehensible to the general public,

---

1. The argument developed here specifically focuses on *economic* performance, i.e., the degree to which goods and services are efficiently produced. There are, of course, other aspects of performance that could be addressed, such as concerns with equity.

the more they control information and the more they are able to recruit professional managers—better and more permanent than the ministry—the less are the differences between them and investor-owned firms. Ministries are not always strong enough to impose policies on reluctant SOEs [state-owned enterprises], and their managers may enjoy more autonomy than officially permitted.[2]

Aharoni's argument is supported by a much earlier report of the *Liberal Industrial Inquiry* of 1928 in the United Kingdom. The committee commented on the problems associated with high levels of political control.

> . . . [W]e are inclined to think that it would have been better if in the first instance the post office, telephones and telegraphs had been in the hands of an ad hoc administrative body detached from the central administration. There are weighty arguments for requiring government undertakings to be conducted in a form analogous to that of joint-stock companies, the capital of which is owned and the directors appointed by the state. This is the present method of administering, for example, the Belgian and German railways and the German post office. Amongst its advantages are a greater detachment from politics and from political influence.[3]

On the other hand, some argue that political control over public enterprise management promotes economic efficiency. Public interest theorists contend that elected officials encourage management practices consistent with the overall interest of society, including economic efficiency. The early proponents of public ownership, such as Labor Minister Lord Morrison of Lambeth, believed that political oversight would ensure that state-owned firms both supplied public goods and operated like an efficient privately owned entity.[4]

Without political oversight, it is argued, bureaucrats will pursue their own personal interests at the expense of the "public interest." As Niskanen has pointed out, the two most likely priorities for public sector managers will be the size of their departments, or enterprises in this case, and the salaries

2. Yair Aharoni, *The Evolution and Management of State Owned Enterprises* (Cambridge: Ballinger, 1986), 71.

3. Cited in C. Ashley and R. G. H. Smails, *Canadian Crown Corporations: Some Aspects of Their Administration and Control* (Toronto: Macmillan Co. of Canada, 1965), 8.

4. John Vickers and George Yarrow, "Privatization in Britain," paper presented at the conference on Privatization in Britain and North America sponsored by the Bradley Policy Research Center, University of Rochester, Washington, D.C., 1987, 151; Ashley and Smails, *Canadian Crown Corporations*, 1.

and perquisites they can accumulate.[5] Unless subjected to the careful scrutiny of political officials, economic efficiency will take second place to the self-interested goals of public sector managers.

In his case study of the French nationalized oil companies, Feigenbaum alerts us to the costs of managerial autonomy for public enterprises.[6] He argues that the large multinational state enterprises, exemplified by national oil firms such as Elf-Aquitaine and ENI, are under little pressure to make "efficient" economic decisions (for example, in terms of pricing and investment behavior) because of the international oligopolistic nature of the industry. As a result, when management is subject to only a minimal amount of political oversight and is given the general directive to maximize profits, we should not expect business decisions that necessarily are in the public interest. In fact, Feigenbaum makes the point that the pricing and investment decisions by French oil companies were decidedly not in the overall interest of the French economy or French consumers. More careful political oversight, he contends, would promote greater economic efficiency. There is some evidence that when political control over management is tightened, economic performance improves. Vickers and Yarrow argue that, in the United Kingdom, the government's decision to impose stricter financial controls on public enterprises in the late 1970s and 1980s had beneficial effects on performance.[7] Ironically, many of France's major corporations performed better after their nationalization in 1982 than they had earlier under private ownership. As the *Financial Times* pointed out, "Of the seven nationalised industrial groups, only one made a profit in 1982; in 1985, only one is likely to have shown a loss."[8] The increased political scrutiny brought on by nationalization under the Socialist government did not inhibit efforts by public sector management to improve its economic performance.

Political Control Varies

Unfortunately, there is no readily available metric indicating the extent of political control over public enterprises. Most distinctions are relatively imprecise. But in order to test propositions regarding political control and performance, it is imperative to impose some precision on the definition and measurement of the independent variable. I propose an ordinal measure that has

---

5. W. A. Niskanen, *Bureaucracy and Representative Government* (Chicago: Aldine-Atherton, 1971).

6. Harvey B. Feigenbaum, *The Politics of Public Enterprise Oil and the French State* (Princeton: Princeton University Press, 1985).

7. Vickers and Yarrow, "Privatization in Britain," 151.

8. "Privatisation à la française," *Financial Times*, 14 April 1986, 48.

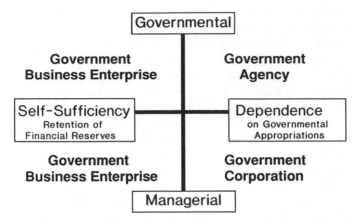

Fig. 3.1. Discretionary authority. (Adapted from John Freeman, "The Politics of Mixed Economics," University of Minnesota, photocopy.)

five distinct categories: private, semiprivate, government business enterprise, government corporation, and government agency. Political control increases as we move from the private to the government agency end of the scale.

The least ambiguous distinction between firms is whether they are publicly or privately owned. AT&T, for example, is 100 percent owned by private shareholders, while the German Bundespost is entirely owned by the state. Even for privately owned firms, the picture is complex. A number of nominally private European telephone companies, for example, are partially owned by their government: the Spanish government has a 30 percent interest in Telefonica, and the British government owns 49 percent of British Telecom. Even with a minority interest, government can frequently exercise effective control.[9] It is therefore appropriate to differentiate between the *privately* and the *semiprivately* owned firm. Private firms are entirely owned by private shareholders. Semiprivately owned enterprises are only partially in the hands of private investors with the state retaining a significant ownership.

Publicly owned firms are also quite heterogeneous. John Freeman suggests a classification scheme that I adopt here and present in figure 3.1.[10] This measure indicates the extent to which management in publicly owned enterprises enjoys decision-making autonomy and is financially independent of government authorities.

9. Aidan Vining and Robert Botterell, "An Overview of the Origins, Growth, Size and Functions of Provincial Crown Corporations," in *Crown Corporations in Canada: The Calculus of Instrument Choice*, ed. M. J. Trebilcock and J. R. S. Prichard (Toronto: Butterworth, 1980), 5.

10. See John Freeman, "The Politics of Mixed Economics," unpublished manuscript.

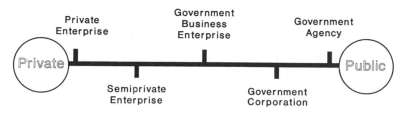

Fig. 3.2.   Private-public continuum

State-owned enterprises with the least autonomy are those categorized as *government agencies;* management decisions are subject to governmental approval, and the firms are entirely dependent upon government appropriations for financing. As examples, Van der Bellen cites the Federal Departmental Agencies in Austria that are integrated within their supervisory ministries and exercise little autonomy (examples include the Austrian PTT and the Federal Railways).[11] *Government corporations* are somewhat more autonomous because their management has a much freer hand in setting policy. These entities have a legal status that distinguishes them from government agencies. Typically, they have their own board of directors, a budget independent of the general governmental budget, and often issue shares, although the government is typically the exclusive shareholder. While management decisions are not subject to direct governmental control, the financing of capital and operational expenditures receives close political scrutiny.

Government enterprises are those publicly owned entities that are financially self-sufficient. For example, they can retain profits for future investment (rather than turning them over to the treasury); typically they are also authorized to raise funds on the open capital markets. While legally subject to political oversight, in practice the government interferes only minimally in their activities. Examples would be the German holding company, Veba, Air Canada, Canadian National Railways, Elf-Aquitaine of France, and British Petroleum.

These five categories can be arrayed on a private-public continuum that represents the degree of managerial independence from governmental control over decision making (see fig. 3.2). In general, management in private enterprises are least restrained by governmental control over decision making and finances. At the other extreme are government agencies that have little financial and managerial independence of governmental authorities. The remaining

---

11. Alexander Van der Bellen,"The Control of Public Enterprises: The Case of Austria," *Annals of Public and Cooperative Economy* 52 (1981): 73–100.

three categories—semiprivate, government business enterprise, and government corporation—fall between these two extremes.

Private-Public Categorization of Telcos

In table 3.1, twenty-three telcos from the OECD countries are grouped by the five categories defined previously. Unless otherwise noted, the categorization covers the period from 1964 to 1986. Assignment to categories is based on secondary materials and information provided by telco officials.[12]

The United States is the only OECD country where telecommunications services are provided primarily by completely private telcos. Prior to 1984, the largest provider was AT&T. Since then the entity has been split up into a long-distance carrier, AT&T, and seven regional Bell Holding Companies— all of which have remained in the hands of private shareholders. The smaller independent carriers, such as GTE and United Telephone, are also private firms.

Six countries fall in the *semiprivate* category. The British and Japanese governments have recently partially sold off their interest in the telephone service provider, although both governments have retained significant controlling interest. Telefonica of Spain has always had important participation by private shareholders—from its founding in 1924 until its nationalization in 1945, it was entirely private. The Spanish government presently controls 30 percent of its capital.

In some countries, public and private entities coexist, serving different regions or communities within the country. Finnish telephone service is provided by the government-owned PTT and by local telephone companies that are privately or cooperatively (i.e., subscriber) owned. Similarly in Denmark, telecommunication concessions are divided between private and state enterprises. In Canada, regional telco monopolies have both public and private shareholders: the largest, Bell Canada, is private, as is the smaller BC Tel. On the other hand, the provincial telephone companies of Newfoundland, Manitoba, Alberta, and Saskatchewan are publicly owned.[13] For the purpose of this analysis these countries are categorized in the semiprivate category because political constraints, in circumstances where public and private coexist, will be similar to those where government shares ownership of a single entity

---

12. Organization for Economic Cooperation and Development, *Changing Market Structures in Telecommunications* (Paris: OECD, 1984); Organization for Economic Cooperation and Development, *Trends of Change in Telecommunications Policy* (Paris: OECD, 1987); Logica, *Communications in Europe—The Changing Environment* (London: Logica, 1983).

13. The Alberta government has recently announced plans to privatize its provincial telephone company in late 1990 and early 1991.

TABLE 3.1.   Classification of Telcos, 1964–86

Government Agency	Government Corporation	Government Enterprise	Semiprivate Enterprise	Private Enterprise
France	Belgium	Sweden	Spain	United States
United Kingdom	W. Germany	Japan	Finland	
(to 1981)	United Kingdom	Italy	United Kingdom	
Ireland	(1981–84)	Greece	(1985–)	
Switzerland		Australia	Canada	
Turkey		(1975–)	Denmark	
Austria		Portugal	Japan (1986–)	
Australia				
Netherlands				
Norway				
New Zealand				
Iceland				

with private investors. The existence of private entities—like the presence of private shareholders—is likely to moderate political oversight. Because of the ease with which consumers and taxpayers can make comparisons between private and public firms, governments are somewhat constrained in the political demands they can place on state-owned telcos. At the same time, such coexistence of public and private will not generate the same degree of independence of these pressures that we are likely to see in the case where service is primarily provided by private entities.

The *government enterprise* category comprises the telcos of Sweden, Japan (prior to the 1986 privatization), Greece, Australia (post-1975), Portugal, and Italy. These are essentially run as private business enterprises with a considerable degree of autonomy from elected officials. In the case of Televerket of Sweden, for example, the company is headed by an independent board appointed by the government. It consists of representatives of the business and scientific communities as well as the political parties. Each year Televerket submits a three-year program to the government for approval.[14] This submission outlines in very general terms the goals and activities of Televerket and includes "a general description of Televerket's activities during the three year period, a plan for investments and how they should be financed, goals for service, productivity, and rate of return."[15] Within this framework, the management of Televerket has considerable leeway in selecting the means for financing its plans. Management generates its own working capital and may borrow freely on capital markets.

14. Organization for Economic Cooperation and Development, *Trends of Change*, 311.
15. Organization for Economic Cooperation and Development, *Trends of Change*, 311.

In contrast to the government enterprise, the *government corporation* is subject to greater degrees of political control. Although government corporations have their own legal status, important budgetary, investment, and financial decisions are often subject to legislative approval. A case in point is the Belgian Régie des Télégraphes et Téléphones (RTT). The Régie is a public corporation under the direct authority of the Ministry (or Secretary) of State. Its budget, which must be approved by Parliament, is funded out of operating income or by borrowing, which also requires parliamentary authorization. Like any other public agency, the RTT is subject to the control of a number of governmental bodies, including the Ministries of the Budget, Finance, and Civil Service.[16]

The telcos of France and Ireland (prior to 1984), Switzerland, Turkey, Austria, Australia (pre-1975), Netherlands, Norway, New Zealand, Iceland, and the United Kingdom (prior to 1981) belong in the *government agency* category. These telcos have no formal independence of the government and no independent legal status; rather, they are departments under the direct authority of a ministry. Consequently, these entities have no independent budgetary authority. Moreover, they typically have no authority to set tariffs or raise funds on open markets. In Ireland, for example, the telephone monopoly (prior to 1984) was the responsibility of the Department of Posts and Telegraphs. This entity had no independence of political control: its budget was subsumed within that of the Ministry for Posts and Telegraph; all decisions relating to tariffs, services, investments, and development had to be approved by the Minister. In 1984, administration of the telecommunications service was transferred to a new state-owned company, Telecom Eireann, which is subject to much less political control.

This five-category scheme for grouping public and private enterprise illustrates two important aspects of the theoretical argument developed earlier: (1) the degree of political control exercised over management varies, and (2) firms can be grouped according to the degree of this political oversight. While this categorization provides important insights into the performance of public versus private firms, to facilitate the data analysis in the next chapter, this categorization is collapsed into two categories.

Variation in Political Control and Performance

Independence of governmental control should reduce the demands made on public enterprises by narrow political interests (e.g., patronage seekers, employees, consumers, and suppliers). The political agenda of the elected government—such as countercyclical macroeconomic policies, employment

---

16. Organization for Economic Cooperation and Development, *Trends of Change*, 188.

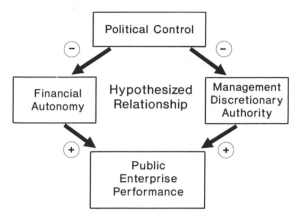

Fig. 3.3.   Political control and economic performance

concerns, trade-related issues, etc.—should also weigh less heavily on decision making by the more autonomous entities. Alternatively, the political
objectives should most heavily affect firms at the public end of the continuum.

Figure 3.3 sketches the hypothesized link between political control and
performance. Two facets of corporate decision making are particularly sensitive to this variable: raising capital and management discretionary authority.
As political control increases, management's ability to raise capital and define
corporate strategy is seriously compromised. Without this autonomy, the *economic* performance of the entity suffers: costs mount, profits decline, and
government subsidies become increasingly necessary.[17] Aharoni cites examples from the developing economies indicating that "in countries in which
SOEs [state-owned enterprises] operate under control structures with less
governmental interference, the financial results were much better."[18] This
section reviews how public corporations in general, and telcos in particular,
vary on these two dimensions and how this variation affects the economic
performance of public enterprises.

Finances

Revenues are the sine qua non of the corporation; a portion is allocated to
operating costs, with the balance typically divided between capital invest-

---

17. R. Kent Weaver, *The Politics of Industrial Change: Railway Policy in North America*
(Washington, D.C.: The Brookings Institution), 168 and 278; Aharoni, *Evolution and Management*, 390.

18. Aharoni, *Evolution and Management*, 189.

ments and profits (dividends or retained earnings). In the short term, firms have a limited number of options available for raising revenues: they can increase the price of their products or services, they can raise funds on the equity markets, or they can borrow money. Without control over the raising and spending of revenues, management's ability to shape corporate strategy is very seriously compromised, and political priorities are likely to override any commercial considerations.[19]

The setting of tariffs and borrowing of funds illustrate the impact of political pressures on the finances of public enterprise.

Tariffs. Obviously, tariffs play a critical role in providing the firm with revenues that cover operating costs and fund capital expenditures. Although these revenue imperatives are universal, firms at the two ends of the private-public continuum respond to very different price-setting cues. At the private end, pricing is dictated by industry demand and the firm's costs. But for firms at the other end of the spectrum, political considerations are likely to be just as, if not more, important than economic factors.[20]

Because tariffs are a sensitive political issue, the more they are subject to government control, the greater the likelihood that public enterprise management will respond to political, as opposed to economic, cues in setting them. One reason is very straightforward: consumers of goods and services produced by state enterprises are also voters, and they may react to higher prices by punishing incumbents at election time.[21]

For the publicly owned sector with large numbers of consumers, such as urban transit, telephone service, electricity, and health insurance, the political fallout from a price increase or service reduction could be very damaging. An interesting case in point is the 1981 decision by the Liberal government in Canada to eliminate one-fifth of Via Rail service—the Crown corporation responsible for passenger train transportation. The decision proved highly unpopular with the electorate and is cited as one of the contributing factors to the government's 1984 electoral defeat.[22] Another Crown corporation, Canadian National Railways, confronted similar political opposition when it attempted to reduce its Newfoundland service.[23] More recently, the New Democratic government in the Canadian province of Manitoba suffered a humiliating defeat primarily, according to public opinion surveys, because the state-owned automobile insurance company hiked premiums just prior to the

---

19. Jeanne Kirk Laux and Maureen Appel Molot, *State Capitalism, Public Enterprises in Canada* (Ithaca, N.Y.: Cornell University Press, 1988), 99.

20. Sam Peltzman, "Pricing in Public and Private Enterprises: Electric Utilities in the United States," *Journal of Law and Economics* 14 (April 1971): 109–47.

21. Aharoni, *Evolution and Management*, 194.

22. Weaver, *Politics of Industrial Change*, 263.

23. Weaver, *Politics of Industrial Change*, 189.

election.[24] The political obstacles to tariff increases or service reductions are likely to be particularly intense during periods immediately preceding elections.

Public enterprises are a potential instrument for controlling inflation. There is considerable evidence indicating that incumbent governments suffer at the polls as a result of rising inflation or declining real income.[25] Since public enterprises account for a significant proportion of GNP in many developed Western countries, they are often enlisted in efforts to dampen inflationary trends.

A number of British studies have documented government efforts to control inflation by manipulating public enterprise prices. Millward compares price and wage settlements in public and private British firms, concluding that price setting in public enterprises is countercyclical while the evidence is much less convincing regarding wage settlements.[26] In the early 1970s when the United Kingdom was experiencing high rates of inflation, the Heath government severely restricted price increases by public enterprises. Pryke points out that "at the beginning of 1973 statutory price control was established and, although this applied to industry as a whole, the nationalized industries were a special case because they were not permitted to raise their prices when trading at a loss because of direct restraint by government."[27]

Clearly the temptation is strong for governments to pressure public enterprise management into maintaining low tariffs. As a result, public enterprises are often unable to raise sufficient revenues to cover their operating and capital investment costs. This, in turn, inhibits capital spending and as a result restricts the development of the country's telecommunication infrastructure. The French telco faced this problem throughout much of the post–World War II period.[28]

Second, political constraints also affect the monopolist's ability to practice price discrimination that involves setting prices according to certain variations in cost and demand characteristics of a good or service. For example, the price of a good can vary because of differences in the cost of providing it. The price of fresh vegetables is higher in certain communities simply because the

---

24. "Canadians to Choose Those They Dislike Least," *Wall Street Journal*, 13 May 1988, 15.

25. Douglas A. Hibbs, *The American Political Economy: Macroeconomics and Electoral Politics in the United States* (Cambridge, Mass: Harvard University Press, 1987); Douglas A. Hibbs, *The Political Economy of Industrial Democracies* (Cambridge, Mass.: Harvard University Press, 1987); Edward Tufte, *Political Control of the Economy* (Princeton, N.J.: Princeton University Press, 1978).

26. Robert Millward, "Price Restraint, Anti-Inflation Policy and Public and Private Industry in the United Kingdom, 1949–1973," *Economic Journal* 86 (June 1976): 226–42.

27. Richard Pryke, *The Nationalised Industries: Policies and Performance Since 1968* (Oxford: Robertson, 1981), 260.

28. L. J. Libois, *Genèse et Croissance des Télécommunications* (Paris: Masson, 1983).

transportation costs are higher. Certain service providers charge peak-load prices when demand levels are very high. This is justified by the extra costs incurred in order to satisfy the increased demand. But pricing strategies that discriminate among various classes of consumers or regions of the country are politically unpopular and, therefore, are avoided by public enterprises.

Historically, governments have strongly promoted universal access to residential telephone service at uniform prices. As a result, telcos have had little flexibility in pricing residential services. They could not, for example, discriminate between rural and urban telephone subscribers even though service in the less densely populated communities is more costly to provide. Governments have also imposed tariffs that subsidized residential subscribers at the cost of business users. These and similar political priorities represent important constraints on telco pricing strategies. More flexibility in designing tariffs could enhance telco revenues. For example, by increasing rates on basic residential service (which is relatively inelastic) and by reducing tariffs for long-distance service (which is considerably more elastic), telcos could raise overall revenues.

From a social perspective, these constraints on pricing might be highly laudable. Nonetheless, it is important to note that they have certain economic costs: they can reduce the amount of funds available for reinvestment in the telecommunications infrastructure. In the longer run, this underinvestment could compromise the ultimate social goal of high quality universal telephone service.

Borrowing. The endpoints of the private-public continuum also distinguish the constraints placed on the borrowing activities of telcos. At the private end, the firm's ability to borrow and its costs of borrowing are determined by the market's evaluation of the company's creditworthiness. Well-managed, profitable firms with solid, long-term prospects will borrow funds more cheaply than firms that are less well managed, are less profitable, and have questionable long-term prospects.

For firms in the public sector, these economic constraints have little relevance to the firm's cost of borrowing. Funds are typically borrowed on very attractive terms because the notes are guaranteed by the state. Political factors replace the market as a constraint on borrowing activities, and they become increasingly important as we move toward the public end of the continuum.

Two political factors play a vital role in shaping borrowing authorizations. First, borrowing by publicly owned enterprises contributes to overall government debt.[29] Governments are concerned about the magnitude of the

---

29. Paul N. Courant, "Fiscal Policy and European Economic Growth," in Robert Z. Lawrence and Charles L. Schultze, eds., *Barriers to European Growth: A Transatlantic View* (Washington, D.C.: Brookings Institution, 1987).

government debt because of its fiscal and political implications. Accordingly, many governments place tight controls on the borrowing activities of public corporations in an attempt to reduce the public deficit.[30] In the United Kingdom, for example, prior to privatization, British Telecom's borrowing activities were considered part of the overall Public Sector Borrowing Requirement (PSBR), and BT could not raise funds without Treasury authorization. Faced with a dangerously high level of government debt, British governments seriously restricted the borrowing of state enterprises in the 1970s. One of the principal reasons for Margaret Thatcher's privatization of British Telecom and other state-owned firms was the desire to free them of the restrictions imposed by the PSBR.[31]

In a similar manner, the borrowing activities of the German Bundespost are reviewed by a government committee that regulates the financing requirements of all nationalized industries. But, in contrast to the BT case, the Bundespost has borrowed extensively on the open market in the last couple of decades. One reason these authorizations differ is that, during the 1970s and early 1980s, the U.K. government had significantly higher borrowing requirements than its German counterpart. Unlike Germany, where government debt was comparatively modest (this has changed more recently), the U.K. government faced serious budgetary difficulties. As a result, British Telecom's borrowing authorizations have been much more restricted than those of the German Bundespost. Because the ability of government enterprises to borrow funds is closely tied to the fiscal priorities of the government, the economic merits of their expenditure plans often are of secondary importance.

Second, to the extent that government officials favor the borrowing demands of one public enterprise over others, the reasons are more likely to be political than economic. As a result, public enterprises commanding greater political resources will receive more generous borrowing authority. The size of a firm's work force represents one political advantage. Political authorities arc more responsive to a firm with a large work force than to a much more capital-intensive firm with fewer employees, regardless of the economic merits of their respective requests.[32] Other political considerations include support from regions where factories are located, the threat of closures and mass layoffs, and appeals to national security. Public enterprises that simply cannot mount the lobbying effort necessary to compete with politically more powerful candidates are disadvantaged in their efforts to raise capital, regardless of the merits of their requests.

30. Aharoni, *Evolution and Management*, 318.

31. Yarrow and Vickers, "Privatization in Britain," 11–13.

32. George Stigler, "The Theory of Economic Regulation," *Bell Journal of Economics and Management Science* 2 (Spring 1971): 3–21.

Management Discretionary Authority

Aside from overseeing finances, governments impose varying degrees of control over the day-to-day management decisions within public corporations.[33] Once again, as we move from the private to the public extremes of the continuum, political influences play an increasing role in shaping management behavior. Five areas of management decision making are examined in this section: purchasing, revenues and expenditures, research and development, employment, and service offerings.

Purchasing. Because the purchasing decisions of large corporations can affect national economies, government intervention is common. At least in the short term, the decision by large corporations to purchase goods manufactured domestically can contribute to job creation, economic growth, and possibly exports (by underwriting initial development costs and providing scale economies). Accordingly, governments have encouraged their public enterprises to "buy national" when at all possible. Examples of this practice span virtually all of the nationalized industries: British Steel and the Central Electricity Generating Board are required to purchase British coal, the SNCF in France only purchases major rail equipment from French manufacturers, and the Airbus partnership subcontracts primarily to European suppliers.

This practice has been well refined by the telecommunications industry where most national telcos have adopted policies that favor domestic manufacturing industries. In order to protect jobs and to promote domestic high technology industry, telcos are encouraged to purchase equipment such as central office switches and customer premises equipment from domestic manufacturers whenever feasible. Governments have also tolerated, if not promoted, product standards that handicap foreign manufacturers and, therefore, constitute effective import barriers. In Europe, for example, this practice has left the market for telecommunications products fragmented because each of the major nations has its own protected manufacturer of telecommunications equipment.[34]

"Buy national" policies are practiced more frequently by public rather than private enterprises. Because national suppliers benefit from such arrangements, they are generally opposed to the privatization of public enterprises. Once privatized, these entities are less reliable instruments of government industrial policy. Recognizing this fact, British suppliers of central office switching equipment expressed "serious reservations" concerning BT's priva-

---

33. Aharoni, *Evolution and Management*, 299.

34. European Community, *Towards a Dynamic European Economy: Green Paper on the Development of the Common Market for Telecommunications Services and Equipment* (Brussels: Commission for the European Communities, 1987).

tization. With government exercising less control over BT purchasing, these protected suppliers were concerned that privatization would mean reduced sales.

Revenues and Expenditures. Governments take a keen interest in the revenues and expenditures of public enterprises because of their public policy implications. At the public extreme of the spectrum, governments can determine what portion of revenues are retained (the balance being turned over to general revenues) and how they are spent. Government agencies are the most vulnerable to arbitrary political decisions regarding retained earnings and capital investments. A government agency such as France Telecom has little autonomy concerning revenues. For example, during the early 1980s, the Minister of Industry shifted profits from France Telecom's telecommunications activities to underwrite government subsidies for the electronics industry.[35] Somewhat more flexible is the government corporation. The German Bundespost is a case in point: it exercises more control over its revenues and their expenditures but nonetheless is expected to turn 10 percent of its annual gross revenues over to the federal government. A government business enterprise like Swedish Televerket is similar to the private firm in that it enjoys almost total control over its revenues and expenditures. Finally, private firms are the least subject to political pressures or overtures.

On the expenditure side, governments can have a very complex agenda. Motivated by industrial policy considerations such as accelerating the development of certain industries or the promotion of exports, governments often impose stringent restrictions on the implementation of investment projects. Governments may insist that only certain contractors and manufacturers be considered for particular projects, and even the location of investments is often determined by political as opposed to economic criteria.

Reelection considerations affect the timing and location of investment projects. Governments often attempt to reap political advantage from large capital investment projects by locating them in districts where the political payoffs are substantial and by timing them to coincide with important electoral campaigns.[36]

Once again, the degree to which government is able to impose these preferences on public enterprise management varies. At the private end of the spectrum, political pressures have less influence on capital investment decisions. As a result, investment decisions are more likely to be based on profitability as opposed to political priorities.

---

35. Jacques Darmon, *Le Grand Dérangement: La Guerre du Téléphone* (Paris: J. C. Lattes, 1986), 136.

36. Raymond Duch, "The Politics of Investment by the Nationalized Sector," *Western Political Quarterly* 43 (June 1990): 245–65.

Research and Development. Private firms have much greater control over their research and development agenda than is the case with public enterprises. Threatening this independence are the research priorities governments attempt to impose on industry. This is evident from the variety of government programs supporting research in such high technology industries as semiconductors, space, aeronautics, and telecommunications.[37]

Firms at the public end of the spectrum typically have little choice but to follow the research and development priorities established by government officials. Public enterprises are often active participants in the decision to promote a particular area of research, and as a result their participation is voluntary and enthusiastic. But this is not always the case. Occasionally, they are forced to participate; on other occasions, they voluntarily cooperate but do not have the option of abandoning projects once they lose their commercial attraction.

In a number of different industries, the research and development priorities of public enterprise are virtually dictated by political considerations. A recent example is government support for the establishment of Direct Broadcast Satellite (DBS) service in Europe. Governments encouraged their telcos to proceed with development and implementation with little consideration of market demand or economic feasibility. As Tydeman and Kelm pointed out:

> The reasons for the national pushes toward DBS are many and varied. France is seeking technological superiority in the aerospace industry, West Germany is aware of the industrial implications and is a willing copartner in the Franco-German industrial development, the United Kingdom wanted to introduce additional competition as well as stimulate industry, and Ireland and Luxembourg could see economic implications if a major DBS or satellite project was coordinated from their respective countries.[38]

Political factors relating to DBS service outweighed any considerations of the economic burden that such an initiative might have on the public enterprises that would implement the policy. The economic feasibility of the technology promoted by the French and German governments (high-powered satellites with a small number of transponders) is dubious. This questionable feasibility earned it the active opposition of France Telecom. But the govern-

---

37. Giovanni Dosi, "Semiconductors: Europe's Precarious Survival in High Technology," in Geoffrey Shepherd, François Duchene, and Christopher Saunders, eds., *Europe's Industries: Public and Private Strategies for Change* (Ithaca, N.Y.: Cornell University Press, 1983), 228.

38. John Tydeman and Ellen Jakes Kelm, *New Media in Europe: Satellites, Cable, VCRs and Videotex* (London: McGraw-Hill, 1986), 103.

ment's research and development agenda prevailed over the reservations voiced by critics. In contrast, private entities in the United States that originally expressed an interest in DBS have all but abandoned the technology today. Unlike their state-owned counterparts, they were under no political obligation to proceed with its development.

A similar situation has evolved in the European civil aeronautics industry. Four major European nations—the United Kingdom, Germany, France, and Spain—have cooperated in a program to promote the development and manufacture of commercial aircraft that could compete with those marketed by leading U.S. firms such as Boeing and McDonnell Douglas. Although the Airbus venture, as it is called, remains unprofitable today, the participation of Aérospatiale, Messerschmitt, and Casa is ensured because they are either entirely or partially state-owned.[39] British Aerospace, the only private entity in the consortium, remains active because of the substantial subsidies it receives from the U.K. government.[40]

Private firms have more flexibility. They are freer to ignore the research and development priorities established by government planners. That is not to say that they exercise this option very frequently. Because governments offer attractive incentives for participation, even private firms tend to support government research priorities. But their involvement is contingent upon the government offering incentives that make such participation commercially attractive (British Aerospace's participation in the Airbus venture is a case in point). It is reasonable to conclude that private European firms such as Olivetti, Siemens, Philips, and British Aerospace have somewhat more flexibility in setting their research and development agenda than their public counterparts such as Aérospatiale, Italtel, Thomson, and Rhone-Poulenc.

Research and development is a very important strategic expenditure. A firm's ability to compete in world markets, including its revenues and profits, are dependent upon the freedom to manage and deploy these assets. Because public firms tend to lack flexibility in this regard, their research expenditures are less productive, their overall costs are higher, and they are less competitive vis-à-vis private firms that are not similarly burdened.

Employment. A firm's ability to shape employment policies decreases as we move toward the public end of the spectrum. In virtually all countries, employment is a very sensitive political issue. As a result, the more closely a firm is controlled by government, the less flexibility management enjoys in

---

39. The German federal government recently divested itself of much of its interest in Messerschmitt. One of the important issues in the negotiations was the liability that Messerschmitt would assume regarding its participation in the Airbus venture.

40. "Airbus Partners Adopt Proposals for Cutting Costs," *Financial Times* (London), 13 April 1988.

hiring and firing. Particularly in periods of high unemployment, governments are likely to oppose large-scale layoffs. In addition, the employees of many public enterprises are often granted civil service status that imposes further rigidity on labor relations. Compared to the private sector, civil servants are typically awarded more generous benefits (health insurance, retirement benefits, and paid vacation, for example), are governed by policies that favor seniority as opposed to merit in promotions, and face stricter tenure rules that make it difficult to dismiss workers. As a result, the labor costs of firms at the public end of the continuum tend to be significantly higher.

Service Offerings. Although all firms, public or private, are subject to government regulation, public firms face a degree of detailed supervision that is unparalleled in private firms. Governments expect service offerings of public enterprises to address social and political priorities. This is frequently the case with utilities such as water, electricity, urban transportation, and telephone service. The government can insist, for example, that these services be made available to all citizens wishing to subscribe, regardless of the costs involved. They may even take an active role in drawing up the minute details of service provision, suggesting what routes should be served by the nationalized railroads or setting guidelines for the programming offered by state-owned broadcasters.

This section has shown in considerable detail why variations along the private-public continuum might affect the economic performance of firms in general and the telcos in particular. First, private firms have more control over the raising of revenues, spending, and corporate strategy than firms at the public extreme of the continuum where political influences play a much greater role. Second, these political constraints compromise the economic performance of the firm because management sacrifices the goals of revenue growth and profit for political priorities imposed by elected officials.

These observations have two important implications for assessing the costs and benefits of public versus private enterprise.

1. The benefits generated by market forces (efficient internal and external allocation of resources) decline as we move from private to pure public ownership.
2. Political constraints are not an effective substitute for market forces— in fact, in the absence of market forces, as political constraints increase, the economic losses associated with public ownership rise.

Some might argue that where the market is not disciplining firms, political oversight is an effective check against poor management. But, as I have discussed earlier, government is a poor taskmaster. Not only is political control an ineffective check on management, but it imposes a wide range of extraneous political goals on management that further undermine economic performance.

Stages of Development

The argument linking political autonomy and economic performance is compelling but the relationship is likely to vary according to the diverse political and economic environments in which firms operate. For example, British Telecom operates under a radically different set of economic constraints than is the case for its counterpart in Botswana, where telephone service is still a luxury.

The argument that the effects of political variables are contingent upon level of development (be it economic, political, or social) has been advanced by many others.[41] For example, Huntington suggests that increasing levels of political participation can have very different implications for democratic stability, depending upon the maturity of a country's political institutions.[42] Some have argued specifically that government-directed industrial policies are likely to be successful in certain sectors of the economy but not in others.[43] Moreover, it has been suggested that some industries, such as utilities and public transportation, operate more efficiently under government ownership than other sectors that are much more sensitive to consumer demands (such as consumer electronics or broadcasting). In short, the relationship of interest, political constraints, and performance will likely vary according to the political and economic context.

It is not feasible to model all of the factors that interact with the political control–performance relationship. We can, though, focus on firms in the telecommunications service industry, which is the empirical focus of the subsequent chapters. The effect of political constraints on the performance of telcos is hypothesized to be neutral or positive at low levels of development and negative as the infrastructure becomes more developed.

---

41. Samuel P. Huntington, *Political Order in Changing Societies* (New Haven, Conn.: Yale University Press, 1968); Gabriel A. Almond and James Coleman, *The Politics of the Developing Areas* (Princeton, N.J.: Princeton University Press, 1960); Frederick Frey, "Communication and Development," in Ithiel de Sola Pool et al., eds., *Handbook of Communication* (Chicago: Rand McNally, 1973); Robert W. Jackman, *Politics and Social Equality: A Comparative Analysis* (New York: Wiley, 1975); J. Roland Pennock, "Political Development, Political Systems, and Political Goods," *World Politics* 18 (1966): 415–34; Ithiel de Sola Pool, "Communications in Totalitarian Societies," in Pool et al., eds., *Handbook of Communication*; Raymond M. Duch and Peter Lemieux, "Politics and the Growth of Communications," unpublished manuscript (1990).

42. Huntington, *Political Order*.

43. John Zysman, *Political Strategies for Industrial Order: State, Market, and Industry in France* (Berkeley, Calif.: University of California Press, 1977).

The development of the industry resembles an S-shaped innovation diffusion curve.[44] These models have three distinct phases: (1) an early stage of high cost and consumer resistance resulting in slow growth rates, (2) a period of low prices, widespread awareness of the service, and consumer acceptance, generating high rates of adoption and an exponential rate of growth, and (3) a saturation stage when growth slows considerably. As figure 3.4 indicates, these three phases capture the developmental trajectory of the telecommunications service industry.

The pre-infrastructural stage is represented by the low penetration, low growth phase of the S-curve depicted in figure 3.4. At this point, development of the telecommunications infrastructure is not a priority. Telephone and telegraph service is available primarily to business subscribers and commercial establishments (such as hotels, restaurants, and retail stores). Penetration rates among residences are comparatively low. As table 3.2 illustrates, most of the developing countries fall into this category. The table compares the distribution of the world's telephones, population, and income between developed and developing countries. Note that the developed countries, with the exception of Europe, account for a higher percentage of the world's telephones than of the world's total Gross National Product (GNP). For example, in 1981 the United States accounted for 37.8 percent of the world's telephones but only 23.4 percent of its GNP. Exactly the opposite is characteristic of developing countries: they account for a higher percentage of the world's GNP than of the world's telephones. Africa has only 0.4 percent of the world's telephones but 2.6 percent of its GNP and 10.2 percent of its population. This suggests that, even after taking into consideration their population and GNP, these countries still have substantially underdeveloped telecommunications systems. They fall in the pre-infrastructural period. Telecommunications in countries falling in the infrastructural and post-infrastructural stages are the subject of this book.

The infrastructural stage represents the accelerated growth phase of the S-curve depicted in figure 3.4. Telephone penetration at the outset is relatively low—in 1964, for example, in a sample of 20 developed nations, the median number of telephones per 100 population was about 20. The United States led with 45 telephones per 100 population. During the 1960s and 1970s (considered the infrastructural period of telecommunications development), developed countries witnessed rapid growth in telephone penetration rates.

The infrastructural stage is a period during which the basic telecommunications infrastructure is built. Growth in diffusion is essentially supply driven, a function of the resources committed by government and the telcos to

---

44. Arthur P. Hurter and Albert M. Rubenstein, "Market Penetration by New Innovations: The Technological Literature," *Technological Forecasting and Social Change* 11 (1978): 197–221.

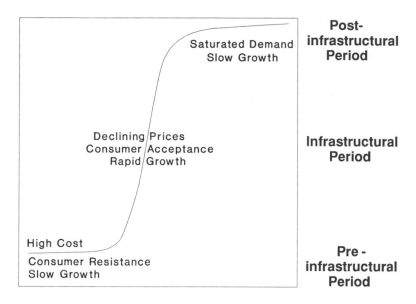

**Post-
infrastructural
Period**

Saturated Demand
Slow Growth

**Infrastructural
Period**

Declining Prices
Consumer Acceptance
Rapid Growth

High Cost
Consumer Resistance
Slow Growth

**Pre -
infrastructural
Period**

Fig. 3.4. S-shaped curve

fund capital expenditures. The industry looks like a traditional utility, providing consumers with a single undifferentiated product (such as electricity, gas, water, and basic transportation).

The telecommunications industry in this infrastructural period had a monopoly structure in virtually every country: government-enforced barriers to entry ensured that telecommunications services were provided by one firm. Needless to say, buyers in such an environment have little power vis-à-vis the monopolist. Their only real avenue of redress is political, because all service providers are either state-owned or state-regulated monopolies. With no threat of competitive entry, very little competition from substitute products, and minimal buyer power, national telcos have been virtually unassailable.

As telephone penetration approaches saturation, the industry moves into a post-infrastructural stage. This is represented by the upper plateau phase of the S-curve in figure 3.4. In this stage the service provider is confronted with challenges to its ironclad monopoly power. First, technological advances introduce new competitors and buyers become more powerful, forcing telcos to be more responsive to their demands.[45] Since they can no longer count on growth fueled by increasing telephone penetration, they must design new

45. Eli Noam, "International Telecommunications in Transition," in *Changing the Rules: Technological Change, International Competition, and Regulations in Communications*, ed. Robert W. Crandall and Kenneth Flamm (Washington, D.C.: Brookings Institution, 1989), 264.

TABLE 3.2. Distribution of the World's Telephones, Population, and Income

	Telephones (1981, millions)	Percentage	Population (1979, millions)	Percentage	GNP (1979, billions of US $)	Percentage
Developed countries						
USA	192	37.8	223	5.3	2,374	23.4
Canada	16	3.2	24	0.6	223	2.2
Japan	58	11.4	116	2.8	1,010	9.9
Israel	1	0.2	4	0.1	16	0.2
Oceania	10	2.0	22	0.5	154	1.5
Europe	190	37.4	788	18.8	4,613	45.4
South Africa	3	0.6	28	0.7	57	0.6
Total	470	92.6	1,205	28.8	8,447	83.2
Developing countries						
Africa	2	0.4	428	10.2	265	2.6
Asia	16	3.1	2,209	52.9	868	8.5
South America	20	3.9	339	8.1	576	5.7
Total	38	7.4	2,976	71.2	1,709	16.8
World						
Total	508	100.0	4,181	100.0	10,156	100.0

Source: Robert J. Saunders, Jeremy J. Warford, and Bjorn Wellenius, *Telecommunications and Economic Development* (Baltimore: Johns Hopkins University Press, 1983).

services and products that increase network usage. Demand for such services and products is much more elastic than was the case for basic telephone service.

Technological advances are making competitive entry an increasing threat to the telcos' effective monopoly.[46] One example is the competition provided by private data networks. Firms offering data processing and data bank services lease private lines from the national telcos in order to serve individual subscribers directly. In effect, this bypasses the national telco's public network, depriving it of revenue. Large international corporations can now lease transponders on satellites or fiber optic networks that permit them

---

46. Alan Baughcum, "Implementations of Technological and Policy Developments for Telecommunications Markets," in *Telecommunications Access and Public Policy*, ed. Alan Baughcum and Gerald R. Faulhaber (Norwood, N.J.: Ablex Publishing Corporation, 1984); Robert R. Bruce, Jeffrey P. Cunard, and Mark D. Director, *The Telecom Mosaic: Assembling the New International Structure* (London: Butterworth, 1988); Marvin Sirbu, "Comparing Alternative Technologies for Local Access," in *Telecommunications Access and Public Policy.*

to create their own private telecommunications systems, bypassing the national telecommunications network.[47]

Countries are now finding themselves in competition with each other in efforts to attract firms with telecommunications-intensive activities. With telecommunications playing an increasingly important role in commerce and business, firms are now locating in areas that offer favorable telecommunications environments. This puts pressure on national telcos to offer services and prices competitive with service providers in other countries.[48]

The demands placed on management are considerably different in these two developmental stages. In the infrastructural stage, a premium is placed on administrative planning. Management is responsible for designing and implementing plans for extensions to the telecommunications network; competition is not a significant threat, nor is the telco much concerned with aggressive marketing.

Because telcos face a different competitive environment in the post-infrastructural stage, a different set of management skills are required. Faced with the threat of competitive entry, management must design new services and tariffs that will appeal to customers and they must become more adept at marketing these services. The premium is no longer merely on planning; in the post-infrastructural period, it is on marketing.

The relationship between political control and performance will be stronger in the post-infrastructural as opposed to the infrastructural period of telecommunications development. Political influences can affect two important telco activities regardless of the developmental stages: (1) the amount of funds available for capital investment projects, and (2) how these funds are allocated. The infrastructural period represented a public works challenge: construct physical plant and connect consumers anxious for access to the public network. In the post-infrastructural stage of development, telco management is faced with a number of new challenges that were not of critical importance in the preceding infrastructural period. Three of these challenges are:

1. responsiveness to emerging competitive threats,
2. responsiveness to new and fast changing technologies, and
3. responsiveness to consumer demands.

As I have pointed out, greater degrees of political control tend to restrict management's flexibility in responding to these new, post-infrastructural

---

47. For a discussion of the implications of these transformations for national telecommunications service providers see Edward Carr, "A Survey of Telecommunications: Netting the Future," *Economist*, 10 March 1990.

48. European Community, *Towards a Dynamic European Economy*.

challenges. Because they lack these qualities, public enterprise performance in the post-infrastructural period is more seriously threatened than it was in the era of structural development. Similarly, Aharoni argues that the " . . . costs of public relative to private operations are liable to be high for activities that are small scale, decentralized, produce nonstandardized products and sell in highly changing or highly competitive markets."[49] Increasingly, the telecommunications services offered in the post-infrastructural period resemble those enumerated by Aharoni.

Conclusion

Public ownership rests on perfectly laudable public policy goals: it addresses the problems of natural monopoly and ensures the provision of certain public goods. Nonetheless, there is a cost associated with public ownership: state enterprises perform less well than firms in the private sector.

The conventional dichotomy between private and public firms, however, is too simplistic given that economic performance varies considerably among state-owned firms. In fact, there are numerous examples of state enterprises that perform just as well, if not better than, those that are privately owned. In the telecommunications sector the example of Televerket of Sweden stands out. In the transportation sector, Canadian National Railways and Lufthansa of Germany are examples of successful public enterprises.[50] The energy sector has a number of well-run and profitable entities such as Elf-Aquitaine of France.[51] There is also some data from the United States suggesting that public utilities have performance levels comparable to those in the private sector.[52] What explains the superior performance of some public enterprises?

I have proposed a political approach to this variation in performance. Public enterprises can be arrayed on a political control scale: at the low end are private and semiprivate entities that exhibit high degrees of financial autonomy and managerial discretionary authority. On the high end of the political control scale, we find declining financial and managerial autonomy as we move from government business enterprises to government corporations, and finally to government agencies. A firm's ranking on this continuum is a much more powerful predictor of performance than a simple private versus public dichotomization. Performance declines as political control rises

---

49. Aharoni, *Evolution and Management*, 32.

50. Douglas W. Caves and Laurits R. Christensen, "The Relative Efficiency of Public and Private Firms in a Competitive Environment: The Case of Canadian Railroads," *Journal of Political Economy* 88 (1980): 958–76.

51. Leslie E. Grayson, *National Oil Companies* (New York: Wiley, 1981).

52. Aharoni, *Evolution and Management*, 196–201.

because financial and management autonomy is compromised and because agency costs increase.

The relationship between political control and performance is not likely to be similar for all national telcos. I hypothesized that the relationship would be stronger in the post-infrastructural phase as opposed to the infrastructural stage of telecommunications development.

CHAPTER 4

An Empirical Analysis of Political Effects

This chapter provides empirical support for the propositions developed in chapters 2 and 3. The results presented here suggest that political control is more powerful than ownership (private vs. public) in explaining variations in performance. Telcos with greater autonomy perform better than those subject to high levels of political control.

Performance is defined as the extent to which national telcos have satisfied consumers' demand for access to basic telecommunications services. Because telephone service is widely accepted as a social good (i.e., universal service), measuring performance in terms of how close a nation approximates such a goal seems relatively noncontroversial.[1] Of course there are other measures of economic performance, in particular profitability and economic efficiency. These measures, unlike universal service, are considerably more controversial because there are serious disagreements over their measurement.[2] Moreover, the cross-national comparison of these measures is very problematic. Even if profitability and cost-accounting data could be obtained from the developed countries, comparative analyses of these data would likely be misleading because governments and government-owned telcos do not employ consistent cross-national accounting methods.

To avoid the problems associated with using noncomparable data and to ensure that the results are based on an adequate number of countries, I have, for the most part, shied away from measures other than the straightforward "access to telephone service." The analyses described below are based on historical data from over 20 OECD nations.

Economic Models of Telecommunications Development

Most models of telecommunications development focus exclusively on socioeconomic determinants, ignoring political factors. One of the earliest ef-

---

1. Measuring the performance of other government-owned entities such as steel manufacturers or oil companies is considerably more controversial.
2. Yair Aharoni, *The Evolution and Management of State Owned Enterprises* (Melrose, Mass: Balinger Publishers, 1968), 161–72.

forts to model the growth of telephones was conducted by Jipp in 1963.[3] In his model of telephones per capita, which included both developed and developing nations, the only independent variable was per capita Gross Domestic Product (GDP). These and similar "wealth" models are able to explain over 90 percent of the variation in telephone penetration.[4] The relative size of the service sector is another important explanatory variable because the service sector (which includes, for example, financial and retail activities) typically has a greater demand for telecommunications services. Countries with larger service sectors should, on balance, have higher telephone penetration rates. Table 4.1 is reproduced from Saunders, Warford, and Wellenius, and provides strong support for this argument.[5]

In their sample of both developed and developing nations, the service sector is without a doubt the largest consumer of telecommunications services. In the United States, for example, this sector is responsible for purchasing over 47 percent of the nation's telecommunications services. The Philippines, where the service sector purchases only 17 percent of the country's telecommunication services, is the only exception. This pattern cannot simply be explained by the magnitude of the service sector because the sample includes a number of developing nations where this sector is relatively small.

Models of telecommunications demand have also incorporated measures of country size. It stands to reason that demand for telecommunications services will be highly correlated with a nation's population. The geographic area of a country may also affect demand for telecommunications services. Countries with a very large geographic expanse and low population densities, such as Canada and Australia, have strong political, economic, and social reasons for promoting an efficient and extensive telecommunications system.[6] We would expect that the area of a country would be positively related to its demand for telecommunications services.

It is customary for economists to incorporate exclusively these socioeconomic variables in their models of the growth of telecommunications demand. This is understandable since these variables—GDP, in particular—account for an overwhelming amount of the variance. Even though the contribution of political variables to explained variance is likely to be relatively

3. A. Jipp, "Wealth of Nations and Telephone Density," *Telecommunications Journal* 30 (July 1963): 199-201.

4. Robert J. Saunders, Jeremy J. Warford, and Bjorn Wellenius, *Telecommunications and Economic Development* (Baltimore: Johns Hopkins University Press, 1983), chap. 4.

5. Saunders, Warford, and Wellenius, *Telecommunications*, chap. 4.

6. Harold Innis, *Empire and Communications* (Oxford: Clarendon Press, 1950); Harold Innis, "Transportation as a Factor in Canadian Economic History," in *Essays in Canadian Economic History,* ed. Mary Q. Innis (Toronto: University of Toronto Press, 1956).

TABLE 4.1. Communications Output Distribution Coefficients (percentage of total sales of telecommunications and postal services purchased by each sector)

Sector	United States (1967)	Japan (1965)	Colombia (1970)	Korea (1966)	Turkey (1963)	Taiwan (1964)	Philippines (1961)
Agriculture	0.55	0.26	1.84	0.33	0.22	0.67	2.71
Mining and manufacturing	15.33	34.82	17.78	18.23	11.05	15.88	48.47
Services	47.30	47.43	51.59	49.88	43.92	71.54	16.60
Other	3.97	5.09	NA	1.49	NA	2.39	NA
Household consumption	32.83	12.40	28.79	30.07	44.81	9.52	32.22

Source: Robert J. Saunders, Warford, and Wellenius, *Telecommunications and Economic Development*, 90.
Note: NA = not available.

small, their *coefficients* can signal a very significant political effect.[7] This chapter proposes a model of national telecommunications performance that incorporates both the socioeconomic factors typically employed by economists and institutional variables emphasized by political scientists.

Political Control

One of the few exceptions to the pure socioeconomic models described above is the effort by Foreman-Peck to assess the impact of institutional variables on the penetration of telephone service.[8] He examines telephone penetration and the volume of telephone conversations for developed countries in 1913. Included in his models is a dummy variable that takes a value of zero for private or mixed ownership and 1 for exclusive government ownership. Population and gross national product per capita are statistically significant in all of his results. Rather surprisingly, the dummy variable for exclusive government ownership is positive in five of the specified models and is statistically significant in three of these specifications. Foreman-Peck also includes in these

---

7. In an earlier study, for example, I examined the impact of political regime and regulatory policies on the penetration of television and radio media. Although these political variables only contributed between 5 percent and 10 percent of the total variance explained, the coefficients suggested that democratic, as opposed to nondemocratic, regimes had very significant differences in media penetration. See Raymond M. Duch and Peter Lemieux, "Politics and the Growth of Communications" (unpublished manuscript, 1990).

8. James Foreman-Peck, "Competition and Performance in the United Kingdom Telecommunications Industry," *Telecommunications Policy* 9 (September 1985): 215–28.

models an interaction term that is the product of the government ownership dummy and gross national product per capita. Here the results conform more closely to expectation: the coefficients are negative and statistically significant in most equations.

Two interesting conclusions can be drawn from the Foreman-Peck analysis. First, in the early period of telecommunications development (1913), government ownership had a positive impact on telecommunications development. This, of course, is consistent with the argument that risk—particularly the likelihood of government expropriation of private telecommunication service providers—meant that government-owned telcos were freer to commit long-term capital expenditures to expand national telecommunications infrastructures. Second, the significant negative coefficient for the interaction terms suggests that continued government ownership retards telecommunications development.

Foreman-Peck decided not to model more contemporary telephone penetration rates because, he argued, there is little variation in the institutional variable: virtually all telephone systems in the post–World War II period are state monopolies. This, of course, assumes that state monopolies are a homogeneous group. As I have argued, state monopolies vary considerably in terms of political control and this is a much more powerful explanatory variable than ownership.

The model estimated below includes a political control variable that is based on the five classifications developed earlier: government agency, government corporation, government business enterprise, semiprivate corporation, and private corporation. Government agencies are subject to the most

TABLE 4.2.   Classification of Telcos for Regression Analysis

Autonomous of Political Oversight	Subject to Political Oversight
Australia	Austria
Canada	Belgium
Denmark	France
Finland	Iceland
Greece	Ireland
Italy	Netherlands
Japan	New Zealand
Portugal	Norway
Spain	Switzerland
Sweden	United Kingdom
Turkey	West Germany
United States	

governmental oversight while private corporations are most autonomous. This is a categorical variable that could only be incorporated into the regression model as four dummy variables. Given the sample size, this would result in too few cases in each category, seriously undermining the reliability of the estimates. To ensure that each of the categories had a reasonable number of observations, the five categories were collapsed into a single political dummy variable. Countries with telcos that are classified as government agencies or government corporations are assigned a dummy variable value of 1. These countries are considered to have relatively high degrees of governmental control over their telcos. A value of zero is assigned to all the other countries that are considered to have relatively autonomous telcos. The distribution of countries is presented in table 4.2. This binary representation of the data has the attraction of having a similar number of cases in each category.

Performance

The firm can be evaluated along a variety of dimensions. Typically, economic performance is judged by such measures as profit, total revenues, revenues or profit per employee, or return on equity. Of greater concern here is the social goal of maximizing access to the telephone system (universal service). More specifically, what factors best account for high versus low levels of telephone penetration in different developed nations? Performance is measured by the number of individuals and businesses subscribing to telephone services.

What economists characterize as telecommunications demand and what I have labeled performance are not necessarily synonymous. The evidence of such a divergence is in the long waiting lines that many countries have for the installation of telephone service. Countries for which socioeconomic models would predict similar levels of demand often have different levels of telephone *penetration*. Underlying demand for the service might be similar, but the *performance* of the telcos could vary significantly, resulting in this discrepancy. I have argued that much of this difference between underlying demand and performance is accounted for by the political variable introduced above.

Two dimensions of performance are examined in this chapter: total telephone lines in service and data transmission services in use. Total telephone lines in service is a measure of the service provider's ability to develop a telecommunications infrastructure. Figure 4.1 presents the 1965 and 1980 telephone main lines-per-capita data for a sample of 21 nations. As I indicated earlier, the 1960s and 1970s were periods of accelerated growth for most developed nations. For most of the nations, telephone penetration was still low in 1965, the beginning of this infrastructural development period.

The post-infrastructural period begins in the late 1970s, when telephone penetration reaches saturation points and telcos were forced to market new

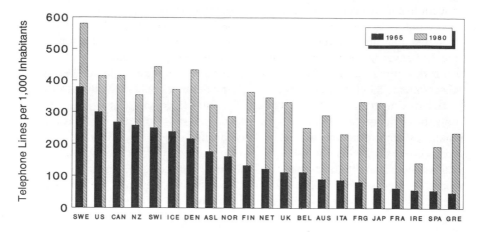

Fig. 4.1. Telephone main lines per capita, 1965 and 1980 (OECD countries). (Data from ITU, *Yearbook of Common Carrier Telecommunications Statistics* [Geneva: ITU, 1986].)

services to ensure continued growth in revenues. By 1980, telephone line penetration increased considerably: the median penetration rate was almost 330 lines per thousand population, compared to only 112 in 1965.

In both 1965 and 1980, telephone main lines per capita for this sample of nations vary considerably. For example, in 1965 Ireland had approximately 57 main lines per thousand population compared to over 300 for the United States. Although the discrepancies narrow somewhat by 1980, variation among countries remains high; for example, while Sweden had 580 telephone main lines per thousand population, there were still countries such as Belgium, Italy, and Spain with less than half that penetration rate.

With the introduction of computers and the digital representation and storage of information, data transmission has become increasingly important. The extent to which countries have developed and stimulated demand for data communications applications (e.g., centralized data bank facilities, transmittal of banking and financial information, credit card verification systems, etc.) and hardware (modems, multiplexers, satellite antennae, switching equipment, etc.) is an indicator of post-infrastructural development. Although more esoteric than the plain, ordinary telephone, data transmission plays an important direct and indirect role in the life of citizens. Data transmission is directly associated with a variety of services that individuals have grown to take for granted: airline ticketing, cable television, computer data banks, credit card verification, automatic teller machines, etc. More important, it has a major indirect impact on consumers because of its growing importance for national economies. Firms are increasingly dependent upon high-speed data transmission facilities and sophisticated application software. For many businesses, such as finance and banking, the quality of a firm's communications facilities is considered a critical competitive asset. The European Commission estimates that by the year 2000, 40 percent of employment will be directly related to a communications-intensive occupation. Underdeveloped data communications facilities negatively affect consumers, jobs, and overall economic activity. This measure of post-infrastructural development ought to be particularly sensitive to the political control variable because it is much more demand driven than basic telephone service. To test this hypothesis, the analysis that follows includes three measures of data communications development. One measure is the number of *data terminals* in use; this includes such instruments as modems, telex machines, and teletex terminals. Information regarding the number of data terminals attached to both public and private networks is made available for 1982 on a country-by-country basis by the ITU.[9] Figure 4.2*a* compares the per capita penetration of these data terminals in a sample of sixteen developed nations.[10] The numbers range from less than one data terminal per thousand inhabitants in Greece to almost seven terminals per thousand inhabitants in Sweden.

In addition to the ITU exhibits, figure 4.2 presents two other measures of data communications: modems (Figure 4.2*b*) and network terminating points (NTPs) in service (Figure 4.2*c*). Modems are the interface between computers and the telecommunications network that permit the transmission and reception of data.[11] *Network terminating points* (NTPs) are used to "indicate the point of connection between a unit of user equipment and a telecommunication transmission facility."[12] Both measures indicate the extent to which the telecommunications network is employed for the transmission of data.

Once again, the disparities among countries are significant. Referring to the modem figures (fig. 4.2*b*), Sweden has almost five modems per thousand inhabitants; Italy, Belgium, the United Kingdom, Austria, and Spain have fewer than two; and Ireland and the Netherlands have less than one per thousand inhabitants. The disparities are even more pronounced for NTPs per

---

9. International Telecommunications Union, *Yearbook of Common Carrier Telecommunication Statistics* (Geneva: ITU, 1986).

10. Total data terminal equipment represents the sum of the following items identified by the ITU: "Number of data terminal equipments on the public telephone and telex networks," "Number of private leased circuits," and "Number of data terminal equipments connected to dedicated public data networks."

11. Eurodata Foundation, *Eurodata Foundation Yearbook* (The Hague: Eurodata Foundation, 1983).

12. Marino Benedetti, "Eurodata '79: The Growth of Data Communications in Western Europe," *Telecommunications Journal* 48 (1981): 14–18.

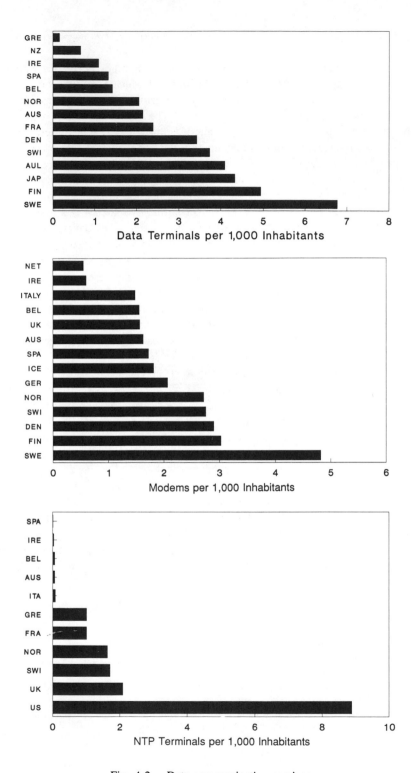

Fig. 4.2. Data communication services

thousand inhabitants. By far, the United States leads in data communications facilities with almost nine NTPs per thousand population. Sweden, Norway, and the United Kingdom fall way behind with about two NTPs per thousand inhabitants. At the very low end of the scale are Belgium, Italy, Spain, Austria, and Ireland with an insignificant number of NTPs. Overall, countries such as the United States, Sweden, Denmark, and the United Kingdom have established a prominent lead in data communication penetration.[13]

Both measures of telco performance, main line penetration and the diffusion of data communications hardware, show considerable cross-national variation in performance. The next section tests the hypothesis that political control, along with socioeconomic variables, explains this variation in performance.

Results

The remainder of this chapter will present the results of a series of regressions predicting the penetration of telephone and data communications service. In all cases, a logarithmic specification of the model is employed.[14] The independent variables in the models consist of the socioeconomic variables discussed earlier (GDP, size of the service sector, and geographic area) and the political variable measuring the extent of governmental control over the telco.

Given the logarithmic structure of the model, the coefficient estimates for the quantity variables, like GDP, measure elasticities. A coefficient value of .50, for example, indicates that a 1.0 percent increase in the associated independent variable would produce a .50 percent increase in the dependent variable. The service variable has the following logit specification:

$$\log \ \frac{\text{Service sector as percent of GDP}}{1 - \text{Service sector as percent of GDP}}$$

The effect of this variable is more difficult to interpret than the other variables. Because of the logit specification, the impact of an absolute change of 1.0 percent in the service sector's share of GDP depends upon the level of the service sector's share of GDP. Absolute changes near the limiting values of 0 percent or 100 percent affect the dependent variable more strongly than do

---

13. It is encouraging to note that the three measures of data communications are highly correlated with each other. The ITU measure of data terminal equipment has a correlation coefficient of .72 with the network termination point data and .91 with the modem data provided by the Eurodata Foundation.

14. Two considerations guided this decision. First, a visual inspection of the data indicated that, at the low and high extremes, penetration rates tend to be more insensitive to changes in the values of the independent variables. Second, after the log transformation, the fit of the equation improved considerably.

TABLE 4.3. Regression Results for Telephone Penetration

Independent Variable	Dependent Variable		
	1965 Telephone Penetration		1980 Telephone Penetration
Intercept	1.90	2.06	1.64
Political control	−0.10	−0.11	−0.13
	(0.07)	(0.06)*	(0.04)**
Log (GDP)	0.89	0.91	0.97
	(0.06)**	(0.04)**	(0.03)**
Logit service	0.15	—	—
	(0.39)		
Log (area)	0.04	—	—
	(0.06)		
R^2	0.97	0.96	0.98
N	20	20	22

Note: Standard errors in parentheses.
*$p = .10$.   **$p = .05$.

changes around 50 percent.[15] Table 4.3 presents the regression results for the penetration of telephone service in 1965 and 1980.

1965 Telephone Penetration

Looking first at the 1965 results, the initial equation indicates that penetration depends almost exclusively on a nation's level of wealth. The other socioeconomic variables in the model are statistically insignificant and the political variable remains below conventional levels of statistical significance. Because of the very high standard errors for the area and service variables, a second equation was estimated that included only the political variable and the measure of national wealth.[16] Dominating the equation is the relationship between wealth and telephone service diffusion, which is essentially linear: a

---

15. The logit specification assumes that it is "harder" for a country to move from 10 percent to 11 percent literate or, symmetrically, 89 percent to 90 percent, than it is to move from 50 percent to 51 percent literate.

16. Since the excluded variables had very small correlations with the independent variables that remained in the model, I do not suspect that their elimination from the model created any serious specification bias. For an excellent discussion, see Peter Kennedy, *A Guide to Econometrics*, 2d ed. (Cambridge, Mass.: MIT Press, 1987), chap. 5.

1.00 percent increase in GDP yields a 0.91 percent increase in the number of telephone main lines.

In this second equation, the coefficient for political control is statistically significant and relatively large. For 1965, countries where telcos were under close political supervision had telephone penetration levels that were only 78 percent ($10^{[-0.11]}$) of those in countries where the service providers were relatively autonomous of governmental oversight. Political control reduces telephone penetration by 22 percent.

1980 Telephone Penetration

The coefficient values for 1980 follow the pattern of the 1965 results quite closely. Once again, the only statistically significant socioeconomic variable is GDP, which actually has an effect that is larger than was the case in the 1965 results. The political effect is virtually identical: countries where the telco is subject to considerable levels of political oversight have penetration rates that are 25 percent lower than in the case of nations without strict governmental control.

Data Communications Development

The political effects reflected in telephone penetration levels should be even more pronounced in the case of new, enhanced telecommunications services. As noted earlier, the new, enhanced services of the post-infrastructural phase represent a significant challenge to telco management. The challenge is no longer simply adding physical capacity to the telephone network but rather designing and marketing services and hardware to specialized user groups.

Estimates for four models, similar to the ones for telephone penetration, are presented in table 4.4. The dependent variable in the first two models is the log of the number of data terminals reported for each nation by the ITU. As for the independent variables, they are identical to those employed in the previous regression analysis.

The first column provides the regression coefficients for the fully specified model with data terminals as the dependent variable. Only the political and GDP variables are statistically significant. The second model drops the insignificant socioeconomic variables. As the GDP coefficient indicates, the relationship between wealth and the penetration of data transmission equipment is very elastic: a 1.0 percent rise in GDP translates into a 1.1 percent rise in the number of data terminals. This is not surprising given that the demand for data transmission services is very much tied to business activity—the wealthier the nation, the more business activity and therefore the greater demand for data transmission.

Also statistically significant in the model is the variable measuring the degree of autonomy from political oversight. The variable's coefficient suggests that nations served by telcos that are subject to a high degree of political control have data terminal penetration levels that are 49 percent ($10^{[-0.31]}$) of those in nations with relatively autonomous telcos.

Similar equations were estimated for the other two measures of the development of data transmission services and their coefficient estimates are also presented in table 4.4. The results for the equation with modems as the dependent variable are different than those for the data terminal equation. Gross domestic product remains an important driving force behind the demand for modems, although its elasticity here is marginally below 1.0. Area is also a statistically significant factor in the demand for modems: nations with a larger landmass have higher levels of demand. In countries where the physical distance between towns and cities is large, transmitting data over the telephone networks is undoubtedly more economical and quicker than other methods that require transporting written material, disks, or tapes.

Unlike the earlier equation, political autonomy is slightly below statistical significance. The variable has a coefficient in the correct direction, -0.16, but the t-statistic is only 1.3. Undoubtedly, one of the factors contributing to its high standard error is the small number of observations used in the analysis (13 countries).

TABLE 4.4.   Regression Results for Data Penetration

Independent Variable	Dependent Variable			
	Data Terminal Equipment		Modems	Network Termination Points
Intercept	2.28	2.34	1.10	2.30
Political control	−0.30 (0.09)**	−0.31 (0.08)**	−0.16 (0.13)	−0.29 (0.17)*
Log (GDP)	1.09 (0.08)**	1.1 (0.08)**	0.97 (0.07)**	0.90 (0.18)**
Logit service	−0.19 (0.44)	—	—	—
Log (area)	0.02 (0.08)	—	0.27 (0.14)*	—
R^2	0.95	0.95	0.96	0.70
N	16	16	13	14

Note: Standard errors in parentheses.
*$p = .10$.   **$p = .05$.

Finally, the fourth equation in table 4.4 expresses the dependent variable as network termination points. The results for this model more closely reflect those for data terminal equipment. As was the case with the first equation, only two variables are statistically significant: GDP and the political variable. Both coefficients are slightly smaller than they were in the first model. Each 1.0 percent increase in GDP translates into a 0.9 percent increase in the penetration of network termination points. Nations whose telcos are not autonomous of political oversight have data penetration rates that are only 52 percent ($10^{[-0.29]}$) of those with autonomous telcos.

Alternative Specifications

The political variable in the preceding analyses was defined by collapsing the five government ownership categories, originally developed in chapter 2, into a binary measure. Because of the small number of cases in the analyses, this ensured that each value of the independent variable would have an approximately equal number of cases.

This specification has certain drawbacks. First, it reduces the amount of information available regarding the independent variable because it transforms an ordinal measure into a categorical measure. Second, this operationalization makes it difficult to determine whether the political variable offers a better explanation of performance than a variable that simply distinguishes between private and public ownership. To address these weaknesses, table 4.5 presents the regression results for models that more fully exploit the information available for the political variable.

Equation 1 tests the traditional argument that performance is tied to ownership: private firms are hypothesized to outperform public enterprises. The Private dummy variable has a value of 1 for all telcos that are entirely or partially privately owned. This includes Finland, Denmark, Spain, Canada, and the United States. For all other countries the variable has a value of 0.

The results offer little support for the traditional argument that privately owned firms outperform those that are government-owned. Note that the Private dummy variable has a coefficient that is not significantly different from 0, suggesting that telcos under private ownership performed no better than publicly owned telcos.

A second issue concerns the representation of private and relatively autonomous public entities as one category (i.e., the collapsing of private, semiprivate, and government enterprise into one category). Are government enterprises sufficiently similar to private entities to justify this strategy? Equations 2 and 3 in table 4.5 address this question by introducing two dummy variables. The Public dummy variable has a value of 1 for all countries where the telcos are government enterprises (Sweden, Japan, Italy, Greece, Aus-

TABLE 4.5.   Regression Results for Telephones, 1980

Independent Variables	Number of Telephones in 1980		
	(1)	(2)	(3)
Intercept	1.51	1.59	1.16
Log (GDP)	0.99	0.98	0.75
	(0.04)**	(0.03)**	(0.15)**
Logit service	—	—	0.16
			(0.12)
Log (area)	—	—	0.52
			(0.73)
Private	0.05	—	—
	(0.06)		
Public	—	0.06	0.03
		(0.06)	(0.06)
Government	—	−0.10	−0.10
		(0.05)**	(0.05)*
R^2	0.98	0.98	0.99
N	22	22	22

Note: Standard errors in parentheses.
$*p = .10.$ $**p = .05.$

tralia, and Portugal) and a value of 0 otherwise. In countries where the telcos are either a government agency (France, United Kingdom, Ireland, Switzerland, Turkey, Austria, Netherlands, Norway, New Zealand, and Iceland) or a government corporation (Germany and Belgium), the Government dummy variable assumes a value of 1, and a value of 0 for all other countries.

In both equation 2 and the more fully specified equation 3, the Public dummy variable has a coefficient insignificantly different from zero. This suggests that there is no difference between countries with private or semiprivate telcos and those where the telcos are classified as government enterprises. As a result, we lose no information by collapsing the two categories.

Alternative Measures of Performance

The analysis has focused on two performance measures that indicate the degree to which consumers are provided with access to telecommunications (voice and data). As I have argued, the extent of universal service is the strongest measure of telco success. Nonetheless, it is conceivable that telcos focus on other objectives beneficial to their public shareholders. One particular objective is efficiency. Rather than promoting universal access at all costs, management might be considerably more sensitive to cost constraints, preferring to maximize the efficiency of providing service. Then, the lower levels of telephone penetration that are associated with political constraints might be compensated by higher degrees of efficiency. This hypothesis is tested in table 4.6 where 1980 revenues per employee (expressed in U.S. dollars) are regressed against the political autonomy variable and GDP per capita. Higher efficiency, here, is equated with the generation of greater revenues per employee. The results suggest no difference between firms facing different degrees of political constraints. This is somewhat surprising, calling in question the relationship between political constraints and performance.

Although this result suggests that other measures of performance might generate different conclusions, there are some very serious problems with the measure, which is the reason that it does not serve as the central indicator of performance. Revenues per employee is a good measure of performance in competitive markets because producers have serious competitive constraints on the prices they can set and, therefore, on the revenues that they can generate. In perfectly competitive markets, increases in revenues per employee reflect increased efficiencies in production. This, of course, is not necessarily the case in monopoly situations where producers can simply increase prices, or reduce service quality, in order to generate higher revenues

TABLE 4.6.   Alternative Performance Models

	Dependent Variables		
Independent Variable	1980 Revenues/ Employees	1965 Investment/ Revenues	1980 Investment/ Revenues
Constant	4,962	1.30	0.50
GDP per capita	3.65* (1.15)	−0.0004* (0.0001)	−0.00 (0.00)
Political control	−105.70 (8,434)	−0.20* (0.13)	−0.03 (0.06)
R^2	0.37	0.40	0.02
N	21	20	23

Note: Standard errors in parentheses; revenues, investment expenditures, and GDP per capita are measured in U.S. dollars.
$*p = .10$. $**p = .05$.

per employee. Because telcos have traditionally been government-protected monopolists, this measure of performance has serious weaknesses.

A possible alternative explanation for cross-national differences in telephone penetration is that they simply reflect varying levels of cultural acceptance. Telcos in different societies might be making similar efforts (always taking into consideration their different levels of economic development), only to face varying levels of consumer enthusiasm for telephone service. This alternative explanation is tested in the last two columns of table 4.6, where effort (measured by total investment as a percent of total telecommunications revenues) is regressed against GDP per capita and the political autonomy variable. The table reports the findings for 1965 and 1980 data. First, the 1965 results are entirely consistent with the findings for telephone diffusion: investment effort declines as political constraints rise. There is no relationship between these variables in the 1980 results, suggesting that once penetration levels reached saturation levels, political variables had a much lower impact.

Overall, the analysis of alternative measures of performance does not seriously call into question the initial conclusions regarding the relationship between political constraints and performance.

Summary and Conclusions

In accordance with most earlier studies this chapter demonstrates that wealth is the driving force behind the demand for telecommunications services. This was the case for regression equations estimated on data from both 1965 and 1980. Moreover, wealth dominates the diffusion equations for both basic telephone service and more advanced data communication services.

Telecommunications development is also affected by institutional factors. A distinction was developed in chapters 2 and 3 between service providers that were relatively autonomous of political intervention and those that were subject to substantial political control. This, I argued, was the critical factor distinguishing telcos' performance levels, rather than the private versus public distinction that is frequently cited. In four of the five models presented in this chapter, the variable measuring political control had a significant coefficient in the predicted direction. Service providers that were organized in such a manner so as to insulate management from political oversight had significantly higher levels of telephone and data communications development.

I have yet to address the magnitude of the political impact on telecommunications diffusion. The size of the effect is important for a number of reasons. First, it permits accurate predictions. Telcos subject to higher levels of political control will have significantly lower levels of telephone and data

TABLE 4.7. Contributions to Explained Variance in Telephone and Data
Services Penetrations from Socioeconomic and Political Factors

	Telephone		Data Terminals		
Factors Included	1965	1980	ITU	Modems	NTP
Both socioeconomic and political	0.964	0.98	0.95	0.964	0.71
Socioeconomic only	0.957	0.97	0.89	0.957	0.63
Difference[a]	0.007	0.01	0.06	0.007	0.08
Political only	0.11	0.15	0.14	0.16	0.04

[a]Difference between the value for all factors and that for socioeconomic factors alone.

communication penetration. If this variable is ignored in forecasting models, the forecasts will either under- or overestimate penetration levels depending upon the extent to which national telcos are subject to political oversight. Second, the size of the political effect signals to policymakers whether the efforts associated with modifying organizational structures would generate commensurate improvements in performance. Finally, the size of the impact is important for testing the hypothesis that political effects would be larger for post-infrastructural services (i.e., the data communication service) than infrastructural service. Two strategies for measuring the magnitude of these effects will be considered.[17]

First, we can evaluate the magnitude of the political effect by its contribution to explained variance. By this method, the impact of the political variable appears to be quite marginal. Table 4.7 reports the R^2 values for three different regressions: one where only the socioeconomic variables are used as explanatory factors; one that includes only the political variable; and finally, one where both sets of variables are included simultaneously.

The floor value for the political effect can be estimated by assessing the additional variance in telecommunication penetration that can be explained beyond that which is accounted for by socioeconomic factors. This method maximizes the effect of socioeconomic variables. The difference between the fully specified equations and those in which the political variable is dropped are presented in the third row of table 4.7. For the 1980 telephone equations, the difference is about 0.01, setting a floor value of variance explained at about 1 percent. This is considerably higher in two of the data equations

---

17. This discussion is based on a similar evaluation conducted in Duch and Lemieux, "Politics and the Growth of Communications," 33.

where the differences are 6 percent and 8 percent. In the case of modems, the difference is 1 percent, as it was in the telephone equations.

These estimates of the floor value of the political effect likely understate its impact because they ignore the possibility that some of the socioeconomic differences across nations may be systematically related to variations in the organizational structure variable. The maximum impact of the political variable, that is, its ceiling value, can be estimated by only including the institutional variable in the equation. As the R^2 values reported in table 4.7 indicate, this results in considerably larger estimates of the size of the political effects, ranging between 11 percent and 15 percent in the case of telephones, and between 14 percent and 16 percent for the data equations. By averaging the floor and ceiling estimates of the political effect, I arrive at a best guess for the size of the political effect in the telephone equations of about 5–8 percent and approximately 8–10 percent in the case of data penetration.

This traditional approach of measuring contributions to explained variance would suggest that political differences play a relatively minor role in determining cross-national variations in telecommunications penetration. But the question I have posed concerns whether the rate of telecommunications development *differs significantly* between countries with high versus low political constraints on their telcos. A much better measure of this political effect is the size of the estimated regression coefficients themselves. These values tell us the expected difference in telecommunications penetration levels when countries with different telco organizational structures are compared.

To illustrate the magnitude of these differences, I have plotted the models' predictions in figures 4.3 and 4.4 as a function of gross domestic product (these are the unlogged predictions of the model). The estimated political effects are substantial. The telephone predictions for 1965 and 1980 are presented in figure 4.3. In 1965 a country with a GDP of about $1,000 billion where the telco was relatively free of governmental oversight is estimated to have about 60 million telephones. This compares to only 47 million in a country with the same GDP where the telco was subject to considerable governmental oversight. As I noted earlier, the difference is about 22 percent. We see a similar political impact in the estimates based on the 1980 coefficients.

The political impact on the penetration of data terminal equipment is even more dramatic. Figure 4.4 plots the predicted penetration of data terminals for a range of GDP values. A country with a GDP of approximately $1,000 billion and a relatively autonomous telco is estimated to have 456,400 data terminals compared to only 227,000 for a country with a similar GDP whose telco is subject to significant governmental oversight. The implication of figure 4.4 is that removing the political constraints on a service provider has the effect of doubling the penetration of data terminal equipment.

Earlier I distinguished two phases of telecommunications development:

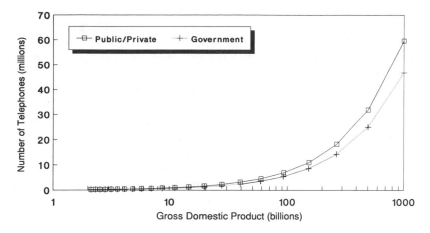

Fig. 4.3.   1965 telephone penetration predictions based on regression estimates

the infrastructural period corresponded with the development of basic telephone service while the post-infrastructural period is represented by the implementation of more innovative, consumer-sensitive technologies. The negative impact of government control, it was argued, would be greater in the post-infrastructural period because of the premium placed on innovation and marketing skills. There is some support for this argument in the regression

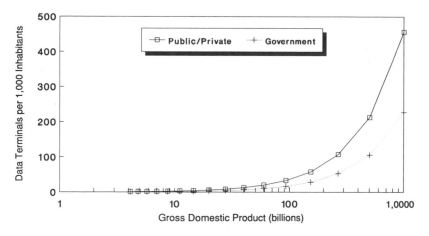

Fig. 4.4.   1982 data terminal penetration predictions based on regression results

results. A visual inspection of figures 4.3 and 4.4 suggests that the spread between countries with autonomous, as opposed to politically constrained, telcos is much higher in the case of data penetration than telephone diffusion. In fact, the difference is twice as large for the data equation as it is for the telephone model.

This chapter provides evidence indicating that ownership per se does not explain performance differentials between private and public enterprises. A much more powerful predictor of performance levels is the extent to which government oversees and controls the management of telcos. Countries in which the service providers are relatively free of government oversight have higher levels of telecommunications development. As the telecommunication industry becomes more demand driven and growth is tied more closely to innovation and marketing, this negative relationship between government oversight and performance increases in magnitude.

In recent debates privatization has been cast as the most appropriate policy for improving the performance of public enterprise. This chapter suggests that, short of full scale privatization, policymakers can significantly improve the performance of public entities by reducing political oversight and control. As a result, management of public entities would be under less pressure to accommodate the political goals of incumbent officials. Policies that might reduce political oversight would include establishing an independent supervisory board, an independent budget, the freedom to borrow funds on the open market, and the authority to set prices.

CHAPTER 5

Institutional and Economic Factors Shaping Liberalization

Competition plays an important role in accounting for public sector performance. The difference in performance between a private and public monopolist might be small in comparison to that between a public monopolist faced with competition and one that confronted no competitive threats.[1] In general, most economists agree that competition, when sustainable, should be encouraged. Historically, policymakers have been skeptical as to whether competition could be sustained in industries such as broadcasting, telephones, and electrical utilities. Recently, both economists and policymakers have reassessed whether these sectors, traditionally considered monopolistic, can actually sustain competition. This chapter examines the traditional rationale for precluding competition and explores recent arguments questioning the appropriateness of government-enforced entry barriers.

There are many markets where policymakers would agree that competition works—examples might include retail trade, consumer electronics, and hotels. The telecommunications service industry, on the other hand, is a sector where policymakers differ considerably on the appropriateness of competition. Some argue that major sectors of the industry remain natural monopolies; therefore competition is unworkable and entry barriers should be enforced. On the other hand, others argue that entry barriers are unnecessary because competition—or the threat of competition—is an effective constraint on established telecommunication service providers.

Natural Monopoly?

Until recently there has been very little competition in the telecommunications industry because governments considered it a natural monopoly that could only be served by one monopolist (either a public or regulated, private monopoly). Because the industry faced declining economies of scale, economists argued that only one firm could serve the market efficiently. In a market with

---

1. John Vickers and George Yarrow, *Privatization: An Economic Analysis* (Cambridge, Mass.: MIT Press, 1988).

declining scale economies, the existence of more than one firm would result in destructive competition because neither firm could sell any quantity of the product at a price equal to or greater than the average cost of production.[2] To avoid this, governments restrict entry into such markets. To prevent monopoly pricing and "uneconomic profits," governments either closely regulate or nationalize these monopoly providers.

In its early stage of development and well into its mature stage, the telecommunications industry clearly exhibits scale economies. An industry has increasing returns to scale when it demonstrates scale elasticities that are greater than one. The scale elasticity measure is simply the ratio of the percentage change in output to the percentage change in all inputs. If the measure is greater than one, this suggests that a 1 percent increase in inputs yields a greater than 1 percent increase in output. Meyer et al. have summarized a number of studies that estimated the scale elasticities for U.S. and Canadian telephone systems—the results are reported in table 5.1.[3] A more recent review by Sharkey concluded that "most writers found [scale economies] to be in the range 1.04 to 1.16."[4] Virtually all of these econometric studies are based on highly aggregated data that can seriously bias the parameter estimates.[5] Nonetheless, it seems reasonable to conclude that scale economies have been, at most, modest in the postwar economies with highly developed telecommunications infrastructures (e.g., Canada, Sweden, and the United States).

There are certain characteristics of the telecommunications industry that lend themselves to scale economies. First, because of the interdependent nature of demand, the more subscribers to the network services, the greater utility of the services to existing subscribers. Moreover, since those who receive messages are not charged for calls, the higher the level of usage, the greater number of calls received and, therefore, the higher the utility for subscribers. Because the addition of subscribers places no real burden on the existing network facilities (and, in fact, increases the utility of the overall service), the marginal cost of adding new subscribers or increasing service continually declines.

---

2. George Stigler, *The Theory of Price*, 3d ed. (New York: Macmillan, 1966), 221.

3. John Robert Meyer, Robert W. Wilson, M. Alan Baughcum, Ellen Burton, and Louis Caouette, *The Economics of Competition in the Telecommunications Industry* (Cambridge, Mass.: Oelgeschlager, Gunn and Hain, 1980), 129.

4. William W. Sharkey, *The Theory of Natural Monopoly* (New York: Cambridge University Press, 1982) 205.

5. See the critical evaluation of these models in Leonard Waverman, "U.S. Interexchange Competition," in *Changing the Rules: Technological Change, International Competition, and Regulation in Telecommunications*, ed. Robert W. Crandall and Kenneth Flamm (Washington, D.C.: Brookings Institution, 1984).

TABLE 5.1. Point Estimates of Scale Elasticity in Telecommunications Systems from Econometric Studies

Telecommunication System	Scale Elasticities
U.S. Bell System[a]	0.74–2.08
U.S. Bell System (excluding one study)[b]	0.98–1.24
Bell Canada[c]	0.85–1.11

Source: John R. Meyer, Robert Wilson, M. Baughcum, Ellen Burton, and Louis Caouette, *The Economics of Competition in the Telecommunications Industry* (Cambridge, Mass.: Oelgeschlager, Gunn & Hain, 1980), 129.

[a] American Telephone & Telegraph Company, "An Econometric Study of Returns to Scale in the Bell System," Bell Exhibit 60, FCC Docket 20003 (Fifth Supplemental Response), 20 August 1976; L. Mantell, "An Econometric Study of Returns to Scale in the Bell System," Staff Research Paper, Office of Telecommunications Policy, Bell Exhibit 40 in Docket 20003; H. D. Vinod, "Application of New Ridge Regression Methods to a Study of Bell System Scale Economies," Bell Exhibit 42, FCC Docket 20003, 21 April 1975; and H. D. Vinod, "Bell System Scale Economies and Estimation of Joint Production Functions," Bell Exhibit 59, FCC Docket 20003 (Fifth Supplemental Response), 20 August 1976.

[b] Excluding American Telephone and Telegraph Company, "An Econometric Study of Returns to Scale in the Bell System," Bell Exhibit 60, FCC Docket 20003 (Fifth Supplemental Response), 20 August 1976.

[c] A. Rodney Dobell et al., "Telephone Communications in Canada: Demand, Production, and Investment Decisions," *Bell Journal of Economics and Management Science* 3 (Spring 1972): 175–219; Melvyn Fuss and Leonard Waverman, "Multiproduct Multi-input Cost Functions for a Regulated Utility: The Case of Telecommunications in Canada," paper presented at the National Bureau of Economic Research Conference on Public Regulation, Washington, D.C., 1977.

Second, if multiple suppliers face significantly different peak periods of demand (as might be the case if one supplier serves residential consumers and another serves business consumers), there would be significant economies associated with monopoly service. Since service providers must construct switching equipment to satisfy peak demand, a merger of two suppliers with different peak periods of demand would considerably reduce total capital equipment costs.

Third, there are economies associated with planning for the entire telecommunications network needs of a country. It allows service providers to route messages more economically, particularly during periods of peak demand. With a fragmented network, different service providers are unable to take advantage of other providers' excess capacity and, therefore, are unable to complete calls during peak periods. As a result, they must construct un-economic switching facilities to accommodate relatively low demand routes.

In its early stages of development, scale economies in the industry are particularly prominent. Saunders et al. suggest that economies are likely to be much higher in less developed countries. Because penetration is low, providers are not burdened with outdated equipment; therefore, while the average cost of service is high (because of the need to purchase new equipment), it declines rapidly as new subscribers are added to the network.[6] A similar argument can be made for the early stages of the telecommunications industry in the developed nations.

At the turn of the century, these substantial scale economies led Holcombe to strongly recommend government entry barriers for the industry. In the short term, he argued, multiple providers of telephone service could survive in individual communities but, because of increasing economies of scale and a steadily declining average cost curve, he believed only one firm would survive in the market. Competition in such a situation would actually increase the cost of the service because no single producer would be able to realize the full extent of the industry's scale economies.[7] With virtually no exceptions, governments heeded this and similar advice by restricting service provision to a single, regulated private or government-owned entity.

Either option, publicly or privately owned monopoly provider, imposes significant costs on society. The costs associated with regulating private monopolists have proven to be considerable because government must invest substantial resources to obtain accurate estimates of the true costs faced by monopoly service providers. Since monopolists are inclined to inflate their estimates of costs and understate expected revenues, government must invest in procedures for verification.[8] Meyer et al. estimate that in 1979 the total annual direct costs of telecommunications regulation in the United States approached $100 million.[9] This is a very conservative estimate—the actual amount, including both direct and indirect costs, was probably much higher.

There is no regulation of nationalized monopolists per se but, as previous chapters pointed out, they also impose costs on society. Lacking competitive pressures, government-owned monopolists tend to be less efficient in their use of resources and often set prices at levels significantly higher than their marginal cost. Rather than continue supporting the costs associated with

6. Robert J. Saunders, Jeremy J. Warford, and Bjorn Wellenius, *Telecommunications and Economic Development* (Baltimore: Johns Hopkins University Press, 1983), 38.

7. Arthur N. Holcombe, *Public Ownership of Telephones on the Continent of Europe* (New York: Houghton Mifflin Company, 1911), 125.

8. Alfred E. Kahn, *The Economics of Regulation: Principles and Institutions* (New York: John Wiley and Sons, 1970), vol I: chap. 2.

9. Meyer et al., *The Economics of Competition*, 145–46.

government-protected monopolists, some argue that entry barriers to these industries can be eliminated *without* the risk of monopolists setting prices at uncompetitive or monopoly levels.

Contestable Markets?

Some economists have questioned the link between scale economies and minimum-cost pricing and therefore the need for government regulation of natural monopolies. Chicago school economists have argued that the inefficiencies of market power are either small or short lived.[10] As a result, extensive government regulation of these markets is unnecessary. Demsetz suggests subjecting natural monopolists to competitive pressures through bidding for monopoly concessions.[11] If government officials were to periodically require that monopoly concessions be opened to bidding by both incumbent and potential entrant firms, this would force incumbents to maintain competitive prices because the pricing of goods and services would be one criterion for evaluating contestants.

More recently, proponents of contestable markets theory have argued that scale economies are an irrelevant criterion for determining whether a monopolist is subject to competitive pressures.[12] Even for industries characterized by significant scale economies, this theory suggests that a monopolist is subject to competitive pressures so long as entry into, and exit from, the industry are possible without a loss of the initial investment. In a contestable market like the airline industry, a new carrier can begin serving a route, undercut the price of the established carrier, make a profit, and then exit from the industry without sacrificing its initial investment (this assumes, of course, access to gate facilities). The threat of such entry would be sufficient incentive for the monopolist to set prices based on marginal cost.

Contestable markets theory makes a number of rather heroic assumptions. First, it assumes that there are no significant sunk costs associated with entry that would prevent easy exit from the industry. In other words, the capital assets necessary for competing in an industry could easily be sold off without taking any significant losses. Second, the monopolist is restrained from responding immediately to entry with prices lower than those of the entrant. Another assumption is the existence of a pool of potential market

10. Richard A. Posner, "Natural Monopoly and Its Regulation," *Stanford Law Review* 21 (February 1969): 548–643; Sam Peltzman, "Toward a More General Theory of Regulation," *Journal of Law and Economics* 19 (August 1976): 211–40.

11. Harold Demsetz, "Why Regulate Utilities?" *Journal of Law and Economics* 11 (April 1968): 55–65.

12. William J. Baumol, John C. Panzar, and Robert D. Willig, *Contestable Markets and the Theory of Industry Structure* (New York: Harcourt, Brace Jovanovich, 1982).

entrants that have the resources to enter an industry relatively quickly and to mount a competitive campaign against the incumbent.

Contestable markets exhibit all the benefits of competitive markets. Inefficient firms cannot survive in contestable markets because their higher prices will eventually encourage entry by more competitive entities. Contestable markets are similar to competitive markets in that they do not easily support cross-subsidies because any activity that is making excess profits will be subject to entry. It has also been demonstrated that pricing in contestable markets is consistent with allocative efficiencies.[13] In other words, goods are priced at or near marginal cost.

This theory suggests that society can reap the benefits of competition in industries with declining scale economies without the need for (and cost of) extensive government regulation. In sharp contrast to its prescribed role under traditional theories of natural monopoly, government is *not* expected to regulate entry into contestable markets; rather, it is expected to eliminate any barriers to entry or exit. The theory does suggest, however, that government regulation continues to be appropriate in those circumstances where the sunk costs associated with a particular industry are considerable, thereby preventing easy exit from the industry.

Detractors of the theory find the assumptions concerning ease of entry and exit, without a price response from the monopolist (i.e., ultrafree entry), to be so extreme that they lack any generalizability. Vickers and Yarrow suggest that, in fact, incumbent firms have a range of strategies that can be implemented to deter entry.[14] Whether there exist potential entrants to industries that require significant resources in order to mount a competitive threat is also questionable. In the case of some industries, such as telecommunications, energy, and transportation, the resources required for entering the market are substantial, considerably reducing the pool of potential entrants. Moreover, from a practical policy perspective, because it is unclear what constitutes acceptable versus unacceptable costs of exiting an industry, policymakers are faced with an imposing task of gauging the contestability of particular markets.

X-Efficiency

Related to the theory of contestable markets is the argument that competition generates productive internal efficiencies or "X-efficiencies."[15] Faced with no

13. Elizabeth Bailey and William Baumol, "Deregulation and the Theory of Contestable Markets," *Yale Journal on Regulation* 1 (1984): 111–37.

14. Vickers and Yarrow, *Privatization*, 61–77.

15. Harvey Leibenstein, "Allocative Efficiency versus X-Efficiency," *American Economic Review* 56 (1966): 392–415.

competition, there is no check on managerial or organizational "slack." Shareholders—be they public or private—have no effective means to evaluate the performance of managers. Competition provides shareholders with a means to judge relative performance and to allocate rewards accordingly. Assuming that competing firms face similar exogenous cost factors, competition provides information about managerial effort.

The X-inefficiencies associated with monopolies are another justification for removing entry barriers. Although society incurs costs because of competitive entry into markets with scale economies, many argue that these are more than compensated by the benefits from internal X-efficiencies. These advocates of liberalization do not deny the existence of natural monopolies, they simply consider their costs smaller than those associated with management "slack."

Evaluating the argument that local telephone service is a natural monopoly, Wenders builds on both the contestability and X-efficiency theories. He concludes that "[e]ven if competition produces, from a theoretical standpoint, an apparently wasteful duplication of plant, this apparent inefficiency is likely to be outweighed by the superior price- and cost-minimizing discipline offered by an unregulated market."[16] As he points out, the political realities of regulated local telephone service have effectively undermined any efficiency in pricing and investment allocations, thereby making competitive entry a much more attractive option from the perspective of economic efficiency.

Many policymakers have been persuaded that the costs of liberalization are relatively small compared to the maintenance of entry barriers, and, therefore, government regulation of entry should be reduced or eliminated. This line of reasoning guided U.S. legislators in their extensive deregulation of industries such as trucking, broadcasting, telecommunications, and air and rail transportation.[17] These ideas have also heavily influenced the thinking of British policymakers under Margaret Thatcher.[18] Government-enforced entry barriers to a number of British industries have been reduced: gas and electricity, some telecommunications services (VANS and customer premises equipment), airlines, coach and bus services, and domestic and international air services. Other countries such as Canada, France, and New Zealand have similarly reduced government-enforced entry barriers.

---

16. John T. Wenders, "Natural Monopoly and the Deregulation of Local Telephone Service," *Telecommunications Policy* 14 (April 1990): 127.

17. For a discussion of deregulation in the broadcasting industry, see Roderick Oram, "U.S. Regulation Shrinks to a Formality as TV Booms," *Financial Times*, 14 October 1988, 3; for further information on telecommunications and air and rail transportation, see Bailey and Baumol, "Deregulation."

18. Vickers and Yarrow, *Privatization;* Dennis Kavanagh, *Thatcherism and British Politics: The End of Consensus?* (Oxford: Oxford University Press, 1987), chap. 4.

TABLE 5.2. Competition in the European Telecommunication Equipment Market

	First Set	PBX	Mobile Phone	Radio Pager	Modem	Terminals			
						Telex	Teletex	Videotex	FAX
West Germany	1	2	3	3	2	3	3	2	2
France	2	2	2	2	2	2	2	2	2
Italy	1	2	2	2	1	1	2	2	2
Netherlands	1	1	1	1	2	1	2	2	2
Belgium	1	2	1	1	2	2	2	3	2
Luxembourg	1	3	3	1	2	3	3	3	3
U.K.	2	2	2	2	2	2	3	2	2
Ireland	1	2	2	–	2	2	–	2	2
Denmark	1	1	2	2	2	1	2	2	2
Greece	1	2	–	1	3	2	–	–	3
Spain	1	2	2	2	1	2	2	2	2
Portugal	1	2	–	–	2	1	–	–	3

Source: European Economic Community, *Towards a Dynamic European Economy: Green Paper on the Development of the Common Market for Telecommunications Services and Equipment* (Brussels: Commission of the European Communities, 1987).

Note: 1 = network operator exclusive provision, 2 = mixed supply, 3 = private supply only, – = none

Variation in Competition Policies

While numerous governments have implemented policies liberalizing entry barriers over the last ten years, a careful examination of different national policy initiatives suggests that they have varied considerably in their enthusiasm for liberalization and in the pace with which they have implemented these policies.

Nowhere is this diversity more evident than in the telecommunications industry, where governments have adopted quite distinct liberalization policies. Table 5.2 and 5.3 profile the range of entry barriers characterizing the European telecommunications industries. In table 5.2 the European Commission (EC) has summarized the extent of competition in nine telecommunications equipment areas as of 1989. With the exception of the United Kingdom and France, European telecommunications service providers had a monopoly on the provision of the first telephone set in each residence.[19] There is considerably more regulatory diversity in the other equipment areas. For example, in the case of radio pagers, the state had a monopoly in the Netherlands, Belgium, Luxembourg, and Greece; there was a mix of state and private competitors in France, Italy, the United Kingdom, Denmark, and Spain; and

19. With liberalization proceeding rather quickly in anticipation of the 1992 economic integration of Europe, these regulations are changing.

TABLE 5.3. Competition in the European Telecommunications Service Sector

| | Basic Service Network | | | | Use of Leased Circuits | | | |
| | | | | | Domestic Share | | International Share | |
	Local	Long-Distance	International	Mobile	Resell	Connect to Public Net	Resell	Connect to Public Net
Belgium	GM-PC	GM-PC	GM-PC	GM-PC	N[a]	N	N[a]	N[a]
Denmark	OM[b]	OM	GM	OM	N	N	N[a]	N[a]
France	GM	GM	GM	GM[c]	N[d]	N[d]	N[a]	N[a]
Greece	GM-PC	GM-PC	GM-PC	PL	N	N	N[a]	N[a]
Ireland	GM-PC	GM-PC	GM-PC	GM-PC	N[a]	N[a]	N	N
Italy	GM-PC	GM-PC	GM-PC	GM-PC	N[e]	N[e]	N[a]	N[a]
Luxembourg	GM	GM	GM	GM	N	—	N[a]	N[a]
Netherlands	GM[f]	GM[f]	GM[f]	GM[f]	N[g]	N[g]	N[a]	N[a]
Portugal	GM-PC	GM-PC	GM-PC[b]	—	N[h]	N[h]	N[a]	N[a]
Spain	OM[i]	OM[i]	OM[i]	OM[i]	N	N	N[a]	N[a]
United Kingdom	RC-LI	RC-LI	RC-LI	RC-LI	Y[j]	Y[j]	N[k]	N[k]
West Germany	GM	GM	GM	GM	Y[l]	Y[m]	Y[l]	Y[n]

Source: EEC, *Towards a Dynamic European Economy*.

Note: GM = government monopoly–government agency; GM-PC = government monopoly–public corporation; PL = partly liberalized; OM = other monopoly; RC-LI = regulated competition with liberalized entry; Y = generally permitted; N = generally prohibited.

[a] Subject to exceptions.

[b] Telecom service providers in addition to PTT on M basis.

[c] Licensing of additional providers to be announced.

[d] Steps toward licensing of private value-added services announced.

[e] New legislation on VANs being discussed in Parliament.

[f] PTT to be converted to limited liability company in 1989.

[g] Usage of VANs to be liberalized.

[h] Currently under consideration in commission.

[i] Telex, telegram, public facsimile, etc. provided by PTT.

[j] Pure resale prohibited until at least 1989.

[k] Pure resale prohibited until at least 1989, subject to additional restrictions.

[l] Shared use permitted, resale prohibited.

[m] Voice-band circuits at one end only.

[n] International fixed connections without restrictions, "flat rate" circuits with restrictions.

there were only private competitive providers of this equipment in West Germany.

Table 5.3 presents a similar profile for the telecommunications service sector. In the basic service network sector—local, long-distance, international, and mobile communications—there were government monopolies in all but three of the twelve EC countries. The United Kingdom had regulated competition with limited entry in all four areas. Greece was the only other country to have liberalized the service sector with its partial liberalization of mobile telephony.[20] There is more variation in the degree to which equipment maintenance has been liberalized. Finally, the shared use or resale of domestic leased circuits had been liberalized in the United Kingdom and Germany but was generally prohibited by the other ten EC countries.

Tables 5.2 and 5.3 present two puzzles. First, how do we explain the decision by virtually all governments to liberalize their regulation of the telecommunications industry? Second, what accounts for the significant differences in the degree of liberalization that has been adopted? The first puzzle is explained by recent technological changes in the industry that have advanced the contestability of telecommunication markets. A growing body of evidence indicates that government entry barriers are unnecessary and likely contribute to inefficiencies.

Countries have adopted quite different regulatory policies for the telecommunication industry: for example, the United Kingdom had dismantled many of its entry barriers while Germany, until very recently, left them virtually intact. Cross-national variations in competition policy is a function of two variables: political constituencies and institutions. There are *political constituents* for both removing and maintaining entry barriers, and their relative importance is likely to vary cross-nationally. The effectiveness of pressure for liberalization is also a function of variations in *institutional constraints* within which political actors must operate.

Communication Policy in Comparative Perspective

Liberalization has accelerated recently in such diverse economies as France, the United Kingdom, the United States, and even in Eastern Europe, raising the possibility that governments will progressively dismantle entry barriers to most industries. To some this suggests that national policies are converging to a norm of increased competition, with political factors playing a relatively insignificant role in shaping economic policies.[21] Similar claims have been

20. Since the EC report was published, a number of areas have been subject to liberalization. For example, the French and German governments have licensed competing private carriers in the mobile telephone sector.

21. An extreme expression of this view is the controversial article by Francis Fukuyama, "The End of History?" *National Interest* 16 (Summer 1989): 3–18.

made for other areas of government activity. Growth in overall government expenditures, for example, is primarily driven by the rate of national income growth; political factors account for a surprisingly small share of the variation.[22] There is a remarkable degree of consensus among nations on the need for state-supported national health insurance and social security.[23] Moreover, evidence would even suggest that communist and capitalist nations differed little in the priorities accorded public expenditures.[24] National competition policies may be the subject of similar forces promoting convergence.

Alternatively, cross-national differences in competition policies may persist and possibly even increase. The substantial variations in levels of deregulation indicated by tables 5.2 and 5.3 presented earlier in the chapter would certainly suggest that this is the more likely outcome. As Eli Noam has very aptly phrased it, the "postal-industrial" complex in most developed countries has very ardently pressured decision makers against any changes to status quo competition policies (most of which are extremely illiberal).[25] The result is that some countries have moved in more liberal directions while others maintain fairly severe entry barriers to the industry.

Four political variables suggest themselves as plausible explanations for these differences: electoral considerations, ideology, policy constituencies, and institutional constraints.

Electoral Explanations

Since virtually all governments covet reelection, this is often a good guide to their policy actions.[26] For example, in order to improve their chances of reelection, evidence suggests that incumbents manipulate macroeconomic policies to generate favorable outcomes such as low inflation, low unemploy-

---

22. James Alt and K. Alec Chrystal, *Political Economics* (Brighton, Sussex: Wheatsheaf, 1983), chap. 9; David Cameron, "The Expansion of the Public Economy: A Comparative Analysis," *American Political Science Review* 72 (1978): 1243–61.

23. Arnold Heidenheimer, Hugh Heclo, and Carolyn Teich Adams, *Comparative Public Policy: The Politics of Social Choice in Europe and America* (New York: St. Martin's Press, 1983).

24. Frederic L. Pryor, "Growth and Fluctuation of Production in OECD and East European Countries," *World Politics* 37 (1985): 204–37; Frederic L. Pryor, *Public Expenditures in Communist and Capitalist Nations* (London: Allen and Unwin, 1968).

25. Eli M. Noam, "Telecommunications Policy on Both Sides of the Atlantic: Divergence and Outlook," in *Marketplace for Telecommunications Regulation and Deregulation in Industrialized Democracies*, ed. Marcellus S. Snow (New York: Longman, 1986); and Eli M. Noam, "International Telecommunications in Transition," in *Changing the Rules: Technological Change, International Competition, and Regulation in Communications*, ed. Robert W. Crandall and Kenneth Flamm (Washington, D.C.: Brookings Institution, 1989).

26. Anthony Downs, *An Economic Theory of Democracy* (New York: Harper and Row, 1957), chap. 4.

ment, and high economic growth.[27] Regulatory policy, on the other hand, typically has very low saliency for much of the electorate and, therefore, is not likely to be a major issue in political campaigns.

Ideology

There can be no doubt that certain governments and political parties are more predisposed to liberalization of entry barriers, just as certain governments are more predisposed to social welfare expenditures.[28] For example, Margaret Thatcher, the Prime Minister of the United Kingdom, is ideologically committed to competition.[29] Nonetheless, just as ideology has been a very incomplete explanation for commitments to social welfare programs and expenditures, ideology is only a partial explanatory factor for variations in competition policies. While it is true that the United Kingdom has enthusiastically implemented liberalization policies, the conservative administration of Kohl in Germany has moved very slowly in this area. By contrast, New Zealand has undertaken very significant steps toward liberalization under a Labour Prime Minister, initiatives that, surprisingly, have been opposed by the Conservative party.[30]

Moreover, partisanship has been a poor historical predictor of policies governing market structure: parties of both the Left and Right have been responsible for initiatives drastically restricting competition. There are numerous examples of governments of the Right in France, Canada, Italy, Spain, Sweden, and the United Kingdom pursuing policies restricting competition and nationalizing private entities. An explanation for policy differences must go beyond the nominal ideological predispositions of incumbent

---

27. Raymond M. Duch, "The Politics of Investment by the Nationalized Sector," *Western Political Quarterly* 43 (June 1990): 245–65; E. Tufte, *The Political Control of the Economy* (Princeton, N.J.: Princeton University Press, 1978); A. T. Cowart, "The Economic Policies of European Governments, Part I," *British Journal of Political Science* 8 (July 1978): 238–311; M. Lewis-Beck, *Economics and Elections: The Major Western Democracies* (Ann Arbor: University of Michigan Press, 1988).

28. Douglas A. Hibbs, "Political Parties and Macroeconomic Policy," *American Political Science Review* 73 (1977): 1467–87; Alt and Chrystal, *Political Economics;* Cowart, "Economic Policies."

29. See Samuel Brittan, "Political Economy of Thatcherism," *Financial Times*, 1 December 1988; Robert Skidelsky, ed., *Thatcherism* (London: Chatto and Windus, 1988).

30. Claudia Rosett, "'Rogernomics' Transforms New Zealand," *Wall Street Journal*, 21 July 1987; Steven Greenhouse, "The Global March to Free Markets," *New York Times*, 19 July 1987. Also, for a discussion of the ambiguous relationship between party and support for privatization in France, see Harvey B. Feigenbaum, "Privatization and Interest Groups in France," paper prepared for the SOG Conference on Government and Organized Interests, Zurich, Switzerland, September 1989. See also, Gary Becker, "Ideology Gets Flexible," *Business Week*, 22 January 1990, 18.

governments. The next section takes us a step further by examining the role of interested constituencies in shaping competition policy.

Policy Constituencies

Although regulatory issues are of little concern to much of the electorate, they are of intense interest to narrow distribution coalitions that are directly affected by the policies. In fact, most scholars have focused on the role played by special interests in shaping regulatory policies and their implementation.[31] Because entry barriers reduce the uncertainties and risks of competition and often allow for monopoly profits, they tend to command the strong support of incumbent firms, labor, and suppliers to the industry.

Most importantly, these special interests have the organizational resources to be formidable proponents of continued regulation. The benefits of entry barriers tend to accrue primarily to the small number of firms that comprise a protected industry (a single firm in the case of a monopoly). On the other hand, consumers, who are usually very fragmented and dispersed (although this is not always the case), bear the costs of such policies. The "tax" imposed on the average consumer as a result of any particular entry barrier is typically very small. As Olson and others have pointed out, these small groups for which the benefits are concentrated and significant will be effective advocates of their interests while large groups that have a very dispersed membership and bear only a small cost of any particular regulation will be relatively ineffective lobbyists.[32] This traditional analysis of interest group support for regulatory barriers to entry is substantially borne out by events in the telecommunications industry.

Table 5.4 identifies five major interests affected by policies regulating entry to the telecommunications industry: government, labor, manufacturers of equipment, business consumers, and residential consumers. Down the rows of the table are listed the principal issues associated with competition policies. Each of the cells of the table indicates whether the particular interest group has a high or low preference for each of the issues along the columns. Two clusters of issue preferences can be identified in the table: government and labor with high preferences in the upper left-hand quadrants of the table and manufacturers and consumers with high preferences in the lower right-hand quadrants.

---

31. Charles Lindblom, *Politics and Markets: The World's Political Economic System* (New York: Basic Books, 1977); Barry M. Mitnick, *The Political Economy of Regulation: Creating, Designing, and Removing Regulatory Forms* (New York: Columbia University Press, 1980); Vickers and Yarrow, *Privatization*, chap. 4.

32. Mancur Olson, *The Logic of Collective Action* (Cambridge, Mass.: Harvard University Press, 1965).

TABLE 5.4.   Issue Preferences of Regulatory Constituencies

	Interest Level				
Preference	Government	Labor	Business Suppliers	Business Consumers	Residential Consumers
Protect employment	High	High	Low	Low	Low
Government revenues	High	High	Low	Low	Low
Preferential purchasing	High	High	High	Low	Low
Low tariffs	Low	Low	Very High	Very High	High
Efficiency	Low	Low	High	High	High
Service	Low	Low	High	High	High

Protect Employment

As is the case with most government-enforced monopolies, telecommunications service providers tend to be overmanned. In two cases where governments significantly reduced entry barriers—the United States and the United Kingdom—the labor force of the former monopolists declined considerably. After privatization, employment at British Telecom declined by about 5,000 per year.[33] AT&T has reduced its labor force by approximately 78,500 non-management jobs in the four years following divestiture.[34] Because lower entry barriers typically translate into employment-level reductions, organized labor will press hard to maintain entry barriers and thereby protect its members.[35] A case in point is the overwhelming rejection by the German Postal Workers Union of a referendum called by union leaders regarding the government's reform proposals for the Bundespost. Of the 83.7 percent participating in the poll, 96.6 percent rejected the proposals.[36]

Government officials are also sensitive to the employment issue—

---

33. "British Telecom: On the Defensive," *Financial Times*, 19 October 1987; Guy de Jonquieres, "Competition Dials up New Range of Services," *Financial Times*, 8 January 1986.

34. Calvin Sims, "Big Charge in Updating at AT&T," *New York Times*, 2 December 1988.

35. See the account of the opposition of British trade union officials to the introduction of competitive contracting for government services by Kate Ascher, *The Politics of Privatisation: Contracting Out Public Services* (New York: St. Martin's Press, 1987), 101–34.

36. "Aktionen gegen Postreform finden Rüeckhalt," *Frankfurter Allgemeine Zeitung*, 9 September 1988.

specifically, the political fallout associated with labor force reductions. As numerous empirical studies have demonstrated, voters respond to fluctuations in employment levels, punishing incumbents they consider responsible for rising levels of unemployment.[37] It is, therefore, often in the political interest of incumbent politicians to support the maintenance of entry barriers.

Government Revenues

With only a few exceptions, telecommunications service providers are entirely or partially government-owned. The revenues generated by these entities are either used to cross-subsidize various telecommunications services or are diverted to the government's general revenues. Dismantling entry barriers and introducing competition invariably reduce these revenues. Because governments very reluctantly give up revenue sources, they will not be enthusiastic supporters of liberalization.[38] Wages and salaries of organized labor also benefit from higher telecommunication revenues, thereby providing another reason for labor's support of entry barriers.

Preferential Purchasing

A third incentive to maintain entry barriers—preferential purchases— commands an even larger coalition of support, encompassing government, labor, and business. Telecommunications service providers are significant consumers of capital equipment. To ensure that their economies realize a maximum benefit from these purchases, governments have required telcos to favor either national manufacturers of this equipment or foreign companies that have local manufacturing facilities.[39] As a result, national telcos often sacrifice price and quality considerations to national industrial policy priorities.

   With the introduction of competition, these entities are forced to pay less attention to the national origins of capital equipment and pay much more

---

37. D. Roderick Kiewiet, *Macroeconomics and Micropolitics: The Electoral Effects of Economic Issues* (Chicago: University of Chicago Press, 1983), chap. 6; and Lewis-Beck, *Economics and Elections*.

   38. For a general discussion of this phenomenon, see James M. Buchanan and Richard Wagner, *Democracy in Deficit* (New York: Academic Press, 1977). More specifically, it is pointed out in Eli Noam's "International Telecommunications" that, as early as the sixteenth century, absolutist European rulers became very dependent upon the revenues generated by the newly formed European postal monopolies.

   39. EC, *Towards a Dynamic European Economy: Green Paper on the Development of the Common Market for Telecommunications Services and Equipment* (Brussels: Commission for the European Communities, 1987), chap. 6.

attention to cost considerations. Because local manufacturers and their employees benefit from preferential purchases, they can be counted on to oppose reductions in entry barriers that threaten their special relationship with the telcos. In addition, governments benefit because the purchase of domestic goods, as opposed to foreign goods, contributes to a number of industrial policy goals—including employment, balance of payments, and the development of local, high-technology industries. They too will be less than enthusiastic about relinquishing a convenient policy instrument.

Reducing Entry Barriers

The policy preferences typically associated with increased competition—lower tariffs, higher efficiency, and better service—have a much more diffuse constituency. Business and residential consumers of telecommunications services and products are the most likely beneficiaries of increased competition.[40] Because the benefits to any particular member of this constituency are quite marginal, they support these preferences with considerably less intensity than the groups discussed above.

Table 5.4 illustrates the asymmetry of interests associated with telecommunications competition policy. Opposing the preferences exhibited by government, labor, and manufacturers in the upper left-hand quadrant are the interests of business and residential consumers of telecommunications services in the lower right-hand quadrant. Consumers—both business and residential—are fundamentally indifferent to employment, revenues, and preferential purchasing issues, but are more likely to favor efficiency, pricing, and service. To the extent that lack of competition results in monopoly pricing (which is not only reflected in actual prices but also in terms of the quality of service received), consumers bear much of the social costs.

Given their intensity of preferences and their organizational resources, the groups represented in the upper left-hand quadrant of the table will likely dominate the decision-making process. Relatively speaking, the membership of this coalition is small, with each member realizing significant payoffs from government-enforced entry barriers.

Consumers, on the other hand, are a large and unwieldy coalition of interests, and the benefits to any particular member are relatively small.

---

40. It is possible, of course, that consumers might be hurt by the reduction of entry barriers. One case in point is the increase in the cost of residential telephone service that both U.S. and British consumers experienced when their governments liberalized their telecommunications industries. In effect, these increased tariffs were not the "result" of liberalization but, rather, were the result of the elimination of cross-subsidies that had been practiced by the telecommunication monopolists. With the elimination of entry barriers, telecommunications firms were free of government pressures to continue this type of cross-subsidization.

Moreover, the interests of business and residential consumers are not, at least in the short term, identical. Entry barriers and monopoly service provision has allowed the cross-subsidization of many residential consumers, often at the expense of business subscribers. The costs associated with organizing consumers and effectively representing their interests are simply too high, while they are significantly lower in the case of the coalition of government, labor, and manufacturers. As a result, over the last century there has been little modification in the entry barriers restricting competition in the telecommunications industry.

Yet even with this rather formidable political advantage on the part of the monopoly providers, a number of countries have recently reduced entry barriers to the telecommunications industry. This change cannot be explained by any radical alteration in the structure of interests affected by telecommunications regulation—they have essentially remained the same. Nor have the organizational costs associated with lobbying activities substantially changed for the two different coalitions. Rather, entry barriers are being dismantled because the "deadweight cost" to both the beneficiaries and to the consumers have increased considerably. I examine this explanation in the next section.

Deadweight Costs

Gary Becker has proposed a model of competition among pressure groups that helps explain these declining entry barriers.[41] Typical models of the regulatory process identify, on the one hand, beneficiaries or protected groups that are subsidized by policies and, on the other hand, taxpayers that must bear the burden of these subsidies through the payment of a tax (typically higher prices). Becker argues that we must also consider the deadweight costs associated with both the taxes and the subsidies. Deadweight costs are the "distortions in the use of resources induced by different taxes and subsidies."[42] The distortion effect of taxes is the depression of demand for goods or services. Subsidies, on the other hand, distort the supply of goods, encouraging, for example, higher levels of investment than would generally be expected without them.

Taxpayers, even given that they are difficult to organize, are not entirely powerless in the face of these subsidies. Their intrinsic advantage is that the deadweight cost associated with subsidies imposes a tax burden on the ordinary consumer. By contrast, this deadweight cost is an intrinsic disadvantage for subsidized groups (i.e., the beneficiaries of these subsidies) because it

---

41. Gary S. Becker, "A Theory of Competition Among Pressure Groups for Political Influence," *Quarterly Journal of Economics* (August 1983): 371–400.
42. Becker, "Theory of Competition," 373.

signals to taxpayers the distortions associated with entry barriers.[43] These subsidized groups are able to maintain entry barriers because "they can overcome their intrinsic disadvantage with an optimal size, efficiency at producing pressure, success at converting pressure into influence, or with characteristics that raise their influence."[44] But as this deadweight cost rises, taxpayers are more inclined to overcome any disadvantages they have at organizing and producing pressure; at the same time, the subsidized groups, since they too incur some of the deadweight costs, have less incentive to support the subsidies.

This model helps explain why entry barriers to the telecommunications industry are being dismantled when the configuration of interest groups remains intact. Becker argues that the deadweight costs of protective regulations rise as supply and demand in an industry become more elastic, providing a signal and an incentive for consumers and taxpayers to press for the reduction of entry barriers. Such a change in supply and demand elasticities has been occurring in the telecommunications industry over the last twenty years. As a result of dramatic technological advances in the telecommunications industry, capital investment costs have fallen, thereby increasing the elasticity of supply and dramatically reducing the cost of services.[45] All of this has, in turn, increased the elasticity of demand. Technological advances that have dramatically reduced capital investment costs include developments of increasingly smaller microprocessors, the introduction of digital technologies, and the availability of satellite and fiber optics networks for voice, data, and video transmissions.

This increased elasticity of supply and demand has raised the deadweight costs of the subsidies associated with entry barriers. Small changes in the cost of supplying products and services can now have a very significant impact on the quantities of goods made available on the market. Similarly, consumers have become increasingly sensitive to changes in the pricing of telecommunications goods and services. As a result, the impact of subsidies on overall industry demand and growth have become increasingly magnified.

Even beneficiaries of these subsidies are affected by the increased costs of entry barriers that might include inappropriate capital investments, slower industry growth, and lower rates of innovation. For example, restrictions on competition in the provision of customer premises equipment represent a subsidy to most national telcos because it allows them to market equipment at

---

43. Becker, "Theory of Competition," 373.

44. Becker, "Theory of Competition," 382.

45. Kenneth Flamm, "Technological Advance and Costs: Computers versus Communications," in *Changing the Rules*, ed. Robert W. Crandall and Kenneth Flamm (Washington, D.C.: Brookings Institution, 1989).

higher prices than would be possible in the case of free entry. The subsidy represents a tax to consumers who must pay inflated prices. Because the demand for this equipment is quite sensitive to price, the result is lower levels of demand. The resulting lower levels of equipment penetration reduce the overall demand for network usage (less customer premises equipment translates into lower calling volume on the network). Entry barriers to the Value-Added Networks (VANs) sector had a similar impact on the growth of the volume of network usage.[46] Restricting the number of service providers reduced network usage and, as a result, protected firms have had less and less incentive to pressure government officials to maintain entry barriers to the telecommunications industry.

Similarly, the deadweight costs of "taxes" have risen with higher levels of elasticity, thereby increasing the incentive for taxpayers to pressure government officials for reductions in entry barriers. Long-distance telephone service is an example. When demand for long-distance service was quite inelastic, reducing entry barriers had little impact on the pricing of service and on the number of subscribers. But with technological advances, costs have dropped significantly and demand has become more elastic. As a result, the number of consumers who benefit from competition and lower prices has risen, and the deadweight costs of inflated prices are therefore much higher.

The tax burden resulting from entry barriers to the industry affects business and residential consumers somewhat differently. For a number of reasons, residential consumers are not likely to be a force for liberalization. Even with increasing incentives for the dismantling of entry barriers, residential consumers continue to have significant organizational handicaps (they are a large, disparate group for whom the free-rider problem remains prohibitive). Moreover, large numbers of residential consumers stand to benefit from government-enforced monopolies because their tariffs are cross-subsidized by other users. For example, rural consumers are often subsidized out of revenues from urban or business subscribers. Also, local residential telephone service is frequently supported by long-distance revenues. Whether any particular residential consumers stand to benefit from liberalization depends upon a variety of factors including their income level, their usage patterns (for example how much long-distance calling they make or the time of the day during which they make calls), and their geographic situation (rural vs. urban, for example). In sum, residential consumers are both difficult to organize and quite heterogeneous, often having very divergent preferences.

Business consumers, on the other hand, face less daunting organizational handicaps. First, they are fewer in number, which makes it much easier,

---

46. Jennifer L. Schenker, "VANs: The Start of a Chain Reaction," *Communications International* (Magazine Supplement), 11 December 1989.

particularly for large businesses, to organize a collective effort to change policies. Second, their interests are much more homogeneous than is the case with residential consumers. For example, most businesses are large users of long-distance service, which means they have a common interest in reducing the long-distance subsidy to local—mostly residential—consumers. Finally, in the case of larger businesses, the savings from the elimination of entry barriers and the reduction of subsidies are typically significant.

Accordingly, business consumers have been the primary group pressing for the dismantling of entry barriers to the industry. In the United States, early pressure for deregulation came from large oil, retailing, and computer companies who were very heavy users of the network for both voice and data transmissions.[47] Pressure for liberalization in the United Kingdom came from the financial community in London and from the computer companies, once again the most heavy users of telecommunications in the country.[48] In Germany, we see similar pressure being brought on the government by multinational corporations that have either moved or threatened to move much of their telecommunications operations out of Germany to European countries with more favorable regulations.[49] Noam argues that a "second" electronics industry—composed of such medium-sized manufacturers as Nixdorf and Olivetti—have aligned with the large business users in their battle against entry barriers.[50]

Although this increased pressure for removing entry barriers is widespread, the policy responses of developed countries are quite different. Part of the explanation is that incentives for maintaining subsidies have varied. For example, the revenues governments realize from maintaining entry barriers vary from one country to another. In the United Kingdom the PTT has been a continual drain on the Treasury, while in Germany the Bundespost has been a significant net contributor to general government revenues. For the British government, there was considerably more to be gained from privatizing British Telecom and realizing the revenues from such a sale, while, in the case of Germany, the government realizes a significant annual stream of revenue by maintaining ownership.

The impact of technological change is not simply the result of cost-benefit evaluations by affected interests. If it were, competition policies would be more similar than is actually the case. As the following section points out, institutional factors also play an important role in shaping the policy response of different nations.

---

47. Alan Stone, *Wrong Number: The Breaking up of AT&T* (New York: Basic Books, 1989), part 3.

48. Jill Hills, *Deregulating Telecoms: Competition and Control in the United States, Japan, and Britain* (Westport, Conn.: Quorum Books, 1986). 79 and 205.

49. "Crossed Lines on the Market View," *Financial Times* (London), 28 September 1987.

50. Noam, "International Telecommunications," 263–65.

Institutional Constraints

All of the developed nations have interests pressing for or against the liberalization of entry barriers to the telecommunications industry (the configuration of interest-group preferences presented in table 5.4 is remarkably similar in most countries). But, their effectiveness varies from country to country because of institutional structures—interest group coalitions, the legislative process, electoral laws, and the courts—that mediate the demands of these affected interests and thereby significantly influence policy outcomes. Institutional structures either raise or lower the costs associated with efforts to change competition policies. An argument is advanced in the next section suggesting that modes of interest intermediation are the primary factor shaping the liberalization of entry barriers.

Pluralism Inhibits Economic Adjustment and Growth

The literature on interest intermediation has primarily focused on the distinction between pluralist and corporatist institutions. Mancur Olson, for example, divides developed countries into those with small numbers of highly encompassing distribution coalitions (e.g., Germany) and those with large numbers of distribution coalitions with relatively narrow bases of support (e.g., the United Kingdom). This division corresponds to the distinction Schmitter makes between corporatist and pluralist nations.[51]

Corporatism can be defined as a system of interest representation in which the constituent units are organized into a limited number of singular, compulsory, noncompetitive, hierarchically ordered, and functionally differentiated categories, recognized or licensed (if not created) by the state and granted a deliberate representational monopoly within their respective categories in exchange for observing certain controls on their selection of leaders and articulation of demands and supports.[52] The policy-making process in corporatist settings is characterized by "private interest government," a process whereby important public-policy decisions are negotiated directly between representatives of social and economic groups outside of governmental or legislative forums.[53]

Pluralist institutions, on the other hand, minimize participatory barriers

---

51. Philippe Schmitter and Gerhard Lehmbruch, eds., *Trends Toward Corporatist Intermediation* (Beverly Hills, Calif.: Sage Publications, 1979) and John R. Freeman, *Democracy and Markets: The Politics of Mixed Economies* (Ithaca, N.Y.: Cornell University Press, 1989).

52. Schmitter and Lehmbruch, *Trends Toward Corporatist Intermediation*, 13.

53. Wolfgang Streeck and Philippe C. Schmitter, "'Community, Market, State—and Associations?' The Prospective Contribution of Interest Governance to Social Order," in *Patterns of Corporatist Policy Making*, eds. Wolfgang Streeck and Philippe C. Schmitter (Beverly Hills, Calif.: Sage Publications, 1985), 17.

and thereby encourage the participation of interest groups in the political process. Coalitions of interests can be assembled relatively freely without requiring any formal recognition by the state or other regulatory authorities. Moreover, there are typically numerous governmental or legislative channels through which coalitions can try to effect policy change. In the United States, for example, the legislative, executive, and judicial branches provide a number of different channels through which interest coalitions can make their demands.

A significant body of literature links pluralism with economic decline.[54] Mancur Olson argues that the proliferation of distribution coalitions in a society inhibits economic growth. Because these groups are small in relation to society, they "have little incentive to make their societies more productive, but they have powerful incentives to seek a larger share of the national income even when this greatly reduces social output."[55] In societies where there are fewer distribution coalitions and where these groups are "highly encompassing" (i.e., they are the exclusive representatives of large numbers of interests), actors are more likely to take account of the social costs (typically, the reduction in social output) associated with their demands (wage settlements, for example).

Olson points out that this proliferation of distribution coalitions "slow[s] down a society's capacity to adopt new technologies and to reallocate resources in response to changing conditions, and thereby reduce[s] the rate of economic growth."[56] Britain, Olson explains, has not been able to adapt to changing economic circumstances and to new technologies because of the proliferation and strength of its distribution coalitions.[57] Germany and Japan, on the other hand, have fewer, although much more encompassing, distribution coalitions. As a result, according to Olson, they have been much more responsive to changing economic and technological circumstances. In short, Olson argues that greater levels of pluralism inhibit economic adjustment and growth.

In a similar vein, Freeman associates pluralism with conflict and "instability," which in turn "creates uncertainty about fiscal and other kinds of policy, an uncertainty that undermines the willingness of private business to undertake long-term investments."[58] Pluralism, according to Freemen's argument, undermines productivity and growth rates. Corporatism, on the other

---

54. Mancur Olson, *The Rise and Decline of Nations: Economic Growth, Stagflation, and Social Rigidities* (New Haven, Conn.: Yale University Press, 1982), 65 and Freeman, *Democracy and Markets*.

55. *The Rise and Decline of Nations*, 75.

56. *The Rise and Decline of Nations*, 65.

57. *The Rise and Decline of Nations*, 78.

58. Freeman, *Democracy and Markets*, 91.

hand, promotes greater certainty regarding such issues as wages and government fiscal and monetary initiatives, thereby yielding high rates of investment and greater levels of aggregate income for workers.

Pluralism Promotes Liberal Competition Policies

The arguments linking pluralism with economic decline and corporatism with growth assume that the appropriate responses to economic challenges (increased foreign competition, economic stagnation, etc.) are incremental and should favor the status quo. While these policies may have been effective during periods when most of the world's economies were relatively closed economic systems (i.e., sheltered from international trade and financial pressures), they are being challenged as the world's economies become increasingly interdependent. There is some evidence, though, that pluralist institutions, both political and economic (i.e., low entry barriers), may be a critical ingredient of economic growth in the period following the 1970s.[59]

Olson's argument that corporatist structures moderate demands by distribution coalitions, contributing to higher levels of productivity and therefore greater economic growth, accurately describes the post–World War II period through the 1970s. But these corporatist institutions stifle competition, and to the extent that competition in an economy promotes efficiency, they may threaten economic growth.

Corporatist countries with small numbers of highly encompassing distribution coalitions will be less responsive to pressures for the reduction of entry barriers and the promotion of competition. First, these coalitions tend to be dominated by the major corporations and labor organizations that benefit from restricted entry (inflated prices and high wages). Second, increased competition threatens the cohesiveness of encompassing coalitions. As competition increases, competing firms will be less likely to cooperate with each other and with labor on sensitive issues such as wage settlements. Because competition is inherently confrontational and risky (in that outcomes such as profitability are uncertain), it is not likely to be encouraged by corporatist institutions that are consensual by nature and place a high premium on stability and predictability.[60] A third consideration is the explicit or implicit designation of specific organizations as the legitimate representatives of inter-

---

59. Peter Murrell, "Growth of West German and British Manufacturing Industries," in *The Political Economy of Growth*, ed. Dennis C. Mueller (New Haven, Conn.: Yale University Press, 1983).

60. Murrell, "Growth of Manufacturing Industries," 13. Evidence of the threat to corporatist institutions posed by reduced entry barriers is provided for the Austrian case by Freeman, *Democracy and Markets*, 258–66.

ests in society. Because these officially recognized groups exercise a virtual monopoly over organizational life, they restrain the formation of new coalitions that challenge the political or economic status quo.

On the other hand, pluralist nations, with large numbers of relatively small distribution coalitions, will be more responsive to pressures for dismantling entry barriers. Lacking the monopolistic powers associated with encompassing distribution coalitions, threatened interests are less able to frustrate the efforts of procompetitive pressure-groups. Second, political institutions in these nations are designed to accommodate narrow and sometimes unorthodox interests, such as those favoring competition, deregulation, and privatization. Pluralist institutions—because they promote the building of new coalitions and because new interest coalitions typically have access to policymakers—are likely to facilitate challenges to existing political and regulatory entry barriers.

This argument can be illustrated at two levels of the policy-making process: in legislative and extralegislative bodies. Roger Noll has a persuasive theory relating legislative institutions to deregulatory policies. He argues that narrow economic interests—such as those pressing for deregulation of telecommunications—will have more success in political systems where the legislative body has considerable decision-making autonomy and in systems with single-member districts elected by plurality vote.[61] Because specific industries or narrow interest groups cannot compete with much broader interests at the national level (such as in a national political party), their success is linked to the ability to assemble a coalition of supporting legislators who can effectively champion their cause. Although the political weight of narrow economic interests may be insignificant at the national level, it can be quite decisive in local elections where the legislator represents a small fraction of the population and the outcome is decided by a simple plurality. The success of a lobbying effort that assembles a supportive coalition of legislators depends on whether legislators are able to act relatively autonomously and thereby initiate legislation on behalf of narrow economic interests.

Legislatures are, of course, not the sole avenue through which interests are mediated. In fact, issues pertaining to competition and regulation are frequently addressed outside the legislative arena. Virtually all countries have extralegislative bodies in which interests are mediated. In some cases the bodies are officially recognized, while in others they are informal but nonetheless very powerful. With respect to the liberalization of entry barriers, two considerations are important. First, as the *number* of extralegislative bodies

---

61. Roger G. Noll, "The Political and Institutional Context of Communications Policy," in *Marketplace for Telecommunications: Regulation and Deregulation in Industrialized Democracies,* ed. Marcellus Snow, 55–57 (New York: Longman, Inc., 1986).

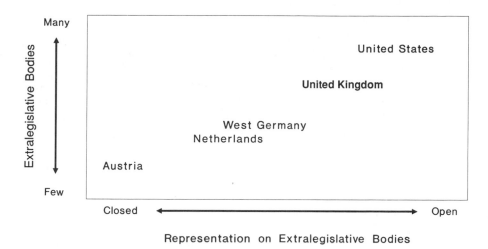

Fig. 5.1.   Categorization of national political institutions

rises, they are increasingly narrow in orientation and, therefore, more likely to respond to pressures from narrow interests. Second, the less restrictive they are regarding *membership* or participation in deliberations, the more responsive they are to narrow interests that might press for changes in the status quo, such as the liberalization of entry barriers.

Figure 5.1 illustrates the argument. There tends to be a positive relationship between the two variables. At the lower left-hand of the quadrant, we find corporatist countries where the policy process is least receptive to pressures from narrow interests—there are few extralegislative bodies and the ones that exist are relatively closed in terms of who can participate. Austria is an excellent example: much of the economic decision making takes place outside of the legislature in officially recognized corporatist entities, and membership in these bodies is restricted to the national representatives of leading social and economic interests in Austrian society.[62]

At the other extreme, in the upper right-hand corner of the quadrant, are pluralist countries in which there are many extralegislative entities and representation before these bodies is very unrestricted. The United States is a case in point. On the issue of telecommunications regulations, for example, the extralegislative bodies preoccupied with the issue include the Federal Com-

---

62. Peter Katzenstein, *Small States in World Markets* (Ithaca, N.Y.: Cornell University Press, 1985).

munications Commission, the Justice Department, the Supreme Court, and the state regulatory bodies (Public Utility Commissions). Representation before many of these bodies, particularly the Federal Communications Commission and the Public Utility Commissions, is virtually without restriction.

Political systems in the upper right-hand of the quadrant have institutional environments that tolerate challenges to the regulatory status quo (politico-economic entrepreneurs have the opportunity to press for the dismantling of entry barriers and often have a reasonable chance of assembling supportive coalitions in these extralegislative bodies). On the other hand, political systems in the lower left-hand quadrant have extralegislative deliberative and decision-making bodies that clearly favor the status quo and provide very few opportunities to narrow interest groups challenging established entry barriers.

Statist Institutions

Certain styles of interest accommodation are neither pluralist nor corporatist but *statist* in nature. Their principal characteristic is the relative ineffectiveness of distribution coalitions, either of the pluralist or corporatist variety. Filling this void are strong centralized state institutions that set the policy agenda and dominate the political process.[63] A good example is France, where the state—backed up by a formidable bureaucracy—is able to impose its will on society.[64] In the Fifth Republic, important policy changes have come at the initiation of technocratic planners rather than from interested groups in society.

Under this style of interest accommodation (or should I say nonaccommodation?), the dismantling of entry barriers will depend upon the initiatives of government. Interest groups are not likely to represent a significant catalyst for policy change. The impetus for change, to the extent that there is any support at all, will come from government policymakers and planners. Because the liberalization of regulatory structures and entry barriers represents a direct threat to the state's control over the economy and, therefore, to the role of policymakers and planners, it is not likely to be embraced enthusiastically by statist regimes. Nonetheless, if government authorities embark upon a policy of liberalization, they are not likely to face much effective resistance from entrenched interests, as would be the case in both the pluralist and corporatist settings.

---

63. Eric Nordlinger, *On the Autonomy of the Democratic State* (Boston: Harvard University Press, 1981).

64. Pierre Birnbaum, *La Classe dirigeante française* (Paris: Presses Universitaires de France, 1978).

TABLE 5.5. Characteristics of Distribution Coalitions

| | Styles of Interest Accommodation | | |
	Pluralist	Statist	Corporatist
Organization	Fragmented	Fragmented	Centralized
Numbers	Numerous	?	Few
Size	Small	?	Large
Policy-making role	Important	Relatively Unimportant	Important
Official recognition	No	?	Yes
Policy-making interventions	Episodic	Few	Regularized

National Styles of Interest Accommodation

Table 5.5 briefly summarizes the characteristics of distribution coalitions in pluralist, statist, and corporatist political systems. No nation falls squarely into any of these categories; rather, nations are characterized as having a predominance of one style of interest accommodation. In most European countries, these institutions were shaped by the post–World War II challenges of economic reconstruction.

Britain
Unlike many other European nations, Britain did not respond to post–World War II economic challenges by forging closer decision-making ties between business, labor, and government.[65] Political conflict seriously undermined any attempts to create corporatist institutions for resolving distributional issues. Such attempts were frustrated by a trade-union movement that was very decentralized and divided between mass and elite workers, two dominant political parties with strongly opposing views on labor's role in the economy, and a narrow focus by both parties on issues concerning wages and the right to strike.[66] At the same time, Conservative governments that dominated policy-

65. See, for example, Andrew Shonfield, *Modern Capitalism, The Changing Balance of Public and Private Power* (New York: Oxford University Press, 1965); Schmitter and Lehmbruch, *Trends;* Peter A. Hall, *Governing the Economy, the Politics of State Intervention in Britain and France* (New York: Oxford University Press, 1986); and Freeman, *Democracy and Markets.*

66. John Zysman, *Governments, Markets, and Growth: Financial Systems and the Politics of Industrial Change* (Ithaca, N.Y.: Cornell University Press, 1983), 173–80; Stephen Blank,

making in the 1950s promoted a liberal model of government-industry relations that maintained an arm's length relationship between the two.[67] Finally,
the British civil service, which exercises overwhelming control over policy
formulation and implementation, has traditionally been an institution of gen-
eralists, with limited independent technical resources and, therefore, dependent on interested parties for information necessary to formulate and implement policies. As a result, the policy agenda is set by individual interested
parties with few constraints imposed by the civil service. Quite unlike other
European countries, this is a model of a relatively passive bureaucracy, react-
ing to their political masters and the pressures of interested parties rather than
forging consensual agreements among major groups in society.[68] In sum, a
pluralist model of government.

The United Kingdom's pluralist style of interest accommodation allows
groups effective access to the policy-making process.[69] In fact, many observers attribute Britain's dismal economic performance in the 1960s and
1970s to the permeability of the political process by narrow interest groups.[70]
Samuel Beer has coined the phrase, "pluralistic stagnation" to describe the
negative impact "new group politics" had on the British economy.[71] Attempts
to overcome this institutional "handicap" have had little success. Efforts by
successive British governments in the 1960s and early 1970s to introduce a
more consensual, corporatist style of mediating between conflicting interests
failed,[72] as have efforts to institute economic planning in the United
Kingdom.[73]

"Britain: The Politics of Foreign Economic Policy, the Domestic Economy, and the Problem of
Pluralistic Stagnation," in *Between Power and Plenty*, ed. Peter J. Katzenstein, 128 (Ithaca,
N.Y.: Cornell University Press, 1987).

67. Zysman, *Governments, Markets, and Growth*; Stephen Blank, "Politics of Foreign
Economic Policy," 101.

68. Shonfield, *Modern Capitalism*, 172–73.

69. Kate Ascher, *The Politics of Privatization*, 57; Samuel Beer, *British Politics in the
Collectivist Age* (New York: Knopf, 1965); Samuel Finer, *Anonymous Empire*, rev. ed. (London:
Pall Mall Press, 1966); Mancur Olson, *The Rise and Decline of Nations: Economic Growth,
Stagflation, and Social Rigidities* (New Haven, Conn.: Yale University Press, 1983), 78.

70. Olson, *The Decline of Nations*; Samuel Brittan, *The Economic Consequences of Democracy* (London: Temple Smith, 1977); Brittan, *Steering the Economy: The Role of the Treasury*, rev. ed. (Harmondsworth: Penguin Books); Finer, *Anonymous Empire*; and Freeman, *Democracy and Markets*.

71. Beer, *British Politics*, chap. 12; Shonfield, *Modern Capitalism*.

72. Samuel Brittan, *Steering the Economy* (Harmondsworth: Penguin, 1970); Shonfield,
Modern Capitalism.

73. Thomas Balogh, "Britain's Planning Problems," in *Beyond Capitalist Planning*, ed.
Stuart Holland, chap. 7 (Oxford: Basil Blackwell, 1978).

Germany

West Germany has a corporatist style of interest accommodation. The most important contributing factors are the concentrated and centrally organized private interests. Since 1945, West German unions have adopted a united, industrywide form of organization compared to the decentralization of U.K. industrial unions.[74] West German business interests have been organized in centralized "peak associations" since 1870, "some 90 years before a similar institution finally emerged in the United Kingdom."[75] The West German financial sector is also characterized by a high level of power concentrated in the hands of a small number of investment banks that control, along with the regional banks of the Federal Reserve, much of the nation's economy. Similar levels of centralization characterize the church and social professions that play an important role in German politics.[76]

This structure of West German peak associations facilitates interelite bargaining on important policy issues. Political institutions in Germany delegate political authority to formal or informal corporatist structures ("private governments" as they are labeled by Katzenstein) that limit participation to elite representatives from centralized peak associations. The "Concerted Action" initiated by the "Grand Coalition" government of the Christian Democratic Union and Social Democratic Party has institutionalized the practice of negotiated agreements between government, labor, and business on important social and economic policies.[77] Similarly, West Germany has a number of parapublic institutions such as the Federal Reserve, the Labor Office, and the Social Welfare Fund, in which elite representatives are able to negotiate policy outcomes and assist in their implementation without the degree of partisan conflicts that might characterize more public confrontations.[78]

Corporatist styles of interest accommodation have enjoyed such success in the German context because of an institutional environment that concentrates representational authority in centralized organizations and a strong tradition of parapublic decision-making bodies.

---

74. Peter J. Katzenstein, "West Germany as Number Two: Reflections on the German Model," in *The Political Economy of West Germany*, ed. Andrei S. Markovits, 201 (New York: Praeger, 1982).

75. Katzenstein, "West Germany," 201.

76. Katzenstein, "West Germany," 201.

77. Ralf Dahrendorf, *Society and Democracy in Germany* (New York: Norton, 1979); Wolfgang Streeck, "Organizational Consequences of Neocorporatist Cooperation in West German Labour Unions," in *Patterns of Corporatist Policy Making*, ed. Gerhard Lehmbruch and Philippe C. Schmitter (Beverly Hills, Calif.: Sage Publications, 1982); Hall, *Governing the Economy*, 236–42.

78. Katzenstein, "West Germany" 202.

France

France falls in the statist category.[79] One of the most important explanations for this grouping is the long tradition of strong, centralized government control over the economy.[80] This tradition has its roots in the efforts of Louis XIV's ministers—Colbert being the most prominent—to effect greater centralized control over the French economy.[81] Second, as Shonfield points out, French governments in the post–World War I era began to play an increasingly managerial and entrepreneurial role in the economy. During this period, we see the birth, on a very large scale, of "mixed enterprises" in which the French state was an active partner with private capital in the formation of national companies such as Compagnie Française des Pétroles and Crédit National.[82]

A third critical factor was the adoption, after World War II, of a centralized Commissariat du Plan that was responsible for directing the rebuilding of France's economy. For most of the post–World War II period, the French government has conducted a very *dirigiste* industrial policy designed by government planners and imposed on industrialists.[83] French government planners are credited with designing, albeit in consultation with French industry, the broad lines of French efforts to rebuild its industrial infrastructure in the 1950s and 1960s. They have also played a key role in the modernization and internationalization of French industry in the 1970s.[84]

A final reason for grouping France in the statist category is the relative powerlessness of its major interest groups. These policies have been imposed on an often reluctant French business and labor community through government's control over state enterprises, government subsidies, and credit allocation.[85] Hennart points out that, in the post–World War II period, French labor,

---

79. This may be changing with the liberalization policies initiated by the French Conservative government. Note, though, that Cohen questions whether there have been any significant changes to the "*etatist* mode of economic policy-making" in S. Cohen, "Informed Bewilderment: French Economic Strategy and the Crisis," in *France in the Troubled World Economy*, ed. S. Cohen and P. Gourevitch, 23 (London: Butterworths, 1982). There are some signs that the Socialist government elected in 1988 intends to assert the power of the state to supervise the rationalization of French industry in preparation for increased liberalization of European trade barriers.

80. Shonfield, *Modern Capitalism*, 71–87; S. Cohen, *Modern Capitalist Planning: The French Model*, 2d ed. (Berkeley: University of California Press, 1977).

81. Shonfield, *Modern Capitalism*, 77.

82. Shonfield, *Modern Capitalism*, 82.

83. Hall, *Governing the Economy*, 54–64; Zysman, *Governments, Markets, and Growth*, 105; John Zysman, "The French State in the International Economy," in *Between Power and Plenty: Foreign Economic Policies of Advanced Industrial States*, ed. P. Katzenstein, 255–94 (Madison, Wisc.: University of Wisconsin Press, 1978).

84. Cohen, "Informed Bewilderment," 23–26; Zysman, *Governments, Markets, and Growth*, chap. 3.

85. S. Cohen, *Modern Capitalist Planning*; Shonfield, *Modern Capitalism*; Zysman, *Governments, Markets, and Growth*.

business, and agriculture—because of internal divisions and poor organization—have had relatively little influence on major economic policy decisions.[86]

This section has distinguished three types of institutional settings in which conflicting interests are mediated: pluralist, corporatist, and statist. The United Kingdom is considered representative of a pluralist regime, West Germany is categorized as a corporatist regime, and France is characterized as a statist regime. This institutional variable is hypothesized to affect the receptiveness of political systems to liberal policy initiatives, with pluralist being the most receptive and corporatist structures the least. There are, in effect, three sets of variables: both pressures for change and the institutional structures that process these demands are the independent variables; the dependent variable is policy change.

It is important to point out that these two sets of independent variables are exogenous and uncorrelated with each other. Second, both concepts are quite distinct from the dependent variable, policy change. As I have attempted to illustrate in this section, each of these three countries have developed very different modes of interest intermediation that have taken shape throughout the post–World War II period but have roots much further back in each country's political traditions. The second set of independent variables, domestic and international pressures to adopt liberal economic policies, has only very recently presented a serious challenge to government decision makers and is quite independent of the institutional variables in this model of change.

A final issue concerns whether nations self-select certain institutional structures because they have certain predispositions to liberal policy change. For example, is Germany a corporatist society because of a general preference for stability and a predisposition against policy change?[87] This possibility obviously cannot be rejected unless we are able to randomly assign countries to these institutional categories and then subject them to equal levels of pressure for change. Moreover, this study of only three cases is not meant to provide any conclusive statistical evidence on the link between institutions and change. Nonetheless, the qualitative evidence suggests that the development of these institutional structures has been entirely independent of any national predispositions toward policy change or liberalism. All three countries, regardless of their institutional structures, have experimented with a

---

86. Jean-François Hennart, "The Political Economy of Comparative Growth Rates: The Case of France," in *The Political Economy of Growth*, ed. Dennis C. Mueller (New Haven, Conn.: Yale University Press, 1983).

87. For an excellent discussion of this and similar problems that face quasi-experimental design, see Christopher H. Achen, *The Statistical Analysis of Quasi-Experiments* (Berkeley, Calif.: University of California Press, 1986).

number of quite radical policy changes in the post–World War II period. The United Kingdom experimented during the 1960s with corporatist institutions, but they failed to take root. Similarly, France, under Chirac, experimented rather unsuccessfully with liberal institutional innovations.

Implications for Competition Policy

The United States has experienced more than a decade of policy changes designed to reduce entry barriers to a number of industries—including telecommunications, airlines, trucking, banking, securities, and broadcasting. Pressures for similar types of initiatives have increased in most of the developed world, leading many to question whether similar deregulation would take root in all developed economies. This is unlikely because of the cross-national variations in institutional factors identified in the preceding section. Countries in which conflicting interests tend to be mediated within pluralist institutions are most receptive to such pressures for liberalized competition policies; countries with statist institutions are less so; countries with a corporatist tradition for interest mediation are least receptive to such policy changes.

As subsequent chapters show in detail, this has been the case with telecommunications policy. The United Kingdom, falling in the pluralist category, has led Europe in dismantling entry barriers to the telecommunications industry. Recent legislation, for example, has allowed the licensing of Mercury as a competitor to British Telecom in the provision of such network services as long-distance calls and private leased-lines. Similar legislation has introduced competition in the provision of Value-Added Network services and customer premises equipment. France, with its statist traditions, has promoted some competitive policies in the area of Value-Added Network services and customer premises equipment but has insisted on maintaining government monopoly control over network facilities. Pressures for the introduction of competition into the telecommunications industry were resisted the most in Germany where, until very recently, the government strongly supported the Bundespost monopoly over network facilities and services.

A similar pattern is evident in areas other than telecommunications. Once entirely dominated by government monopolies, the European broadcasting industry is becoming increasingly competitive. Of the three countries under study here, the British have the most competitive television broadcasting industry, followed by the French who have recently liberalized the industry and, in turn, followed by the Germans who have maintained the state monopoly over television broadcasting.

The United Kingdom was the first of the European countries to adopt private competition in the broadcasting industry—the independent television network (ITV) began competing with the BBC in 1955. More recently, Channel Four was licensed as a private broadcaster in the United Kingdom. Prior to 1980, only Italy had followed the British example of introducing private competition to the government's broadcasting monopoly. In many respects, though, the British broadcasting industry retains certain monopolistic features. Because the BBC relies entirely on licensing fees for support and ITV has a monopoly on advertising, the two networks do not compete directly with one another for revenue. Concerned about this duopoly situation, a government study, the Peacock Report, recently proposed a number of measures that would further increase competition in the industry.[88] Overall, broadcasting has been much more competitive in the United Kingdom than in other European nations.[89]

French broadcasting, on the other hand, has only recently begun to experiment seriously with competition.[90] Prior to 1980, television broadcasting was the absolute monopoly of the French government. Liberalization began during the Socialist administration in the early 1980s. The Socialist government licensed a private over-the-air television station (Canal Plus) and awarded private licenses for the Fifth and Sixth UHF channels. Under the Conservative government of Chirac, liberalization has gone even further. In addition to reassigning the licenses for the Fifth and Sixth channels, the Conservatives privatized TF1, one of the three state networks.[91] By privatizing TF1, the government created a strong private competitor to the remaining two government-owned networks. All told there are now five television networks, three in the hands of private interests and two state-owned.

Germany, as the institutional argument predicts, has been least receptive to pressures for liberalizing the broadcasting industry.[92] The two television networks in Germany, ARD and ZDF, are both government-owned. Only recently have some of the *Länder* governments been considering candidates for private broadcasting licenses.[93] Corporatist institutions are the chief bulwarks against the introduction of competition from the private sector. Under

---

88. "Comfortable Duopoly Under Fire, but Quality Programmes Praised," *Financial Times* (London), 4 July 1986, 9.

89. Chantal de Gournay, Pierre Musso, and Guy Pineau, *Télévisions déchaînées: La Dérèglementation en Italie, en Grande-Bretagne et aux Etats-Unis* (Paris: La Documentation Française, 1985).

90. B. Miege, P. Pajon, and J. M. Salaun, *L'industrialisation de l'audiovisuel: Des programes pour les nouveaux medias* (Paris: Editions Aubier, 1986).

91. "De l'Art d'Arbitrer entre Plusieurs Amis," *Le Monde*, 20 February 1987, 10; "French Broadcasting Reforms Come to a Vote," *Financial Times* (London), 13 August 1986, 2; "Le Choc des Projects," *Le Monde*, 25 February 1987.

92. Friedrich Karl Fromme, "Befüerchtungen und Erwartungen zum privaten Rundfunk," *Frankfurter Allgemeine Zeitung*, 23 June 1988, 2.

93. "Special Section: West Germany," *Economist*, December 1986.

the present situation, the major interests in German society, including the political parties, are guaranteed positions on the boards that oversee the operation of the television channels. Their role is to ensure that television programming reflects opinions and attitudes in German society. The introduction of private television threatens the control exercised by distribution coalitions in Germany and, therefore, has been resisted by the political parties and by major interest groups in the country.[94]

Finance is a third area that is experiencing increasing pressures for liberalization.[95] The financial services sector is growing in importance in most developed nations, and governments are under pressure from domestic firms to deregulate the industry and promote competition in order to maintain the nation's competitiveness in attracting financial business.[96] Although the pattern of policy differences is less dramatic, it confirms the contention that pluralist environments are considerably more supportive of competitive policies than statist and corporatist settings are.

In October 1986, the United Kingdom implemented the Financial Services Bill that radically liberalized regulations governing its financial services industry. Regulations that prohibited commercial banks from providing investment banking services (such as the underwriting of securities) and also prevented firms from offering banking and brokerage services were eliminated. Firms are now permitted to offer clients a full range of financial services, including commercial banking, investment banking, underwriting, and brokerage services. Restrictions on foreign participation in the banking and securities industries were abolished. Most important, membership on the London Stock Exchange was opened up to both British and foreign members, and fixed commissions on securities transactions were abolished.

This is another example of the United Kingdom taking a leadership role among developed nations in the elimination of entry barriers and the promotion of competition. The original intention of the Financial Services Bill was simply to abolish fixed brokerage commissions. It was pressure from a variety of different interests in London's financial community that successfully convinced the government to expand the scope of the legislation. The omnibus Financial Services Bill is the result of incorporating a variety of conflicting demands by rather narrow special interest groups such as the Bank of England, securities firms, commercial and investment banking, insurance and pension funds, and multinational financial service firms. Liberalization of the

---

94. Arthur Williams, "West Germany: The Search for the Way Forward," in *The Politics of Broadcasting*, ed. Raymond Kuhn (Worcester, England: Biling and Sons, 1985).

95. For a review of recent policy initiatives in Europe, see "Europe's Capital Markets," *Economist*, 16 December 1989.

96. "New Barriers for Old in the Major Markets," *Financial Times* (London), 22 May 1986, 3.

French and German financial markets has proceeded at a slower and more controlled pace.

Part of the statist tradition in France is the tight control the government exercises over financial institutions. For example, unlike the United States and Britain, which have attempted to control monetary aggregates through central bank lending and reserve requirements, France has a long history of credit controls and the rationing of borrowed funds.[97] The Socialist administration was responsible for initiating efforts to promote competition in the industry. Until 1984, only the three largest French banks were involved in major corporate financing. The Socialists eliminated barriers to this industry by establishing a market in commercial paper and thereby allowing corporate treasurers to borrow directly from institutional funds. The same government opened up a market in certificates of deposits (CDs).

The election of the Conservative Chirac government ended credit rationing. Rather than seeking to control interest rates through credit rationing, the Banque de France would operate like other central banks and seek to influence such rates through the interbank market (the cost of funds lent among banks).[98] Policies have also been adopted to open up the securities industry. Banks can now compete in some areas of the securities industry—once the monopoly of state-licensed brokers. Recently, the first futures market was established in France for trading in bonds and short-term instruments, and both banks and brokers are allowed to trade.[99] Previously, banks were not allowed to trade in any type of securities. Similarly, brokers have gained increasing entry to the financial industry; they are now allowed to trade in the certificate of deposit market.

West Germany has also liberalized its financial markets. Recent government initiatives have created a number of new financial instruments (such as DM denominated certificates of deposit), reduced restrictions on foreign participation in government debt consortia, and abolished the 25 percent withholding tax on securities.[100] It is important to note, however, that the country's financial sector has a history of relatively liberal entry barriers and has not been excessively burdened with government restrictions and controls. Unlike most other countries (the United Kingdom, the United States, and France, for example), West German banks have not been restricted to lending activities and prohibited from underwriting securities. Under the "universal

---

97. Zysman, *Governments, Markets, and Growth*.

98. "The Right Wants France out of the Banking Business," *Business Week*, 7 October 1985, 45.

99. *Economist*, 29 November 1986.

100. "Foreign Banks Make their Mark," *Banker*, April 1987, 41; "West German Banking, Finance, and Investment," *Financial Times* (London), 7 July 1986, sec. 3; "A Survey of Television," *Economist*, 6 December 1986, 23.

banking" concept, German banks have also been permitted to take unlimited equity interests in nonbanking enterprises—something severely restricted in countries like the United States or the United Kingdom. These liberal banking regulations shaped the close relationship that has evolved in West Germany between the banks and major corporations. By nurturing this close relationship, banking regulations have significantly contributed to the corporatist character of decision making in West Germany. As a result, the leading banks in Germany (Deutsche Bank, Dresdner Bank, and Commerzbank, in particular), through their equity interest in major German corporations, play a significant role in shaping industrial policy.[101]

Liberalization of the German financial sector has not posed the same threat to corporatist institutions as it has in telecommunications and broadcasting for two major reasons. First, the financial sector has a history of liberal regulations; in this context, the deregulation initiatives taken by the Kohl government in the last couple of years are not radical departures from tradition (unlike France, where the liberalization initiatives represented significant changes in policy). Second, liberal regulations have served corporatist institutions well by promoting the centralization of economic power in the German banking sector.

This brief overview of liberalization in the telecommunications, broadcasting, and finance industries illustrates the extent to which institutional structures can either inhibit or promote the introduction of competition. Subsequent chapters provide more in-depth evidence of this link, drawing upon evidence from the telecommunications industries of France, the United Kingdom, and Germany.

Conclusion

As chapter 4 pointed out, there is a growing body of economic literature suggesting that government-enforced entry barriers—even in industries traditionally considered to be natural monopolies—should be eliminated. This chapter presents a political explanation for the very different competition policies adopted by the Western democracies.

We have seen, over the past decade, an increased interest in the liberalization of certain industries, the result primarily of technological advances that increased the demand and supply elasticities for products and services traditionally provided by monopolists. This increased sensitivity to prices and costs made both consumers and monopolists much more aware of the "tax" burdens associated with the subsidies resulting from government-enforced entry barriers. As a result, consumers were more likely to press for policy

---

101. "German Banks Maintain Corporate Grip," *Wall Street Journal*, 30 September 1987.

changes that reduced entry barriers, and monopolists had less incentive to lobby for their maintenance.

Although we note a general acceptance of reduced entry barriers, countries vary considerably in terms of their commitment to increased competition. Part of the explanation is the configuration of interests supporting and opposing increased competition in each country. I have identified three critical variables in the case of government controlled telecommunications monopolies. The more profitable the national telco, the less likely that governments would be willing to reduce revenues by introducing competition. A well-organized labor union representing employees from the national telco would inhibit efforts to introduce competition because of the threats to employment levels and benefits. Finally, the more highly concentrated the firms supplying equipment to the national telco, the less likely that the government would relax entry barriers.

Also important is the variation among nations in the institutional structures through which changes in competition policies are enacted. Certain institutional structures facilitate reduction in entry barriers while others inhibit such policy changes. Pluralist institutions are most conducive to these changes because they make it relatively easy for new entrants to challenge established policies. Countries such as France that are dominated by statist institutions lack the organizational infrastructure that might successfully challenge established entry barriers. Nonetheless, once governments commit themselves to the implementation of policies promoting competition, they face little effective opposition. Corporatist institutions are least receptive to policies reducing entry barriers because they tend to concentrate political power in the hands of established interests that benefit substantially from these restrictions.

CHAPTER 6

Germany: Telecommunications in a Corporatist Context

The history of telecommunications development in Western Europe is rich in data regarding the link between institutional structures and the dependent variables of interest here: economic performance and liberal policy initiatives. Although the case studies of Germany, France, and the United Kingdom that follow are not rigorous empirical tests of the hypotheses introduced earlier, they furnish important insights into how political institutions shape the performance of public enterprises. Moreover, the three studies span a hundred-year period during which many policy modifications were both proposed and implemented, providing qualitative evidence for the arguments that relate styles of interest intermediation and change.

I begin with Germany, where telecommunications policy outcomes pose a number of interesting questions that seem to be inconsistent with traditional economic and political models.

In the early years of German telephony, we find the state-owned telco outperforming its private counterparts in other European countries. Ironically, political constraints were lower in public, as opposed to private, telcos. Because government ownership eliminated the risk of nationalization, the climate for investment and growth was more favorable in Germany than in France and the United Kingdom, where the telecommunications industry was dominated by privately owned entities.

After World War II, the German case raises an entirely different question. Why did the country's telecommunications infrastructure develop so slowly compared to its counterparts in other developed nations? Any simple explanation based on economic ownership is clearly insufficient because a number of state-owned firms outperformed the German telco (France and Sweden, for example) during this period. Once again we must look to political institutions for an explanation. Since the interwar years, the German telco has been governed by corporatist structures that institutionalized the influence of labor and manufacturers while excluding consumers—both residential and business—from the telecommunications policy process. Political control by this select group of interests inhibited post–World War II growth by keeping costs, and therefore prices, high.

A third question concerns the hesitancy with which Germany moved toward liberalizing its telecommunications policies. Once again we seek an explanation in the corporatist policy-making institutions that proved a very effective bulwark against change, both with respect to liberalization of industry entry barriers and to the reorganization of the telco's structure. Interests that would benefit from such changes—residential and business consumers in particular—had no effective channel through which to pressure decision makers. They were not part of the corporatist coalition that controlled policymaking and therefore had little opportunity to affect it.

This chapter addresses three major periods in the development of German telephony: the pre-infrastructural period that preceded World War II; the infrastructural period that followed the war; and the recent post-infrastructural period that began in the late 1970s.

Pre–World War I: Government Ownership and Political Risk

The interesting puzzle of pre–World War I telephony is the strong performance of the state-owned German PTT compared to France and the United Kingdom where *privately owned* telcos played such an important role. The explanation (initially introduced in chap. 2) is that arbitrary government policies, such as confiscatory taxation or uncompensated nationalization, increase risk and discourage capital investment by private entities. This absence of risk is in contrast to the French and British cases, where private telcos were continually threatened by impending nationalization.

In the latter part of the nineteenth and early twentieth centuries, private telecommunications service providers in Europe faced very high levels of political risk. Postal and telegraph authorities in virtually all of Europe saw the telephone as a direct competitor. In an effort to protect their substantial investment in telegraph plant and equipment, and to maintain their control over telecommunication services, these state monopolies lobbied hard to bring telephone service under their authority. The threat to private telecommunication firms was obvious: they would lose their franchise and might not receive reasonable compensation for their investments.

Government ownership of the telephone monopoly gained increasing political support during this period. As Holcombe pointed out, a strong consensus had developed in many academic and governmental circles that telephone service was a natural monopoly and, therefore, should be publicly owned, similar to the government postal service.[1]

---

1. Arthur N. Holcombe, *Public Ownership of Telephones on the Continent of Europe* (New York: Houghton Mifflin Company, 1911), chap. 24.

With the exception of the United States and, possibly, Canada, private investors had every reason to fear that their licenses to provide telecommunications services might be revoked. Concern regarding nationalization reduced capital investments which, in turn, impeded the growth in the telephone network.[2] As long as major political parties and respected opinion leaders advocated nationalization of the telephone system, private entrepreneurs would withhold investments in telecommunications. A public monopoly was thus the policy option most conducive to capital investment in telephony.[3]

Unlike France and the United Kingdom, Germany never permitted competition or private ownership of its telecommunications *service* industry. With the invocation of section 48 of the Imperial Constitution of 1871, Heinrich von Stephan, the postmaster general, categorically rejected all applications and inquiries regarding the construction of private telephone networks.[4] The first public telephone exchange was established in Berlin in 1881 and, during the same year, the Imperial Council declared that telephone service was the exclusive responsibility of the Telegraph Administration. The Telegraph Act was amended in 1892 to reflect the exclusive prerogative of the Telegraph Administration to provide telephone service.[5] To this day, the German PTT retains a monopoly on voice telecommunications *services*.

Because the government assumed responsibility for telephone service, the German telephone system was not beset by the *immobilisme* that characterized capital investment in France and the United Kingdom.[6] Under the stewardship of the Reichspost, capital investment in exchange facilities—both local and long-distance—increased on a regular basis throughout the latter part of the nineteenth and early twentieth centuries.[7]

Figure 6.1 provides a comparison of European telephone penetrations in 1887. As early as 1885, Germany had more telephone subscribers than any other European nation—almost twice the number found in France. By 1887 its lead increased even further and Germany had more than twice the number of subscribers as France. On a per capita basis, the country had 3.1 subscribers per ten thousand inhabitants compared to 1.9 in France.[8]

---

2. Herbert Laws Webb, *The Development of the Telephone in Europe* (London: Electrical Press Limited, 1910), 18.

3. We see a similar pattern in certain contemporary industries such as nuclear power and waste management whereby the threat of government actions greatly reduces the levels of private investment and increases the likelihood that these services will be provided by public, as opposed to private, firms.

4. Gerhard Basse, "100 Jahre öffentlicher Fernsprechdienst in Deutschland," *Archiv für deutsche Postgeschichte* (Frankfurt/Main: Gesellschaft für deutsche Postgeschichte, 1981).

5. Basse, "100 Jahre," 128.

6. Webb, *Telephone in Europe*, 52.

7. Webb, *Telephone in Europe*, 67.

8. See John E. Kingsbury, *The Telephone and Telephone Exchanges: Their Invention and*

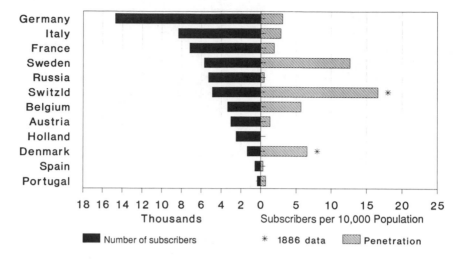

Fig. 6.1.   1887 telephone development levels. (Data from John F. Kingsbury, *The Telephone and Telephone Exchange; The Invention and Development* [London: Longmans, Green and Co., 1915]; *European Historical
Statistics 1750–1975*, 2d rev. ed. [New York: Facts on File, 1980], 29.)

This preemptive move by von Stephan to place telephone service within
the Telegraph Administration helps explain the initial success of German
telephony. By the early part of the twentieth century, most of the private
telephone service providers in Europe were nationalized, eliminating the political disincentive for investment.

The Interwar Years: Political Oversight Hinders Growth

Early government ownership promoted the growth of telephony in Germany.
But these benefits were short lived. As the cost of expanding the telecommunications infrastructure began to mount, political factors played an increasingly important role in the allocation of investment resources. Politicians paid

---

Development (New York: Longmans, 1915), 271. Note that, here, the comparative figures are
telephone subscribers. Subsequent comparisons will use number of telephones and number of
telephone main lines. When at all possible, I have attempted to employ only telephone main lines
as the measure of telecommunications development. Nonetheless, because of data availability,
particularly for earlier periods, I have drawn comparisons employing other measures. For the
most part the different measures are highly correlated and, therefore, I do not believe that any one
definition biases the conclusions that are drawn.

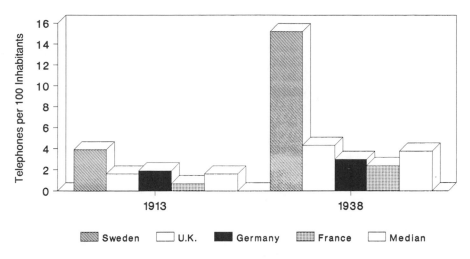

Fig. 6.2. Growth of telephone infrastructure. (Data from AT&T, *Telephone Statistics of the World* [New York: AT&T, 1950].)

increasing attention to expenditures on telephony. Political pressures made the availability of capital funds more unreliable and, as a result, growth in penetration stagnated. These two interwar trends—increased political control and declining rates of growth for telephone penetration—are documented in this section.

Growth rates began to slow down with the onset of World War I. This stagnation persisted throughout much of the interwar period and during World War II. The telephone penetration data in figure 6.2 compare Germany with the United Kingdom, France, Sweden, and the median penetration rate for a sample of developed countries. In 1913, Germany had a telephone penetration that slightly exceeded the median for developed countries and was higher than that of the United Kingdom and France. In 1938, Germany ranked below the median figure for European nations and below the United Kingdom.

Figure 6.3 documents the relative slowdown in Germany's telephone growth. The graph shows two important junctures where growth stopped and then resumed at a somewhat lower rate of growth. These occurred in 1917, when World War I was at its peak, and in 1929. The slowdown in development is even more evident from the series in figure 6.4 that plots the total number of local calls over the same period. Until 1911, call volume increased at a very steady pace. It assumed a much flatter rate of growth in the subsequent years because the network expanded at a slower rate. As figures 6.3 and 6.4 indicate, German telephone penetration continued to grow throughout the

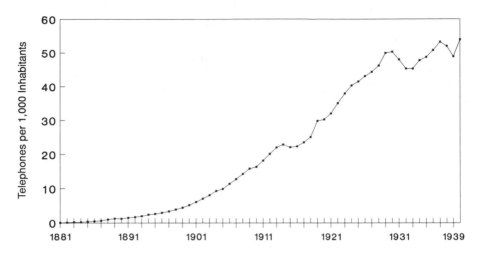

Fig. 6.3. Network density, 1881–1940. (Data from Karl Sautter, *Geschichte der Deutschen Post. Vol. 3: Geschichte der Deutschen Reichspost (1871–1945)* [Frankfurt/Main: Bundesdruckerei, 1951].)

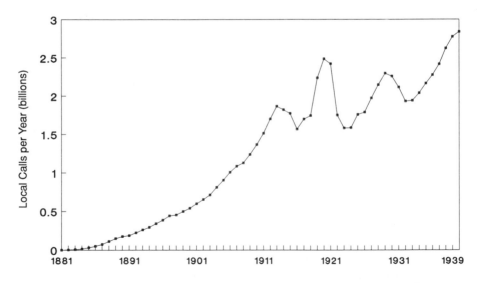

Fig. 6.4. Utilization statistics, 1881–1940. (Data from Sautter, *Geschichte.*)

interwar period, although at a slower pace than previously and at a slower rate than many other developed nations.[9]

Germany's inability to maintain its relatively strong growth in the diffusion of telephony is not explained simply by economic factors. Throughout most of the early twentieth century Germany was one of the more prosperous European nations. As figure 6.5 illustrates, Germany's GNP per capita exceeded the European median and, with the exception of the United Kingdom, ranked among the highest for European countries. It is interesting to note that Germany was consistently wealthier than Sweden, which nonetheless had significantly higher telephone penetration rates than Germany.

Growth in German telephony slowed because politicians were reluctant to invest in infrastructure development. With management strictly accountable to elected officials, funds for capital expansion depended upon political considerations that were not entirely favorable at the time.

During this period, the German telco was essentially a government department with virtually no financial or planning autonomy. With the signing of the Treaty of Versailles in 1919, the Weimar government moved quickly to consolidate all telecommunications authority under the Federal Reichspost (previously, Bavaria and Württemberg operated separate PTTs). The highest administrator was the Reichspostminister (the Imperial Postal Minister) who was fully accountable to the Reichstag. As a government agency, the Reichspost was subject to formal statutes passed by the Reichstag and to governmental decrees. Moreover, the entity's finances were treated as part of the national government budget; this meant that all surpluses were turned over to the treasury and all borrowing was prohibited. As a result, telco investment policies were carefully tailored to the government's political priorities.

For much of the German telco's early history, political pressures primarily concerned tariffs. Until 1900, relatively high uniform rates generated substantial profits for the PTT.[10] Smaller towns argued against paying the same rates as larger cities because the service was less valuable and less costly to provide. Political pressures from smaller towns led to the introduction of a new rate plan in 1910. Rates were graduated by size of city and measured service was also introduced.

With the exception of the tariff issue, the agency attracted little political attention and, therefore, was permitted considerable independence in its efforts to expand the telephone network. This changed after World War I, when the telco's spending plans became subject to careful political scrutiny.

---

9. German territorial expansion during this period caused a small decline in telephone penetration. I estimate that annexed population growth was responsible for a drop of about 2 percent in telephone penetration.

10. Gerald W. Brock, *The Telecommunications Industry: The Dynamics of Market Structure* (Cambridge, Mass.: Harvard University Press, 1981), 141.

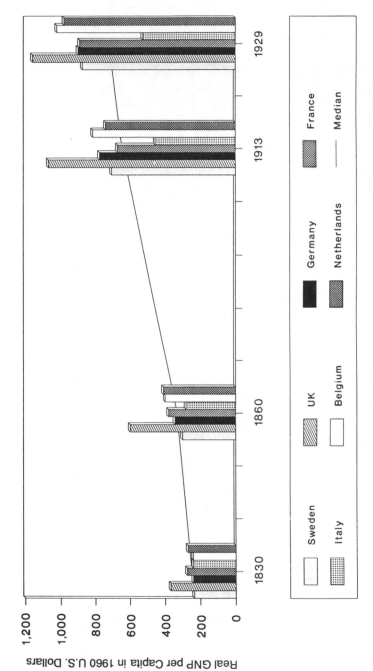

Fig. 6.5. Comparative GNP growth. (Data from Paul Bairoch, *Disparities in Economic Development Since the Industrial Revolution* [New York: St. Martin's Press, 1981].)

After World War I, the costs of expanding the network increased dramatically, straining the government budget. Costs rose because of efforts to extend service to increasingly smaller communities, to broaden the toll service, and to upgrade switching equipment from manual to automatic exchanges. More important, the uncontrollable inflation of the post–World War I period meant that revenues were constantly falling below the Reichspost's operating and capital expenditures.

The liabilities of political control became evident with this increased scarcity of investment funds. In a period of hyperinflation, firms must increase prices regularly, simply to cover their rising costs. As a government agency, the Reichspost had very little control over tariffs; all increases required legislative approval. The approval process was cumbersome and never quick enough to ensure that revenues covered costs and capital investment requirements. As a result, the Reichspost became increasingly dependent upon the federal budget, requiring annual subsidies, in contrast to the revenue it had contributed to the treasury prior to the war.[11] Faced with a rapidly rising budget deficit, the government was under increasing pressure to slash expenditures and reduce borrowing. It seriously cut back its subsidies for telco capital investments. In effect, political forces stymied the Reichspost's efforts to raise revenues: the legislature was slow to approve tariff increases while the only other source of funds—government subsidies—was scarce because of the need to reduce the deficit.

It became clear to policymakers that so long as the telco was closely tied to government funding and control, growth in the telephone network would suffer. The government moved to liberalize telco management from the constraints of political control by passing the Imperial Postal Finances Act (*Reichspostfinanzgesetz*) in 1924 as part of its effort to deal with the demands made by the Reichspost on the government budget. This initiative granted the PTT financial and management independence. In return, it could no longer count on subsidies from the treasury. The act provided for separate accounting and required the Reichspost to meet its expenses and liabilities out of its own revenues. Henceforth, the postal and telegraph administration was to operate as an autonomous enterprise under the name *Deutsche Reichspost* (German Imperial Post) with the cooperation of an Administrative Council.[12]

The act also greatly increased the power of the Administrative Council. Prior to the reform, the Reichspost's activities were subject to close parliamentary scrutiny. As a result of the *Reichspostfinanzgesetz*, the Administrative

---

11. Karl Sautter, *Geschichte der Deutschen Post*, vol. 3: *Geschichte der Deutschen Reichspost (1871–1945)* (Frankfurt/Main: Bundesdruckerei, 1951), 17.

12. Sautter, *Geschichte*, 3:178.

Council, a body composed of representatives of major interest groups, was accorded many of the supervisory responsibilities that had previously been exercised by parliament. Its authority included the Reichspost's budget, user regulations, tariffs, personnel, wages and salaries, borrowing, and other areas of administrative policy. The Administrative Council acted as both a consultative and a supervisory body and could promptly be convened to deal with current issues and problems.

The attraction of this "liberalization" was that it relieved the government of any financial obligations to the PTT. This, in fact, has been one of the prime motivations for much of the privatization occurring today. Governments hope to reduce the political exposure associated with pumping tax revenues into money-losing public enterprises. In the case of the Reichspost, this initiative significantly reduced the political constraints imposed on management and provided a model for the Bundespost, which assumed responsibility for telecommunication services in the post–World War II period.

Reorganization of the PTT had little opportunity to affect telephone penetration, however. In 1933, Hitler assumed power and Germany began preparing for war. During the period of Nazi rule, the Reichspost lost much of its independence. Hitler eliminated the Administrative Council, replacing it with a powerless consultative body. The *Reichspostministerium* (the Imperial Postal Ministry) answered directly to the Führer. Reichspost financial decisions, which formerly required the authorization of the Administrative Council, were subject to approval by the Minister of Finance. With the collapse of the Third Reich, the Reichspost ceased to exist and its infrastructure was taken over by the allied powers.

In summary, the pre–World War II period exhibited a slowdown in the growth of telephone penetration because political control exercised over telco management made it increasingly difficult for the entity to finance capital expansion. In a climate of scarcity, the government was not willing to subsidize telecommunications development. Finally, recognizing the negative impact of political constraints on the PTT, German legislators reorganized the entity, giving it much more independence of governmental direction and responsibility for its own finances.

Infrastructural Stage

For most of the developed countries, the telephone gained widespread consumer acceptance and experienced rapid growth in the post–World War II period. German telephony expanded at a comparatively slow rate during this period, never reaching the levels of penetration one would expect, given the country's wealth. A major reason is the "corporatist" coalition, consisting of representatives of government, labor, and equipment manufacturers, that shaped telecommunications policy during this period. Their interests were not consistent with the widespread diffusion of telephony.

Comparative Measures of Performance

A combination of slow growth in the pre–World War II era and devastation from the war itself left Germany with a relatively poor telecommunications infrastructure. As figure 6.6 indicates, in 1950 Germany had only 4.4 telephones per hundred inhabitants, compared to 6.6 for France and 10.2 for the United Kingdom. But after the war, the German telco rebuilt and expanded its telecommunications infrastructure at a rate superior to many of its European counterparts. By 1955 West Germany had about 13.2 telephones per hundred inhabitants, very similar to France with 11.09. Both lagged behind the United Kingdom with 17.4 telephones per hundred inhabitants. By 1980, with a German telephone density of 45 telephones per 100 inhabitants, Germany had a telephone density similar to that of the United Kingdom and France.

These comparisons are misleading because they do not take account of the relative wealth of the three nations. Earlier regression analyses indicated that a significant amount of this variation in growth rates is accounted for by levels of wealth. For example, much of the United Kingdom's unimpressive telephone growth rate can be attributed to the country's poor economic performance over the 1950–1980 period. For 1965 and 1980, I have estimated a simple bivariate regression with the log of telephones as the dependent variable and the log of GDP on the right hand side of the equation. Table 6.1 shows the predicted scores, actual scores, and residuals for a sample of developed nations. In 1965 Germany had the second highest *negative* residual; in 1980 it still had a sizeable negative residual. This suggests that once we control for economic wealth, the performance of the German telco ranks very poorly compared to other developed nations. The purely economic model predicts that Germany should have many more telephones than is actually the case.

Germany's lackluster performance in this sector, signaled by the large negative residuals in the model, has a political explanation. Throughout the post–World War II period, telecommunications policy was shaped by a corporatist coalition dominated by representatives of the major manufacturers and of labor. Management of the Bundespost was unable to undertake any significant initiatives without their consent. As a result, the policy preferences of labor and manufacturers dominated telco policy decisions, while those of other interests, such as residential and business consumers, were decidedly underrepresented. As a result, the prices of the telco's goods and services to the public were excessively high, and growth of demand and penetration were stifled.

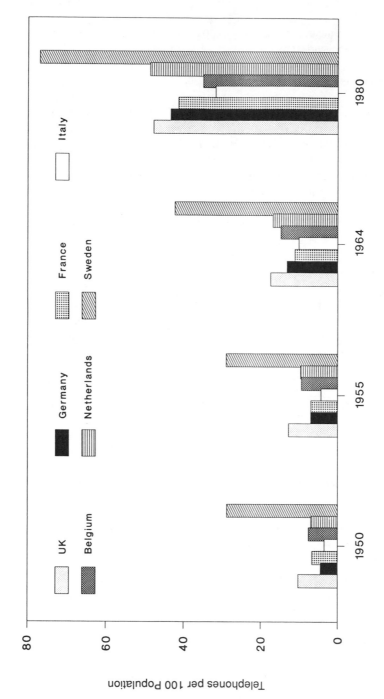

Fig. 6.6. Telephone penetration levels. (Data from AT&T, *Telephone Statistics of the World, The World's Telephones*; AT&T Communications, Overseas Marketing Department, *The World's Telephones: A Statistical Compilation as of January 1, 1987* [Morris Plains, N.J.: AT&T Communications, 1982].)

TABLE 6.1. Observed and Predicted Values for Log Model with GNP as Independent and Telephones as Dependent Variables

Country	1980			1965		
	Observed	Predicted	Residual	Observed	Predicted	Residual
Norway	7.07	7.51	−0.44	6.40	6.36	0.04
Belgium	7.81	8.23	−0.42	6.97	7.15	−0.18
France	9.67	9.94	−0.27	8.03	8.81	−0.78
Ireland	6.18	6.43	−0.25	5.11	5.45	−0.34
West Germany	9.93	10.15	−0.22	8.49	8.96	−0.46
Iceland	4.44	4.65	−0.21	3.82	3.89	−0.07
Switzerland	7.95	8.08	−0.13	7.29	6.99	0.30
Austria	7.69	7.81	−0.11	6.48	6.63	−0.15
Netherlands	8.50	8.59	−0.09	7.32	7.32	0.00
Australia	8.46	8.44	0.02	7.61	7.46	0.15
Italy	9.47	9.44	0.03	8.42	8.39	0.03
Denmark	7.71	7.66	0.05	6.94	6.70	0.24
Finland	7.46	7.41	0.05	6.41	6.51	−0.10
Spain	8.89	8.82	0.07	7.48	7.47	0.01
United Kingdom	9.83	9.73	0.10	8.71	8.83	−0.12
United States	11.45	11.34	0.11	10.97	10.64	0.33
Japan	10.56	10.42	0.14	8.75	8.74	0.01
Canada	9.21	9.03	0.18	8.57	8.23	0.34
Sweden	8.48	8.28	0.20	7.98	7.41	0.57
Portugal	6.90	6.69	0.21	NA	NA	NA
New Zealand	7.01	6.66	0.35	6.52	6.14	0.38
Greece	7.73	7.15	0.58	6.03	6.20	−0.17

Note: NA = not available.

The Tradition of Semipublic Institutions

Semipublic institutions are a part of the German corporatist tradition that encourages consensual agreement among representatives of peak associations.[13] Responsibilities for government functions that directly concern the major social partners are often assumed by these semipublic institutions (examples include social welfare administrations, the central bank, unemployment commissions, cultural agencies, etc.). These bodies are typically governed by representatives of the country's principal social partners. Issues of major concern to groups in society are resolved by consensual bargaining

---

13. The term *semipublic institution* and its application to the German case is from Peter J. Katzenstein, *Policy and Politics in West Germany: The Growth of a Semisovereign State* (Philadelphia: Temple University Press, 1987).

among representatives appointed to a governing board.[14] Semipublic institutions have a long tradition in German public administration. For example, many of Bismarck's social policy programs of the late nineteenth century were implemented by semipublic institutions.[15] Although agents of the state, the predominant representation of labor and business on their governing boards ensured they would act quite independently of government direction.[16]

Successive German regimes have built on Bismarck's early initiatives. We see this in the legislative recognition accorded national associations that organized and represented the interests of individuals and other groups spread throughout the German federation. Introduced during the Weimar Republic, the Law of 1926 supported the development of *Verbände* (interest associations). *Spitzenverbände* (top associations) were actively supported and reinforced under the Nazi regime.[17] They played an active role in policy development and implementation and often functioned as the exclusive agents of the German government.

A number of contemporary German institutions reflect this merging of public and private bureaucracies while maintaining a significant independence from government authorities. The most prominent example is the Bundesbank, which is governed by appointees of both Federal and Länder governments. Although nominally an agent of the German government, as Shonfield notes, " . . . the central bank is very much a law to itself."[18] It is not under the supervision of any federal ministry and is not subject to the general political objectives of the government. The Bundesbank is much more autonomous of political authorities than virtually all other comparable institutions in the developed economies.[19] It has a history of successfully implementing monetary measures even though they clearly contradict the preferences of incumbent government officials.

Another example is the Federal Employment Office, a self-governing corporation with standing under public law but which, nonetheless, is under the supervision of the Labor Ministry.[20] The Employment Office is governed

---

14. This is not to say that politics no longer matters but rather that its importance has been reduced by taking responsibility for decision making out of forums dominated by partisan political actors.

15. Katzenstein, *Policy and Politics*, 172.

16. In fact, as Katzenstein points out, with a two-thirds voting majority on these boards, union representatives exercised a degree of political leverage that was "unintended and unforeseen" by the conservative authors of the legislation (Katzenstein, *Policy and Politics*, 172).

17. Shonfield, *Modern Capitalism: The Changing Balance of Public and Private Power* (New York: Oxford University Press, 1965), 242–43.

18. Shonfield, *Modern Capitalism*, 269.

19. Katzenstein, *Policy and Politics*, 61.

20. Katzenstein, *Policy and Politics*, 69.

by a tripartite board of representatives that ensures a considerable degree of political autonomy.

Two characteristics of these semipublic institutions stand out. First, they are virtually always governed by an independent board composed of representatives from the major interest groups in German society. Second, semipublic entities are accorded considerable independence in the performance of their mandated tasks. The goal is to favor technical decision makers (engineers, bankers, economists, etc.) and minimize the pressures from elected political officials. We see many of these traits in the historical development of the German PTT.

With the formation of the Reichspost after World War I, corporatist influences began to assert themselves. Chambers of commerce and industry and the handicraft guilds played important roles in shaping local development of telephone service.[21] In Bavaria and Württemberg, advisory councils including representatives of agriculture, industry, and commerce already had been established for consultation concerning railroad service. Since railroads and telegraphs were administered by the same entities in the two South German States, they provided a natural forum for an exchange of views on telephone service.

At the national level, these discussions were institutionalized in the form of the *Verkehrsbeirat*, a tripartite board of overseers that the Reichspost was required to consult before implementing or changing regulations and tariffs.[22] The new entity initially consisted of twenty-five members drawn from all sectors of the economy, the Reichs Finance Administration, and the parliamentary assemblies. Eventually, the number of members was raised to sixty-seven. Although only consultative, these early institutional arrangements were precursors to subsequent initiatives instituting semiprivate, as opposed to governmental, oversight of the German PTT (for example, the Bundespost's Administrative Council). The passage of the *Reichspostfinanzgesetz* in 1924 strengthened the power of the independent Administrative Council and further institutionalized the representation of major social partners in the telecommunications decision-making process.

The Bundespost After World War II

After the war, supervision of the Bundespost assumed even more of a corporatist character. Rather than directly controlling the public telco through traditional lines of command (Ministry officials and legislative committees), this task was assumed by a coalition of major interested groups. However, rather

---

21. Holcombe, *Public Ownership of Telephones*, 44.
22. Sautter, *Geschichte*, 3:16.

than insulate telco management from political pressures, these corporatist structures appear to have institutionalized control by selective political groups. Representatives of labor, the major manufacturers, and the government had ironclad control over Bundespost policies, preventing other interests from asserting themselves.

Between the fall of the German Reich in May 1945 and the formation of the Federal Republic in 1949, responsibility for postal and telecommunications was assumed by separate entities in each of the occupation zones.[23] On 1 April 1950 the Federal Republic created a new PTT, the Deutsche Bundespost, which in many ways resembled the Reichspost of the later Weimar period.

Two groups have dominated telecommunications policy-making in Germany since then: labor and the major equipment manufacturers. Not only is the Bundespost the largest employer in Germany, but the German Post Workers' Union (DPG) is one of the country's most powerful unions. It has been a staunch opponent of most proposed changes in the Bundespost's monopoly because of concerns over employment losses.

Telecommunications equipment manufacturers represent the other important interest group. There are approximately six to ten firms that are consulted regularly on telecommunications policy issues. They are formally represented by the communications technology subassociation of the *Zentralverband der Elektrotechnischen Industrie* (ZVEI). Siemens is by far the most prominent member of this group.

On the other hand, Bundespost business users, who are represented by a number of different groups, have not been particularly effective. There is an association of Bundespost users called the *Verband der Postbenutzer*. More recently, Deutsche Telecom has served as an important voice for major telecommunications consumers. The peak associations of business, such as the *Deutscher Industrie- und Handelstag* (the German Chamber of Industry and Commerce), also represent the interests of user groups.[24] But there have been serious disagreements among the business community regarding telecommunications policy issues. Firms such as Siemens, which is a major supplier to the telco, have opposed significant changes while others, such as the *Verband Deutscher Maschinen- und Anlagenbau* (the Association of the German Mechanical Engineering Industry)—which includes Nixdorf (prior to its acquisition in 1990 by Siemens) and IBM—have been very critical.

---

23. Hans Steinmetz and Dietrich Elias, *Geschichte der Deutschen Post*, vol. 4: *1945 to 1978* (Bonn: Bundesdruckerei, 1979), 218.

24. Kevin Morgan and Douglas Webber, "Divergent Paths: Political Strategies for Telecommunications in Britain, France, and West Germany," *West European Politics* 9 (October 1986): 72.

Germany is unique among the three case studies in that oversight of the telco and responsibility for telecommunications policy initiatives are tasks performed, to a large extent, outside of the typical legislative and administrative processes. Although the Bundespost is a government agency, it has many of the characteristics of the unique German semipublic institution. Until the 1989 reforms, the Bundespost was governed by an Administrative Council that operated like a board of directors. The Administrative Council consisted of ten representatives from the Bundesrat and the Bundestag, five from the *Deutsche Postgewerkschaft* (DPG, the German Post Workers' Union), five from the economy at large, and one each from the community of financial experts and the community of telecommunications experts (typically a Siemens representative).[25] It was responsible for approving the Bundespost's financial statement and any changes in regulations governing the use of the telecommunications network. The council also played an important informal role with respect to legislative proposals concerning the industry.

Second, major telecommunications policy initiatives were determined by informal tripartite negotiations between Bundespost and Post Ministry officials, on the one hand, and the DPG and the traditional telecommunications equipment manufacturing industry on the other.[26] The DPG was most influential in the area of personnel policy, while the manufacturers played an important role with respect to technical issues.

Telecommunications policy is shaped by negotiations between government (primarily represented by the Minister of the PTT), labor, and the manufacturers. Both the federal cabinet and the Bundestag have traditionally avoided any initiatives that might alienate the coalition of labor and manufacturers. Even the Post Minister has felt seriously constrained by the prominent policy-making role played both informally and formally (in the Administrative Council and the *Zentralverband der Elektrotechnischen Industrie*) by labor and manufacturers.[27] Although this structure affords Bundespost management and technical staff considerable autonomy and flexibility in running the German PTT, it also ensures that labor and the major manufacturers have veto power over important policy initiatives.

On employment issues, management is very sensitive to the demands made by the DPG. Employees of the Bundespost have civil service status and are therefore covered by the *Bundesbeamtengesetz*, the federal civil servants

---

25. Robert R. Bruce, Jeffrey P. Cunard, and Mark D. Director, *From Telecommunications to Electronic Services: A Global Spectrum of Definitions, Boundary Lines, and Structures* (London: Butterworth, 1986), 549.

26. Morgan and Webber, "Divergent Paths," 69.

27. The *Zentralverband der Elektrotechnischen Industrie* is a thirty-member council of Bundespost equipment suppliers (see "Telecommunications Survey," *Economist*, 23 November 1985, 28).

law. The statute lays out very detailed rules regarding hiring, promotion, and job security. This restricts the Bundespost's efforts to recruit managerial and technical personnel because it carefully regulates the salaries and promotion possibilities candidates may be offered. Any initiatives threatening to change the Bundespost's civil service status or to significantly reduce the entity's work force have been strongly fought by the DPG.

The major telecommunications equipment manufacturers exercise considerable influence over decisions concerning technical issues, pricing, and investment plans. Siemens is the dominant member of this group, followed by ten to fifteen medium-sized firms including Standard Elektrik Lorenz (SEL), DeTeWe, and Telenorma. Bundespost procurement, which is sizeable, has traditionally favored a small number of German manufacturers: Siemens and SEL in the case of central office switching equipment; and Siemens, DeTeWe, and Telenorma in the case of private branch exchanges. The Bundespost selects its discussion partners based on its assessment of each firm's market and technical prowess.[28] German manufacturers are comfortable with this arrangement and have opposed any significant structural or regulatory changes.

Corporatist structures institutionalize the preferences of certain social partners at the expense of others. The three major social partners that participate in the oversight of Bundespost policies—manufacturers, labor, and government representatives—have each imposed their own policy preferences on Bundespost management. Equipment manufacturers have been preoccupied with the purchasing policies of the Bundespost, government representatives focused on tariff policy, and labor unions closely oversaw initiatives affecting employment. At the same time, other interested parties, such as business users, service providers, computer manufacturers, and foreign telecommunication equipment manufacturers, have been shut out of the decision-making process.

This coalition has controlled telco policy-making throughout the post–World War II period. Pressures from this coalition have favored higher tariffs that depressed demand and inhibited telecommunications development. Manufacturers have a direct interest in high tariffs for equipment sales and leases because this obviously increases their revenues. More generally they have favored high Bundespost tariffs because they generate surplus revenues that subsidize high-priced, domestically manufactured switching and plant equipment.

Labor also had strong incentives to maintain high telecommunications tariffs. Because of the Bundespost's monopoly and the relative price inelasticity of demand for telecommunication services, higher tariffs translated into

---

28. Morgan and Webber, "Divergent Paths," 69.

higher revenues, which meant the telco could afford to maintain generous wage levels and working conditions. The requirement that the Bundespost be self-financing meant that tariffs were a critical source of revenue; revenue shortfalls created by overly generous wages or benefits could not be covered by government subsidies.

Government also has an interest in maintaining high telecommunications tariffs because they represent a valuable source of revenues. Bundespost tariffs are a form of indirect taxation. First, revenues raised by the telco have cross-subsidized the loss-making postal office. As table 6.2 indicates, the telecommunications activities of the Bundespost have generated large surpluses: in 1984, telephone services made a profit of 3,506 million DM. In contrast, the postal services of the Bundespost lost 1,771 million DM in 1984. Second, the Federal government also benefits directly from higher revenues because of a requirement that the Bundespost turn over 10 percent of its gross revenues to the general treasury.

As noted earlier, there are political attractions to raising revenues through the pricing actions of state-owned enterprises rather than directly levying a tax. Direct taxation is much more transparent and, therefore, more likely to generate political opposition. The link between government revenues and the pricing strategies of publicly owned enterprises is less obvious and therefore less costly from a political perspective.

Corporatist arrangements make it very difficult for excluded groups to have any significant impact on policies. Neither residential nor business consumers were actively represented in the policy-making process. They, of course, would be the most ardent advocates of lower prices and less restrictive barriers to competition. In the United States, for example, large business users were the prime advocates of lower toll rates and increased competition.[29]

Two facts are quite clear from the analysis to this point: German telco performance in the post–World War II period has been mediocre and the political coalition overseeing Bundespost management had strong short-term incentives to maintain high tariffs. The coalition's success at maintaining high tariffs accounts for the relatively slow growth of German telephony. An examination of Bundespost tariffs during this period suggests that manufacturers, labor, and government, acting in concert, were successful at maintaining high rates.

First, German telephone tariffs are among the highest in Europe. Table 6.3 compares German, French, U.S., and British rates for a variety of services in 1986 and 1987. German long-distance rates (both national and international) are much higher than those in most other European countries and are

---

29. Alan Stone, *Wrong Number: The Breakup of AT&T* (New York: Basic Books, 1989).

TABLE 6.2.   Cost Recovery by DBP Tariffs in Various Service Categories

Category	1977	1978	1979	1984
Postal services	−2,376.8	−2,619.8	−1,740.4	−1,771
Money services	−631.5	−658.5	−589.4	+55[a]
Postal travel service	−108.5	−79.8	−97.4	NA
Money order services	−43.5	−19.8	+4.5	NA
Postal savings service	+461.1	+504.2	+431.4	NA
Telegraph services	+111.0	+128.7	+103.3	+62
Telephone services	+4,951.5	+6,278.2	+4,447.5	+3,506
Other telecom services	+161.2	+194.2	+153.9	−269
Total	+2,491.3	+3,727.4	+2,713.3	+1,582

Sources: 1977–79 figures: Bernhard Wieland, assisted by Jürgen Müller and Karl-Heinz Neumann, Wirtschaftliche Aspekte der neuen Informations- und Kommunikationstechniken (Berlin: Deutsches Institut für Wirtschaftsforschung, 1982), 228; 1984 figures: Federal Republic of Germany Ministry of Posts and Telecommunications, Deutsche Bundespost Annual Report (Bonn: Ministry of Posts and Telecommunications, 1985), 34.

Note: Surplus/deficit in million DM.

[a]The 1984 figures provided by the DBP did not provide a breakdown of Postal banking services that corresponded to the information provided by Wieland, Müller, and Neumann.

certainly higher in comparison to the United States. Telex rates have also been comparatively high, although they were reduced in 1987.[30] With such high rates for business and long-distance service, we might expect that cross-subsidies would result in lower tariffs for local telephone service.[31] But this is not the case: local telephone rates in Germany are just as high as those in France and the United Kingdom and are 60 percent higher than U.S. tariffs.

Business users have been particularly heavily taxed by Germany's high telecommunications tariffs. As table 6.3 illustrated, long-distance tariffs (both

---

30. Michael Tyler, "After the Telecom Earthquake: Were Telco Monopolies Cracked, Shaken, or Only Stirred?" Communications Week, 19 October 1987, 4, notes that:

During the 1970's, telex rates from West Germany and some other European countries on long distance international routes to the Far East were very high compared with those offered in other parts of Europe. Sending a telex message from West Germany to Britain for forwarding to Hong Kong was substantially cheaper than sending the telex directly from Germany to Hong Kong. A whole new business, known as telex refiling (economists would call it "arbitrage") came into being to exploit this anomaly. (5)

31. See Karen Neuman, The Selling of British Telecom (New York: St. Martin's Press, 1984), 23–24; Karl-Heinz Neuman, "Economic Policy Toward Telecommunications, Information, and Media in West Germany," paper presented at the Research Workshop on Economic Policy Toward Telecommunications, Information, and Media Activities in Industrialized Countries, Washington, D.C., 1986, 145.

TABLE 6.3. Comparative Telco Service Tariffs

Country	Local Telephone Calls	Trunk Telephone Calls (> 200 miles)	International Calls	International Telex Calls	Local Telex Calls
			1986		
Germany	0.082	1.230	7.860	4.310	0.643
France	0.083	1.210	4.840	3.460	0.484
United Kingdom	0.088	0.410	1.860	1.740	0.097
United States	0.053	0.810	2.420	2.860	0.700
			1987		
Germany	0.082	1.230	3.930	2.570	0.643
France	0.080	1.190	3.150	3.260	0.448
United Kingdom	0.110	0.350	1.850	1.740	0.104
United States	0.053	0.590	2.420	3.360	1.020

Source: National Utility Service.
Note: Tariffs are quoted in British pounds.

national and international) rank among the highest in Europe. These tariffs affect the entire range of business users, irrespective of size. Large firms with significant telecommunications needs typically lease dedicated lines in order to handle their traffic. Table 6.4 compares the cost of these leased-lines for five European countries. Germany is by far the most expensive country for leased-line facilities.

TABLE 6.4. Leased-Line Charges

Country	Circuit Length 10km	100km
West Germany	$129	$841
France	25	275
Sweden	24	244
Switzerland	46	283
United Kingdom[a]	59	75

Source: Logica Tarifica.
Note: Monthly rent for normal quality, two-wire voice-band private circuit. Connection charge extra. Local currencies converted at rates of 31 March 1985.
[a]Plus 15 percent value-added tax.

The postwar experience of the Bundespost illustrates the impact political factors can have on government controlled telcos. Yet the dynamics of this link between politics and performance is very different in Germany than in the United Kingdom or France. This is explained by the significantly different political institutions responsible for overseeing the provision of telecommunications services in each country. One of the major factors impeding the growth of telephony in France and the United Kingdom was political constraints on capital expenditures. This was not the case in Germany, where the political coalition overseeing Bundespost activities was actually highly supportive of capital expenditures. Unlike France and the United Kingdom, where tariffs were often maintained at low levels (for reasons unique to the two countries), political constraints produced high tariff levels in Germany, resulting in relatively slow growth in telephony *demand*.

The Post-Infrastructural Period

Telecommunication service providers in most of the developed economies have now moved beyond the infrastructural phase in which their primary goal was to establish universal access to the telephone network. They have entered the post-infrastructural stage that is distinguished by innovative service offerings. Their performance is measured less in terms of telephone penetration than in terms of scope and diversity of value-added services.

Germany lags behind many other advanced economies in developing these post-infrastructural services because of industry entry barriers and the reluctance of policymakers to modify entry barriers and the telco's rigid structure.

The Bundespost Challenged by the
Telecommunications Revolution

Industry is not static: market structures evolve, the nature of consumer demand is subject to change, and technology is constantly progressing. In the 1970s, the telcos changed dramatically with the emergence of innovative telecommunications technologies. This opened the way for service enhancements such as various messaging services, electronic mail, voice mail, data base services, toll-free calls, local area voice and data networks, etc. Unlike the basic telephone service, for which demand was rather inelastic, demand for these new, enhanced services is much more sensitive to price levels and customized software features. While some government monopolies have performed quite well in markets where the product is relatively undifferentiated and demand is comparatively inelastic (this is the environment faced by the Bundespost through much of the post–World War II period), in industries with very differentiated products, where demand is much more elastic and success depends on marketing finesse, government monopolies have been much less successful.[32]

Throughout the 1980s, both British and French policymakers have experimented with policies designed to create a more favorable environment for these innovations. To varying degrees, the French and British have liberalized regulations and reduced entry barriers. Throughout this period, Germany firmly resisted modifications in the Bundespost monopoly or in state ownership: Regulations that prohibit or discourage entry into the industry were retained and the government did not modify the Bundespost's organization or reduce entry barriers until the very end of the decade.

This reluctance to adopt more liberal policies cannot be accounted for by an absence of pressure from users.[33] Larger telecommunication users in Germany have lobbied aggressively for changes in these regulations. In addition, the U.S. government has pressured German officials to reduce entry barriers in both service and equipment markets.

The German Bundespost argued that its practices were among the most liberal in the world and that its telecommunications service ranked just as high, if not higher, in quality and range of choice as those of the most developed nations.[34] Recent evidence suggests the contrary. The reluctance of German authorities to liberalize entry negatively affected the Bundespost's performance, which has had serious repercussions for consumers. Tariffs and value-added network services (VANs) illustrate the point.

Tariffs

With telecommunications assuming an increasing proportion of corporate budgets and becoming a source of competitive advantage for many firms, they are seeking more innovative and cost-effective options to satisfy their needs. Demands for increased choice and lower prices conflict with the Bundespost's goals of maximizing revenues and controlling entry into the industry. The Bundespost has little incentive to promote entry. For example, in the case of private networks, the telco can earn greater returns by forcing users to direct their traffic over the public network, where charges are based on volume.[35]

---

32. John Zysman, *Political Strategies for Industrial Order: State, Market, and Industry in France* (Berkeley, Calif.: University of California Press, 1977).

33. John Davies, "Resistance to Change Remains Strong," *Financial Times*, 6 January 1986, 7.

34. "A Look Inside the Deutsche Bundespost," *Telephony*, 26 January 1987, 41; Christian Schwarz-Schilling, "Guidelines for the Development of Public Networks and Services in the Federal Republic of Germany," *Computer Networks* 12 (1986): 209–15.

35. There are, nonetheless, some pressures on the Bundespost to be competitive in terms of price and service offerings. In particular, the telco is sensitive to the fact that high volume telecommunication users often have the option of relocating to European nations that have more competitive pricing and a wider range of delivery media.

There is no incentive for monopolists to offer services that are likely to result in revenue losses. As a result, many innovative telecommunications services that might reduce user costs—such as value-added network services that involve reselling of leased-line capacity—are slowly introduced because they threaten the Bundespost's monopoly profits. As long as these barriers persist, German consumers will not benefit from the diversity of delivery options and competitive pricing that characterize the more liberal telecommunication markets of the United States, the United Kingdom, and Canada.

Bundespost tariffs are not cost based because political pressures favor cross-subsidies and uniform prices. Liberalization of entry barriers would result in a closer alignment of prices with costs. Faced with competition, telcos must adjust prices so that they reflect costs, or face a loss of market share for overpriced services (typically business users and long-distance service). This also has the effect of reducing cross-subsidies, thereby forcing telcos to raise the prices of services that were priced below their actual cost (typically residential and local telephone service). Such readjustments minimize the welfare losses to society. But, determined to protect its revenue base and maintain cross-subsidies, the Bundespost has resisted liberalization, leaving business users with the burden of very high tariffs.

Although the Bundespost resisted realigning tariffs with actual costs, it made some effort to modify tariff structures in order to prevent any erosion of monopoly revenues. The telco promoted the "harmonization" of tariffs by equalizing prices of services that are substitutes for each other.[36] In effect, harmonization efforts target services that can be bought from the Bundespost on a wholesale basis and then resold to consumers. These resale activities represent competition for the retail services the telco offers over the public, switched network. By raising the prices of these wholesale services, the Bundespost hoped to prevent resale efforts. The Bundespost concentrated on reducing the opportunities for arbitrage and cream-skimming that might threaten its revenue stream throughout the 1980s. Its most conspicuous action in this regard was the introduction of usage-based pricing for leased circuits.[37] To the extent that private entities are allowed to lease circuits for resale, the usage charges imposed by the Bundespost prevent any attempt to undercut telco tariffs.

By rejecting liberalization of entry barriers and by harmonizing tariffs, the Bundespost and the German government have ensured that tariffs of existing and any new services will remain comparatively more expensive than those in other countries with more liberal regulations. Tables 6.3 and 6.4 compared West German telecommunications tariffs with those of other Euro-

---

36. Bruce, Cunard, and Director, *Telecommunications*, 557.
37. Bruce, Cunard, and Director, *Telecommunications*, 558.

pean countries, leaving little doubt that Germany has been one of the most expensive telecommunications markets in Europe.

At least in the short term, most West Germans benefit from entry barriers and high tariffs. As noted earlier, high tariffs for business users subsidize residential telephone service, rural telephone users, and the postal service (but even with these subsidies, residential telephone subscribers in Germany pay some of the highest tariffs in Europe). But these cross-subsidies do have long-term costs for the entire society. For one, they tend to distort the decision making of firms. High tariffs for leased-line service discourage firms from operating centralized processing facilities because they inflate the cost of transmitting data to and from district offices. This, in turn, encourages de-centralized data processing capabilities. To the extent that such decentraliza-tion increases the firm's cost of doing business, it reduces the overall effi-ciency of German industry.

Tariffs also affect the location decisions of firms. If Bundespost tariffs are comparatively high, firms with telecommunication-intensive activities will simply avoid locating these activities in Germany. Because there are a number of European countries with more liberal entry and pricing policies, most larger firms can be selective regarding the location of their European offices and plants. A number of multinational firms, particularly in the financial and services industries, have avoided Germany because of Bundespost tariffs and regulations. In 1985, Bank of America and National Semiconductor, for ex-ample, moved some of their telecommunication-intensive activities out of Germany for this reason.[38] This has the obvious implication of reducing economic growth and job creation. It also deprives the country of business activities that tend to be in high-growth areas (data processing, financial services, etc.). High tariffs also increase the costs of doing business for firms already in Germany, which may undercut their international competitiveness.

Value-Added Network Services (VANs)

Another dramatic change sweeping the telecommunications industry is the proliferation of specialized services now available to consumers.[39] The emer-gence of these new, enhanced services has fundamentally changed the nature of the telecommunications industry. When telecommunications service was primarily defined as a single, undifferentiated product, a good case could be made for the natural monopoly model. Technological changes, however, have significantly increased the range of telecommunications services and have

---

38. "Multinationals Fed up with the Bundespost," *Business Week*, 18 November 1985, 62.
39. Mathew Kusinitz, "Measuring the Quake," *Communications Week*, 19 October 1987, 5.

dramatically reduced the sunk costs associated with their introduction. For many sectors of the telecommunications industry, the natural monopoly model is no longer appropriate.

The telephone network has become the medium for delivering a broad range of Value-Added Network Services (VANs) that address specific consumer needs. VANs include electronic mail services, videotext services (such as France's Minitel), financial data base services (such as those provided by Reuters), and data processing services (such as those offered by Geisco and IBM). German entry barriers have actually inhibited the development of this new sector of the industry.

There are a number of reasons entry barriers retard the development of VANs. First, their demand is highly price sensitive. Competition tends to drive prices down, thereby stimulating demand. Second, industry growth is fueled by the development of innovative application software that tends to thrive in a competitive environment. Finally, VANs products are highly customized to fit unique applications. Entry barriers are likely to reduce the range of end-user applications offered and thereby inhibit industry growth.

Throughout the 1980s, German telecommunications regulations represented very serious entry barriers to prospective VANs companies. These regulations allowed shared use of leased circuits, such as airline reservation systems or brokerage houses, but prohibited third-party services such as credit card verification systems and online data base systems. VANs operators prefer to lease circuit capacity from the Bundespost and then provide their customers with direct access to value-added services via dedicated, leased circuits. This type of control is considered important for a number of reasons: pricing, technical, and security factors are the most important. In Germany, the costs of offering VANs have been relatively high because operators have been required to use the Bundespost's public network (VAN-Datex-P) that has volume-sensitive tariffs and restricted capacity. They could not lease lines to provide services because this would constitute resale, which was not permitted. While protecting the monopoly revenues of the Bundespost, these regulations impeded the development of the VANs industry.

Because of stringent restrictions on VANs providers, during the 1980s Germany lagged behind other developed nations in this rapidly growing service industry.[40] In the United Kingdom, which has the most liberal VANs policies, these services generated $919 million in revenue during 1989, compared to $666 million in France, and only $428 million in West Germany.[41] A confidential study prepared by McKinsey for the Bundespost confirmed these

---

40. Terry Dodsworth, "Value-Added Data Networks: Even More Message in Store," *Financial Times*, 19 October 1987, 23.

41. These figures are from Frost and Sullivan Ltd., as reported in John Blau, "Germany Lags in VANs," *Communications Week International*, 4 June 1990, 10.

estimates, noting that Germany had fallen seriously behind other industrialized countries in the provision of new data-based services.[42]

Efforts by the Bundespost to enter the VANs industry have been disappointing. The industry is driven by demands for data-related services from a wide variety of often very narrow user groups. Success in this industry is much less dependent upon engineering prowess than it is on marketing expertise and competitive acumen. The industry is demand driven, rather than supply driven. A state monopolist that has never vigorously competed for market share is at a disadvantage in areas where marketing skills are the key to success. One indication of the failure of the Bundespost to properly market VAN services, particularly to large companies, is the strong interest in the German market since the 1989 VANs liberalization on the part of international VAN operators who hope to capitalize on the underdeveloped state of the industry.[43]

Bundespost's efforts to develop a videotext service (called *Bildschirmtext*) illustrate the problems of a state monopoly in a very demand-driven industry. Bildschirmtext allows subscribers to access a variety of data from centralized, Bundespost-managed data banks; retrieve information; and have it displayed in their home on a modified television screen. At its introduction in 1983, the Bundespost projected 1 million subscribers by 1986. Of the 400,000 Bildschirmtext modems initially ordered by the Bundespost, 320,000 were still in storage as of 1987.[44] Estimates from 1989 indicate there are about 180,000 subscribers.[45]

Bildschirmtext has not been very successful because its implementation was entrusted solely to the German monopoly telco. The Bundespost's skills at operating a basic utility have not served it well in its videotext undertaking. Preliminary market feasibility tests were conducted, but they set prices significantly below the tariffs that were eventually implemented.[46] The Bundespost

---

42. "Bundespost Weaknesses Need Strong Medicine," *Business Week*, 4 May 1987, 3.

43. In a recent evaluation of the German VAN market, Blau notes that "Many private network operators are eager to capitalize on DBP Telekom's perceived deficiency: customer service. IBM, GE Information Services, Reuters Holdings, PLC, and Eucom [a Franco-German joint venture] are among the leading players." See John Blau, "Germany Lags in VANs"; also see John Blau, "Germans Wait for EDI to Develop," *Communications Week International*, 11 December 1989, 15.

44. Wernhard Möschel, "Die Telekommunikation braucht den Wettbewerb: Ein Plädoyer für die Deregulierung der Post- und Fernmeldedienste," *Frankfurter Allgemeine Zeitung*, 23 May 1987, 15.

45. Istuan Sebestyn, "Public Text and Data Services in the FRG," *Computer Communications*, 4 August 1987, 202; "Bildschirmtext ist immer noch kein Medium für den privaten Markt," *Frankfurter Allgemeine Zeitung*, 4 October 1989.

46. Godefroy Dang Nguyen and Erik Arnold, "Videotext: Much Ado about Nothing?" in *Europe and the New Technologies*, ed. Margaret Sharp, 148 (Ithaca, N.Y.: Cornell University Press, 1986).

failed to develop a strategy that would create a demand for this new service. Setting high equipment and utilization tariffs for a brand-new service, virtually unknown to most Germans, did anything but encourage widespread subscribership.

Bildschirmtext inherited another characteristic of the telco's monopoly structure: for political reasons, the Bundespost insisted that all data base services be made available from a centralized computing facility under its control. Pricing, billing, promotion, and access would be handled by the Bundespost. A more decentralized system that left all of these functions to the individual service providers would have encouraged more competition and aggressive marketing, thereby promoting growth. These smaller, more entrepreneurial entities that actually developed the data base services would have a greater incentive to price competitively and promote their products.

This contrasts with the French implementation of their much more successful Minitel videotext service, which has over two million subscribers. Recognizing that the implementation of videotext posed a much different marketing challenge than providing basic telephone service, the DGT adopted policies very different than those of the Bundespost. First, the Minitel terminals were initially provided to subscribers at no charge and later for only a small fee. This had the obvious effect of stimulating consumer demand. Second, the videotext service was offered at reasonable and flexible rates. Initially, the telco offered three different pricing schemes that it hoped would encourage utilization of the videotext service.[47]

Also in contrast to Bildschirmtext, Teltel, the telco subsidiary responsible for Minitel, decentralized the provision of data base services to encourage competition, aggressive marketing, and innovation. In effect, it fashioned the videotext network as a common carrier. The data base services ("servers") are privately owned (there were over 2,500 in 1986) and are not centrally controlled by Teltel. Subscribers access these services via the Teltel network, but all pricing and marketing are the responsibility of the services themselves.[48]

In contrast to the Bundespost, France Telecom has shown more flexibility in the organization of new VAN services and in its tolerance for competition. This has contributed significantly to Minitel's success.

The marriage of communications and computing technologies has radically transformed the telecommunications industry. Recent software and hardware developments have produced a wide array of new telecommunications services that can be offered. Germany has lagged behind in the development

---

47. Bruce, Cunard, and Director, *Telecommunications*, 517; Link Resources, *World Wide Evaluation: Videotext Systems and Services* (New York: Link Resources, 1986), 18.
48. Link, *World Wide Evaluation*.

of these new telecommunications services because of the reluctance of the Bundespost and the German government to reduce entry barriers and decentralize the telco's structure.

The Political Economy of Liberalization in West Germany

West Germany represents one of the most successful and dynamic capitalist economies of the post–World War II era. Its political and economic institutions have been credited with effectively channeling public and private savings during the reconstruction that followed World War II.[49] More recently, scholars have argued that the corporatist arrangements that promote centralized negotiations between business, labor, and government played a critical role in Germany's economic growth during the difficult years of the 1970s.[50] We have a picture of German political and economic institutions effectively promoting the necessary adjustments to economic change. Yet with respect to liberalization or deregulation of markets, Germany's politico-economic institutions constituted a major barrier to change.

This is well illustrated in the case of telecommunications, where West Germany has lagged behind its Western counterparts in the adoption of new technologies and services. This, along with some of the highest tariffs in Western Europe, has discouraged businesses from locating telecommunication-intensive activities in West Germany. The cost to business subscribers of maintaining these tariffs and entry barriers has escalated, producing pressure for change from German businesses and from some political groups. Pressure has also come from the United States, the European Commission, and other European governments, which argue that these entry barriers and regulations violate free-trade agreements. Liberalization of industry entry barriers has been strongly urged by expert commissions appointed by the government itself. Nonetheless, throughout the past three decades German political institutions have significantly impeded liberalization of the industry.

The Problem Diagnosed

In the debate over liberalization of the industry three predominant issue areas have been singled out for attention.

1. Should the telco be privately, as opposed to publicly, owned and operated?

---

49. Shonfield, *Modern Capitalism*, chap. 11.

50. Mancur Olson, *The Rise and Decline of Nations: Economic Growth, Stagflation, and Social Rigidities* (New Haven, Conn.: Yale University Press, 1982).

2. Who should assume regulatory responsibilities for the industry?
3. Which of the telco's lines of business should be subject to more competition?

The debate that emerged in the Bundestag in the 1960s concerned the organizational character of the Bundespost; essentially, how could it be reorganized so as to operate more along the lines of an independent, profit-making business.

A commission established by the Bundestag on 16 April 1964 concluded that a far-reaching reform of the Postal Administration Act was necessary to improve and safeguard the economic health of the Bundespost. It recommended transforming the entity from a federal administration into a public enterprise operating on business principles, with a management that would be largely independent of political pressures.[51] At the very least, the commission argued, the Bundespost needed to be relieved of political burdens—for example, subsidizing local telephone service that was uncompensated by the federal government. The government and the Bundespost accepted the need to reorient Bundespost operations according to business principles and reduce political pressures on management (primarily through the strengthening of the Administrative Council), but throughout the 1960s, legislative efforts in this direction never succeeded.

In May 1970 another commission report, "Act on the Business Constitution of the German Bundespost," recommended that the telco be reorganized to resemble an independent business enterprise. The report indicated that the Bundespost is *not* so much an instrument of federal regulatory policy as it is a government service enterprise, whose operations should be guided by business principles, as opposed to political considerations.[52] At the same time, the report recognized that the Bundespost had certain social welfare obligations. Efforts to pass legislation implementing these concepts failed in the sixth, seventh, and eighth sessions of the German legislature.

The first commissions that addressed telecommunications regulatory issues were primarily interested in the impact of public ownership on the telco's performance. They sought organizational changes that would reduce political control and thereby enhance economic performance. By the end of the 1970s, these recommendations had made no progress toward legislative enactment.

In the wake of telecommunications deregulation by the Ford and Carter administrations in the United States, Germany commissioned two major in-

---

51. Steinmetz and Elias, *Geschichte*, 4: 727–33.
52. Steinmetz and Elias, *Geschichte*, 4: 727–33.

quiries into the regulation of the telecommunications sector: the Monopoly Commission Report and the Witte Report.[53]

The Monopoly Commission's goal was to determine which telecommunications activities ought legitimately to remain a monopoly of the Bundespost. Its main Commission Report defended the basic concept of the Bundespost monopoly on two grounds: Telecommunications was a natural monopoly and, therefore, it was inevitable that only one firm would provide goods and services in an economical manner. Second, the government had a public welfare obligation, embodied in the constitution, to provide universal telephone service to the nation. The Commission's arguments were based on these two fundamental principles.

The question of privatization was never seriously addressed by the commission. It was taken for granted that the Bundespost would remain in government hands and its monopoly would be preserved. On the issue of regulation, the commission recommended that the Bundespost retain its responsibility for approving terminal equipment for sale in Germany. It argued that because of the Bundespost's familiarity with the network, they were the best positioned to determine whether equipment would prove harmful to the network.

With respect to lines of business, the Monopoly Commission was somewhat more liberal. In some areas it concluded that competition was feasible and would not affect the quality of service. The commission argued that the Bundespost should relinquish its responsibility for pricing and selling customer premises equipment and should increase its approval of special networks (i.e., VANs). They also encouraged the Bundespost to open up its procurement process, until then dominated by Siemens and SEL, to include other competitors.

On the other hand, citing the natural monopoly argument and its public welfare obligations, the commission recommended that much of the Bundespost's business remain protected from competition. The commission was unconvinced by arguments that the Bundespost's monopoly over the telecommunications network and voice services should end, asserting that the network was a natural monopoly and competition would simply result in a deterioration of service quality. Customer premises equipment installation and servicing, it argued, should remain part of the Bundespost monopoly because of economies of scope. Because the telco already had the responsibility for maintaining the network, it could provide installation and maintenance at a much lower cost than other entities.

---

53. Alan Baughcum, "Implementations of Technological and Policy Developments for Telecommunications Markets," in *Telecommunications Access and Public Policy*, ed. Alan Baughcum and Gerald R. Faulhaber (Norwood, N.J.: Ablex Publishing Corporation, 1984), 70–75.

As part of the commission's inquiry, three expert reports were prepared. One of these reports, *The Role of Competition in the Telecommunications Sectors*, presented a particularly forceful argument in favor of competition. The authors, Knieps, Müller, and von Weizsäcker, advocated that the Bundespost's activities be clearly separated into monopoly sectors versus competitive sectors.[54] Unlike the Monopoly Commission, these authors suggested that economies of scope were also an important consideration in determining which activities should remain a Bundespost monopoly. They recommended that the public network remain a monopoly activity, but that the provision of enhanced services be open to competition.[55] Regarding terminal equipment, the authors advocated competition between the Bundespost and private vendors. This contrasted with the Monopoly Commission's recommendation that the Bundespost stop marketing terminal equipment.

Four years later, the Federal government formed another commission under the directorship of Professor Eberhard Witte to review the status of telecommunications regulations and the Bundespost monopoly. Unlike previous commissions, the Witte Report did address the issue of privatization. The option was rejected outright with the explanation that such a move would involve considerable constitutional risk. Article 87 of the Basic Law stipulates that the DBP is to be operated as a federal administration with its own administrative apparatus. But the commission did recognize the benefits of a more supple telco organization. It suggested that the post and telecommunications responsibilities of the Bundespost be divided into different organizations, with separate budgets. In addition, it advocated separate subsidiaries for the telco's different lines of business and encouraged the new entities to undertake joint ventures with the private sector. Although stopping far short of advocating privatization, the Witte Commission did recognize the need to relax the Bundespost monopoly and to encourage closer ties with private firms.

On the question of regulation, the commission recommended separation between the telco and the telecommunications regulatory agency. Approval of terminal equipment would be the responsibility of an independent authority reporting directly to the Federal Minister of Posts and Telecommunications. The commission gave no clear indication as to how regulated services—those where both the telco and private firms could compete—would be supervised.

With respect to the Bundespost's lines of business, the Witte Commis-

---

54. G. Knieps, J. Müller, and C. von Weizsäcker, *Die Rolle des Wettbewerbs im Fernmeldebereich* (Baden-Baden: Nomos, 1981).

55. Marcellus Snow, "Telecommunications and Media Policy in West Germany: Recent Developments," *Journal of Communications* 32 (1982): 10–32.

TABLE 6.5. Recommendations of Principal Expert Commissions, 1960–88

Commission	Ownership Structure	Regulatory Responsibility	Network	Basic Voice Service	VANs	Terminal Equipment
1964 Commission Report	More autonomy, less political control	Maintain monopoly	NA	Maintain monopoly	Maintain monopoly	Maintain entry barriers
Monopoly Commission	Little change	Maintain monopoly	Maintain monopoly	Maintain monopoly	Liberalize entry	Relinquish responsibility for pricing and selling terminal equipment
Knieps, Müller, and von Weizsäcker	Little change	Separate licensing from other activity	Maintain monopoly	Maintain monopoly	Liberalize entry	Separate DBP subsidiary for terminal equipment and full competition
Witte Commission	Government ownership, separate subsidiaries, joint ventures with private sector	Divest of regulatory functions	Maintain monopoly	Maintain monopoly	Liberalize entry	Separate DBP subsidiary for terminal equipment and full competition

sion identified five types of activities: the network, monopoly services, regulated services, unregulated services, and terminal equipment. The telco would retain a monopoly over the network "as long as it provides leased-lines (fixed connections) on fair and competitive conditions and in line with quality and quantity requirements."[56] Every three years the telco would be evaluated, and if it did not live up to these expectations, the federal government would permit the establishment of competitive networks.

Basic telephone service—defined exclusively as voice communications—would be the only monopoly service. All other services would be opened to competition (some with and others without regulation). The commission made clear that private service suppliers (VANs) should have liberal interconnection rights for the network. Finally, the commission recommended that the Bundespost remain a competitor in the market for terminal equipment but that all entry barriers be dismantled (including the provision that gave the Bundespost the monopoly on the first instrument in all subscriber residences).

Table 6.5 summarizes the major changes that have been recommended by expert commissions in the post–World War II era. None of the commissions have recommended privatization, although the 1964 Commission and the Witte Report recognized the importance of modifying the telco's organizational structure in order to make it more flexible, less subject to political control, and, therefore, more similar to a private firm. Second, over the course of the last twenty-five years there has been a growing recognition of the need to separate the Bundespost's regulatory responsibilities from its operational activities.

With the exception of the 1964 Commission, there has been considerable agreement on the extent to which the telco's lines of business should be liberalized. With respect to the telecommunications network (both local and long-distance) and basic voice telephone service, all the commissions have advocated maintaining the monopoly. On the other hand, with the exception of the first 1964 Commission, they have all advocated liberalized entry to the VANs and terminal equipment markets.

Reluctance to Change

Important changes to German telecommunications policy did not occur until passage of major legislation in 1989. From a comparative perspective, Germany distinguishes itself by its hesitancy in adopting liberal policies for its telecommunications industry. This is particularly surprising given the number of expert commissions that have advocated reform. Table 6.6 summarizes the

---

56. Eberhard Witte, *Neuordnung der Telekommunikation: Bericht der Regierungskommission Fernmeldewesen* (Heidelberg: G. Schenck, 1987), 10.

changes that have actually occurred since the 1964 Bundespost Commission made its first recommendations. The entries represent the significant government initiatives that were inspired by the commission reports indicated along the rows of the table.

For twenty-five years, while other countries experimented with new organizational policies, the Bundespost structure remained unchanged. During the 1965–76 period, a number of bills were introduced in the German Bundestag aimed at strengthening the Administrative Council, providing far greater managerial independence from political influences, and promoting more flexible business decisions by management. These legislative proposals did not have the necessary political support to win passage—they either died in committee when the legislative sessions ended or were defeated. After a ten-year hiatus, the structural issue was once again addressed by the Witte Commission. In response to the Witte Commission's recommendations, the legislation enacted in July 1989 created a new government enterprise, Telekom, with the status of a public corporation rather than a government agency. This initiative by the government represents a major step toward reshaping the telco into a more commercially oriented and competitive enterprise.

Redefining the regulatory responsibilities of the Bundespost has moved forward rather slowly. In response to the recommendations of the 1981 Monopoly Commission, the Bundespost took responsibility for equipment type approval out of its *Fernmeldetechnisches Zentralamt* (its major research and development operation) at Darmstadt and assigned it to a separate, newly created entity, the *Zentralstelle für Zulassung im Fernmeldewesen* (ZZF)—the new central approval office for telecommunications equipment.[57] The government's 1989 legislation goes somewhat further in removing regulatory responsibilities from the telco. Nonetheless, the regulatory agency remains under the authority of the Ministry of Posts and Telecommunications, which in turn controls the new Telekom. Many observers believe that this does very little to resolve the conflict of interest problems.[58]

Liberalization of the telco's lines of business has also proceeded slowly. First, the government has relentlessly insisted that the telco's monopoly over the telecommunications network and basic voice service is inviolable. The constitutional problems associated with giving up this monopoly make it unlikely that the government will change its opinion in the near future.

The government has also been very reluctant to liberalize access to VANs. Although this step was recommended by the 1981 Monopoly Commission Report, the government's response actually increased entry barriers by

---

57. Bruce, Cunard, and Director, *Telecommunications*, 551.

58. David Goodhart and Hugo Dixon, "Fortress Rhine Lowers the Drawbridge," *Financial Times*, 30 June 1989.

TABLE 6.6. Regulatory Changes Initiated by German Authorities, 1960–88

Commission	Ownership Structure	Regulatory Responsibility	Network	Basic Voice Service	VANs	Terminal Equipment
1964 Commission Report	Number of bills introduced 1965–76, all died or were defeated	Not addressed in report	No change	No change	No change	No change
Monopoly Commission	Not addressed in report	Establish ZZF— separate DBP agency for type approval	No change	No change	Introduce usage-sensitive rates on leased-lines, raises entry barriers	No change
Witte Commission	Government bill splitting DBP into three separate enterprises	Bill creating separate regulatory agency within Ministry	Separate monopoly operator—Telekom	Separate monopoly operator—Telekom	Competitive international common carrier; phase out usage rates	Independent type approval; streamline type approval

imposing usage-sensitive tariffs for private VANs vendors that leased lines from the Bundespost. The Witte Commission recommendations prompted a more liberal response by the government. The 1989 legislation calls for a gradual end to usage- and time-based tariffs on leased domestic lines. They will also remove restrictions on fixed connections to international circuits for data transmission at below voice-grade levels.[59]

Finally, with respect to terminal equipment, little change has occurred in regulations during the postwar years. Bundespost and government officials have argued that entry barriers to the market are already low, compared to most other countries. Christian Schwarz-Schilling, Minister of Post and Telecommunications, contends that the terminal equipment market in Germany has been liberalized for over twenty years, considerably longer than it has been in the United States.

Most observers, however, maintain that de facto entry barriers are significant. In particular they point to type certification standards and procedures that are extremely demanding and expensive for non-German manufacturers. Moreover, the Bundespost continues to maintain very close research and development ties with a small group of German equipment suppliers. This gives these local firms a clear advantage when the Bundespost sets specifications for the equipment it purchases. In response to the Witte Commission recommendations, the government has reduced some of the strict technical requirements enforced on manufacturers (this will make it easier for foreign manufacturers to adapt their products to the German market), ensured the independence of the type approval process, and streamlined licensing procedures.[60] The government has also recently eliminated the Bundespost monopoly over modems.

To some extent the protestations by German government officials are correct; there has been liberalization of the country's telecommunications market, particularly since 1989. But on a comparative scale, policy changes have been very gradual, occurring well after similar moves were adopted by other major developed nations. The 1989 changes are quite conservative compared to the changes that were implemented some time ago by the United States, the United Kingdom, Japan, and even France. Moreover these are policy changes that the government's own expert commissions have been advocating for almost twenty-five years.

---

59. "West German Government Outlines Plan for Liberalizing Services," *Communications Daily* 8 (4 March 1988): 1.

60. *Communications Daily,* 8:1.

Institutional Barriers to Change

This German reluctance to reduce entry barriers is not confined to the tele-communications industry. Liberalization of German markets, a process that has accelerated recently in most Western economies, is frustrated by the corporatist institutions that mediate conflicting interests in the country. First, major policy initiatives tend to be shaped by consensual bargaining among highly centralized and cohesive groups (typically labor and management along with government) and responsibility for the regulation of markets is often assumed by semipublic institutions.

Liberalization of entry barriers is unattractive to the social partners in these consensual decision-making institutions for a number of reasons. First, liberalization policies represent an economic threat to major distributional interests: firms protected by entry barriers (for example, Siemens, SEL, and smaller firms like Krone and DeTeWe) face the prospects of losing important market share. Labor representatives may see wage settlements decline as profits are squeezed by competition.

Second, liberalization represents a challenge to the political status quo: representatives from business and labor, traditionally dominant in these consensual policy-making forums, find their authority undermined by new entrants into the industry. Lower entry barriers raise the possibility that new industry entrants might not participate in these forums and could challenge their legitimacy. This is of particular concern when the industry is opened up to foreign competition. Similarly, competitors new to the industry might include nonunionized employees or unions that simply do not recognize the authority of the major social partners that dominate the consensual policy-making forums. Faced with these risks, representatives of established firms and labor organizations are likely to oppose any efforts to reduce entry barriers that could threaten their policy-making cartel.

These risks of employment reductions have raised the opposition of the major social partners. DPG, the industry's principal labor union, strongly opposes liberalization because of the threat competition poses for the Bundespost's 500,000 employees. They correctly sense that increased competition will likely result in a smaller labor force and reductions in wage increases and benefits.

Siemens, probably the dominant participant in the telecommunications policy-making process, would likely lose market share in Germany if procurement and the terminal market were liberalized. The company's dominance of its home market has played a strategic role in its efforts to increase its share of the global telecommunications equipment market. A captive home market has provided the company with a customer base, scale economies, and revenues from which it could launch its products into foreign markets. Not surprisingly, Siemens has been lukewarm, if not antagonistic, toward proposals for dismantling entry barriers.

Finally, even within the third leg of the social coalition, government, serious concerns have been raised regarding liberalization. Although the conservative Kohl government is favorably predisposed toward deregulation, one element of his coalition has expressed reservations. Because Siemens is the largest supplier to the Bundespost and because many of these jobs are found in Bavaria, job losses from increased competition is certain to affect the region. As a result, the Christian Social Union, which receives much of its electoral support from this region, has publicly challenged the proposals for liberalizing the Bundespost.

The opposition by the major social partners shaping telecommunications policy in itself represents a formidable obstacle to liberalization. But there is also a second important contributing factor: the serious divisions among the social partners that might have supported liberalization.

The greatest of these schisms has been within German big business, a major consumer of telecommunication services. Some of the major German businesses have adopted completely opposing views on the issue. Much of the Bundespost's procurement expenditures benefit two companies: Siemens, one of Germany's largest corporations, and Standard Elektrik Lorenz (SEL), an Alcatel subsidiary. As a result, they have been decidedly antagonistic toward liberalization because it threatens their very profitable close ties to the Bundespost. In contrast, Nixdorf, the large German computer manufacturer, has been an adamant supporter of further liberalization.[61] The computer manufacturing and data processing industries have traditionally supported liberalization because demand for their products and services increases as a result of lower telecommunication tariffs and flexible regulations governing value-added network services. In Nixdorf's case, the company had additional grounds for backing liberalization because it was excluded from the small circle of Bundespost equipment suppliers. Also strongly supporting liberalization were the large foreign multinationals (such as IBM and Citibank) that had heavy volumes of domestic and international telecommunications traffic. These divisions prevented business from forcefully advocating liberalization in negotiations with other major social partners.

Even within the governing coalition of CDU/CSU and FDP there have been serious differences of opinion on the issue of liberalization. The FDP has been a strong proponent of liberalization and many of its members, such as the Minister of the Economy, Mr. Bangeman, have spoken out in favor of

---

61. At least this has been its position prior to its acquisition by Siemens in 1990.

eliminating the Bundespost monopoly. At the other extreme is the CSU, which has opposed any changes in the Bundespost's monopoly.[62]

As Olson points out, these corporatist arrangements increase the sensitivity of the actors to the social costs of certain actions and facilitate constructive agreements on major policy concerns.[63] In the case of liberalization of entry barriers to the telecommunications industry, exactly the reverse has occurred. First, because of the risks and uncertainties of competition, a number of the major social partners are diehard opponents of any liberalization. Second, the government is reluctant to take any action because the interest coalitions are divided on such legislation.

Given all these institutional barriers, how do we explain the liberal policies ultimately enacted by the German government in 1989? First, the legislation passed in July 1989 does not entirely abandon the interests of the major social partners: labor and the manufacturing industry. Schwarz-Schilling, the Minister of the Post and Telecommunications, was careful to craft a bill that explicitly incorporated the demands of the telecommunications trade union and their allies in the Social Democratic Party. Although the legislation was strongly opposed by labor and the SDP, it received their support once a compromise was agreed upon. The reorganization of the Bundespost was of major concern to labor and it is clear from the final legislation that Schwarz-Schilling conceded to many of their demands: Labor retains an important role in the supervisory council that oversees the management of Deutsche Bundespost Telekom and they will preserve their status as civil servants, entitling them to salary scales and benefits similar to those of the public sector. Most important, from labor's perspective, was the protection of jobs and their status as civil servants.

The 1989 bill reduces entry barriers for both services and equipment and this certainly represents a threat to German industry. Nonetheless, it is clear that the major manufacturers, Siemens in particular, favored a significant symbolic gesture toward opening up the German telecommunications market. Increasingly, they were faced with the possibility of retaliatory action on the part of countries where they hoped to establish a presence. In particular, the company hoped to make significant inroads into the United States, but was threatened with trade sanctions if U.S. companies were not afforded similar access to the German market.

There is some chance that this concession by German industry was merely symbolic. The legislation does not seriously challenge the close research and development relationship that exists between Siemens and the

---

62. Möschel, "Die Telekommunikation braucht den Wettbewerb."
63. Olson, *Rise and Decline of Nations.*

Bundespost. Moreover, a number of the seats on the supervisory council are reserved for German industry and there is little doubt that Siemens will maintain an important role in shaping Telekom's purchasing policies.

The argument regarding the link between styles of interest intermediation and liberal policy initiatives does not suggest that such changes are impossible, simply that they are likely to be adopted more gradually than in other institutional environments. This is precisely what has occurred in Germany. Compared to other countries, such as the United States, the United Kingdom, and France, liberal policies have lagged considerably. The United States began aggressive liberalization in the late 1960s, the United Kingdom initiated similar moves in 1979, and France began experimenting with different organizational and regulatory strategies in the 1970s. Katzenstein argues that "This convergence between experimentation and continuity is the most striking political characteristic of West Germany in the 1980s. The big change which Chancellor Kohl and his new government called for in 1983 has not occurred. But innumerable small changes are transforming West Germany's economy and society." He labels this the "convergence of flexibility and stability."[64]

Finally, the legislative initiative of 1989 illustrates the extent to which traditional corporatist institutions are being undermined by pressures outside the traditional German policy process. Structural changes have traditionally been the exclusive concern of national institutions. Increasingly, demands for *structural* change are being externally imposed on German policymakers. The legislative initiatives of 1989, which may ultimately undermine traditional corporatist institutions, were to a large extent imposed on Germany by its major trading partners, the EC and the United States. Decisions by Directorate XIII of the European Commission mandated important liberalization of the German telecommunications industry. Moreover, the U.S. government had been strongly pressuring the German government to dismantle entry barriers to the industry. This is quite different from the *economic* challenges faced by German policymakers during the 1970s and early 1980s.

Conclusion

Why, with the exception of the very early years of telephony, did the German public telco underperform for most of the twentieth century? I rejected the economic explanation because GNP growth, in fact, predicts a much higher degree of telephone penetration in Germany than was achieved throughout most of this century. The argument that public ownership was the cause of its poor performance is not entirely convincing since there are examples of some public enterprises strongly outperforming the German telco—Sweden, for

---

64. Katzenstein, *Policy and Politics*, 307.

example—and others that have performed considerably worse—France, for example.

This chapter's examination of the German case supports the conclusions drawn from the earlier regression analyses: political control (as opposed to ownership per se) is negatively related to performance. Nonetheless, Germany exhibits a number of interesting variations on this theme. First, the nature of political control and its implications for performance vary. During the interwar years, the German telco faced a fairly traditional set of political demands: as part of the German federal government, the PTT, lacking any financial autonomy, was seriously affected by hyperinflation and the government's budgetary crisis. As a result, capital expansion was underfinanced. In the post–World War II era, political control passed on to a small group of very influential interested parties—government, the manufacturers, and labor. Underfinancing was no longer a problem—the interested parties all had a significant stake in expanding capital plant and equipment. Growth in the penetration of telephone service, however, was hindered by the reluctance of this "triumvirate" to advocate the reduction of tariffs—it simply was not in their short-term interest to do so.

Another important lesson from the German context is that the prospects for modifying political control over a public entity vary according to certain institutional characteristics. Germany had evolved a highly respected corporatist system for overseeing the activities of certain public entities, one of which was the Bundespost. Because these corporatist structures institutionalize the market power of a small number of highly organized interest groups, significant reform of the industry, that is, reductions in industry entry barriers, is a difficult proposition.

CHAPTER 7

The Paradox of the French Telephone

The French have had a distinct love-hate relationship with the telephone: as recently as the 1960s, General DeGaulle considered it a gadget and a fad that would eventually lose popularity, while President Giscard d'Estaing envisaged France leading the *télématique* revolution with its telecommunications and computer technology.[1] The development of telecommunications in France reflects this policy-making schizophrenia. On the one hand, for almost an entire century, French telecommunications languished behind developments in other nations. Poor telephone communications in France was, in fact, a joke shared by international visitors. Yet in the 1970s, the French engineered a dramatic improvement in the quality of telecommunications service, expanding the subscriber base rapidly, and French manufacturers became world leaders in telecommunications technology and equipment.

The French case raises three questions regarding ownership and market structure. First, the history of French telecommunications throws into question the hypothesized link between ownership and performance. When the technology was initially introduced in France in the late nineteenth century, telephone service was entrusted to private firms under which telephone penetration advanced very slowly in comparison to the publicly owned systems in neighboring Germany and Switzerland. Nationalization was not a solution: under public ownership, telephone service was poorly administered for almost a century. But this changed in the 1970s when the nationalized telco undertook a spectacular effort to modernize the entire French telephone network. There is no clear pattern of performance associated with ownership. Neither public nor private ownership can be uniquely associated with good or poor performance.

Private ownership did not succeed because political pressures—specifically the threat of nationalization—seriously undermined capital investment. Once nationalized, government authorities accorded telephone service a very low priority, the telco never received adequate budgetary authorization for capital investment, and, as a result, service deteriorated. After a century of neglect, the political fortunes of the telephone improved. Under President

---

1. "Telephones in France: Very Francophone," *Economist*, 28 January 1978.

Giscard d'Estaing, telecommunications became a top political priority and, as a result, capital investment and telephone penetration accelerated dramatically. The French case attests to the irrelevance of ownership per se in shaping the performance of the telco while highlighting the extent to which its fortunes are tied to political priorities.

A second puzzle concerns the liberalization policies adopted after the successful modernization of the French telephone service. Why, after the demonstrated success of the public monopoly, did government policy move toward reduced entry barriers and limited privatization? The costs to society of inaction mounted in France, as it did in the other developed nations, because of technological advances and increasing international competition. But unlike Germany and the United Kingdom, group pressures played little part in the government's policies, giving rise to a distinctive process of de-regulation and liberalization.

Finally, the French responded to the rising costs of entry barriers very differently than the British and the Americans, where governments adopted radical liberalization policies, or than the Germans, where the government was reluctant to make any changes in market structure or ownership. Government authorities adopted a mini-max strategy that minimized their loss of control over the industry while maximizing the benefits from liberal policies. As a result, liberalization has a distinctly statist hue in France. Barriers were lowered, but entry remained under the control of government authorities. Outright privatization was rejected as an option for reducing political constraints; decision makers preferred the creation of independent subsidiaries that, while less subject to political manipulation, ultimately remained under state control.

An Overview of the French Telco's Performance

The early years of the telephone era were not auspicious ones for the French telco. Table 7.1 shows the comparative expansion of the infrastructure for France, Europe, and the United States. Between 1881 and 1890, the number of telephones in France increased tenfold compared to thirtyfold in Europe as a whole. Throughout this early period, France lagged seriously behind other European countries.

Until the end of the 1960s France maintained its slow rate of infrastructure development. In 1938, it had 24 telephones per thousand population, compared to a figure of 30 for Germany (a difference of 17%); France ranked ninth out of the twelve countries for which data were available.[2] By 1965 the

---

2. AT&T Communications, Overseas Marketing Department, *The World's Telephones: A Statistical Compilation as of January 1, 1982* (Morris Plains, N.J.: AT&T Communications, 1982).

TABLE 7.1. Comparative Number of Telephone Subscribers, 1881–1890

	1881	1886	1890
United States	47,900	155,800	211,500
Europe	5,600	77,000	177,000
France	800	5,789	9,129

Source: Louis-Joseph Libois, *Genèse et Croissance des Télécommunications* (Paris: Masson, 1983), 62.

difference had widened to 63 telephone main lines per thousand population in France compared to 82 in Germany, a 30% difference. Of the twenty developed countries in this sample, France still ranked eighteenth. The difference narrowed by 1980 when France had 295 telephone main lines per thousand population, compared to 334 for Germany.

During the period prior to 1970, the French telecommunications infrastructure grew at a snail's pace, primarily because the service provider did not invest in its development. Historical accounts suggest that the low priority accorded the telecommunications sector was directly related to its political status. As a government agency, capital expenditures were set by the intensely political budgetary process. For almost an entire century, as Libois points out, the telephone was simply not a salient political issue.[3] Without political support, major expenditures on improvement of the telecommunications infrastructure were never undertaken.

In contrast, during the 1970s and 1980s, telecommunications gained increased political stature with the result that France rapidly achieved one of the highest telephone penetration rates in Europe (see fig. 7.1).

This chapter is organized around four central themes: the failure of private ownership in the early period of telecommunications development; a century of neglect under public ownership; the state-owned enterprise as the champion of economic modernization; and state-guided liberalization.

The Failure of Private Ownership

Government jurisdiction over the telephone was formally recognized in 1879. In responding to the introduction of telephony, the government pursued two primary objectives: minimize its investment in developing the telephone service and protect the revenue stream generated by the existing telegraph monopoly. These were the political constraints imposed by the serious indebtedness of France after its disastrous war with Prussia in 1870–71. Capital

---

3. Louis-Joseph Libois, *Genèse et Croissance des Télécommunications* (Paris: Masson, 1983).

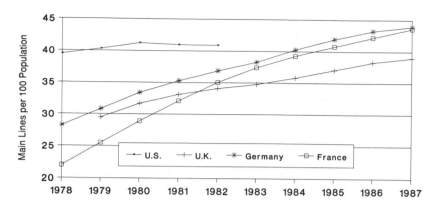

Fig. 7.1.   Comparative telephone diffusion rates, 1978–87. (Data from ITU, *Yearbook of Common Carrier Telecommunications Statistics* [Geneva: ITU, 1989].)

expenditures that added to the public debt were prohibited, except in the case of national defense. As a result, it was extremely difficult to procure capital funding for telecommunications investment projects.

Faced with such a serious budgetary constraint, governments of the Third Republic opted for private, as opposed to government, development of "public" services.[4] Rather than commit scarce public funds, local authorities granted concessions to private providers of gas, electricity, and water distribution. The decision to award private concessions, as opposed to funding public investments in these areas, was not based on any evaluation of economic efficiency or equity but rather political expediency—the state simply could not afford to raise the necessary capital to fund the development of these projects.

To promote telephone service, starting in 1879, private investors were granted *cahier des charges,* concessions to establish local exchanges. These concessions lasted five years, they were restricted to cities approved by the telegraph authorities, and the concessionaires paid the government 10 percent of their gross receipts. Eventually all of the concessionaires were merged into one company, the *Société générale des téléphones* (SGT), which had 8,459 subscribers in sixteen exchanges by 1988.

Should the technology prove a success, government policymakers argued that they could regain control of the telephone exchanges after the

---

4. There is an interesting parallel between the situation faced by governments of the Third Republic and by contemporary governments that have decided to privatize public enterprises in an attempt to reduce the size of government debt.

concessions expired. The private sector would, in effect, underwrite the development costs of this new technology and assume the risks of failure. In the short term at least, the government's objective of minimizing its commitment of public funds was met.

Long-distance telephone service, on the other hand, directly threatened the state's investment in its monopoly telegraph service. To minimize this threat, the French government, in 1885, began construction of long-distance lines rather than turn the service over to the private sector. As Holcombe pointed out, long-distance service was introduced in France at a rate that would "prevent an excessively rapid depreciation of the public investment in the telegraphs."[5]

Both of these policy decisions—private concessions for local service and publicly provided long-distance service—slowed the development of the French telephone infrastructure. The terms of the *cahier des charges* discouraged rapid growth in telephone penetration because concessionaires were unsure about their renewal and were concerned with the extensive public nationalization of private telephone concessions. As a result, concessions were forced to price the service to recoup all of their investment in a relatively short period. State-owned telcos in Germany and Switzerland—for whom there was no risk of losing their concessions—charged lower rates, which in turn generated high growth and raised penetration levels.[6]

Private ownership failed in France, as it did in virtually all of the European countries, because government actions inflated the riskiness of investment: concessions were granted for short periods of time with no certainty of renewal, restrictions were imposed on construction of long-distance facilities, and there was a serious threat of nationalization. In countries such as the United States, where private concessions were not limited to short periods and did not face the threat of nationalization, investment and penetration growth were much higher than virtually any European country.

The Politics of Nationalization

With the *Société générale*'s concession ending in September 1889, the French legislature was under pressure to decide how the industry would be structured and regulated. It had two very broad options: regulated monopoly (either a single national monopoly or regional monopolies) or public ownership. In 1889, the French National Assembly voted for the nationalization of the telephone service in France and ownership of the *Société générale* was trans-

---

5. Arthur N. Holcombe, *Public Ownership of Telephones on the Continent of Europe* (New York: Houghton Mifflin Company, 1911), 276.
6. Holcombe, *Ownership of Telephones*, 272.

ferred to the French Post and Telegraph Administration.[7] Why did the concept of public, as opposed to private, monopoly prevail?

We often think of public ownership as a response to a market failure or as an ideological statement—neither seems to apply here. First, although policy-makers may have considered the industry a natural monopoly, there was by no means a consensus that the monopoly should be government-owned. In fact, there was support among both the public and some elected officials for the establishment of a regulated private monopoly.

During this period of French history, laissez-faire policies were very influential, generating considerable skepticism regarding government owner-ship. The two major reports on the future of the telephone—the Cochery Rapport and the Ducret Rapport—both questioned whether state ownership would be appropriate.[8] Legislation introduced in 1887 by Granet, the minister in charge of the telegraph, favored private monopoly, for at least thirty-five years, after which the State could assume control. The proposal was even-tually defeated in the legislature. If anything, during this period there was a strong ideological current opposing government ownership.

Why then did the French proceed with nationalization of the industry? As chapter 2 pointed out, government ownership generates political benefits for elected officials. In this case, protecting government revenues was the pivotal benefit leading to the nationalization of the French telco. Elected officials, under very serious budgetary constraints, opted for public ownership because any other policy would have seriously threatened the receipts raised by the state-owned telegraph service. Nationalization of the telephone service was expected to protect government revenues in two ways. First, public ownership ensured that the government could slow down the introduction of long-distance telephony—which posed the greatest threat to the telegraph—and better amortize its investment in telegraph plant and equipment. Second, to the extent that there was revenue loss to telephony, the state, rather than private firms, would be the direct beneficiary.

Pre–World War I

Because of the government's indebtedness, once the telco was nationalized, financing the construction of new exchanges and long-distance lines became a very serious problem. By 1889, funds for the construction of telephone ex-changes and long-distance plant had been depleted and the government was unwilling to commit further funds for capital projects. As a result, com-

7. A. R. Bennett, *The Telephone Systems of the Continent of Europe* (London: Longmans, Green and Co., 1895), 139.

8. Holcombe, *Ownership of Telephones*, 268–80.

munities that wanted local or long-distance telephone service were forced to provide their own financing. The Laws were passed by the French Assembly in 1889 and 1890 that placed the burden of constructing local exchanges and long-distance plant on local authorities.[9] Once the plant was constructed, the post and telegraph administration would take possession and assume the expenses of operation and maintenance.[10]

In the short run this policy was quite effective: Holcombe reports that in the first five years after the laws were adopted, the number of exchanges in operation increased by more than a factor of ten.[11] Overall, however, this policy retarded the development of the French telephone system.[12] First, it exacted significant financial sacrifices from local authorities, offering no opportunity to receive income generated from the operational telephone systems. Second, this local initiative policy was unsuccessful at encouraging local authorities to upgrade and extend the telephone plant. Finally, this system of funding, while reasonably effective for construction of long-distance plant between neighboring communities, did not contribute to the development of main trunk lines between smaller communities and larger centers such as Paris.

As a result of the government's nationalization of the telephone service and its subsequent refusal to fund capital construction projects, the French telephone infrastructure was dramatically underfunded, compared to other systems in Europe. Between 1889, when telephone service was nationalized, and 31 December 1902, the total capital expenditures for the telephone system amounted to 40 million francs. This represented an expenditure of 1 franc per person stretched over thirteen years.

Government ownership along with strict political oversight put the French telco at the mercy of its political masters. Although telephony commanded a certain amount of political attention during the pre–World War I period, the penury of the French state resulted in little funding for capital expenditures.

Public Ownership in the Interwar Years

The interwar years witnessed a growing concern over the relative backwardness of French telephone service. Some critics, such as Laffont, the deputy secretary of the Post and Telegraph Administration, called for the privatization of the service, arguing that the state was simply incapable of operating a

---

9. Holcombe, *Ownership of Telephones*, 288.

10. Holcombe, *Ownership of Telephones*, 287–90. Holcombe provides two informative accounts of such initiatives taken by the towns of Nimes and Limoges.

11. Holcombe, *Ownership of Telephones*, 290.

12. This discussion is based on Holcombe, *Ownership of Telephones*, 292–95.

TABLE 7.2.   Telephone Density, 1938

Country	Telephone Density[a]
United States	15.27
Sweden	12.47
Denmark	11.64
Switzerland	10.71
Norway	8.04
Great Britain	6.74
Germany	5.20
Belgium	5.02
Netherlands	4.96
France	3.79
Italy	1.43

Source: Libois, Genèse et Croissance, 83.
[a] Telephones per hundred population.

commercial entity such as the telephone service.[13] The question of poor telephone service was addressed in the Assembly in 1921, resulting in a bill that called for reorganization of the Post and Telegraph Administration and the establishment of a separate budget for the department. In 1923, the bill was finally passed, marking an important turning point in the Post and Telegraph's history.

The legislation was designed to improve the national network and redress some of the financial problems faced by the telco. But before concrete progress could be made, the depression and World War II intervened, and funding for infrastructure improvement simply became unavailable.

By the end of 1938, development of the telecommunications infrastructure in France trailed behind most other developed countries. Telephone penetration figures are presented in table 7.2 for eleven developed countries. Note that France ranks tenth, followed only by Italy. With the government preoccupied with the war effort, the Post and Telegraph Administration never received adequate funding that might have narrowed the gap between France and other developed nations.

Public Ownership in the Postwar Years

After World War II, telecommunications once again was put low on the government's list of investment priorities. In the postwar period, the French initiated a series of plans, developed by the Commissariate au Plan. These plans established the investment priorities for French industry over a five-year

---

13. Libois, Genèse et Croissance, 70.

period. Since the French government maintained tight control over the availability of credit, sectors not given high priority received little funding for capital investments.

The First Plan that shaped postwar investments in the French economy included six priority areas; telecommunications was not one of them. Subsequent plans continued to accord low priority to telecommunications investment. It was not until the Fifth Plan, covering 1966–70, that telecommunications was elevated to a priority sector.

As a result, French telephone service in the early part of the 1970s was seriously deficient. Darmon pointed out that the average waiting period for a new installation was six months and that the *Direction générale de télécommunications* (DGT) had over 1 million requests that were not processed.[14] The social and economic implications were serious: whole communities were virtually isolated because of poor telecommunications and multinationals avoided France because of the poor state of telephone service.

State-Sponsored Modernization

The most recent period of telecommunications development in France represents a very significant break with past patterns. As figure 7.1 illustrated, telephone penetration in France increased dramatically in the 1970s and 1980s. It was the Fifth Plan that signaled the government's change in telecommunications policy. The telecommunications sector assumed critical importance in the government's efforts to promote exports and reduce France's technological lag.

Table 7.3 summarizes the investment amounts targeted for telecommunications by successive plans. Note that the Fifth Plan's annual commitment to telecommunications investment is double that of the preceding plan. An even more important factor for the sector's development was the decision by planners to authorize the DGT to borrow funds on outside markets (previously the DGT was expected to be entirely self-financing). As a result, DGT indebtedness rose from zero in 1969 to over 50 billion francs in 1981.

The Fifth Plan increased the annual investment commitment for the 1971–75 period to about 2 billion francs. This represented more than a doubling of the Fourth Plan's commitment. Investment commitments by the Seventh Plan were even more remarkable. A total of 110 billion francs was to be spent over the 1976–80 period, 22 billion francs annually, a tenfold increase over the annual commitment by the Fifth Plan.

In a matter of ten years, France dramatically improved the state of its

---

14. Jacques Darmon, *Le Grand Dérangement: La Guerre du Téléphone* (Paris: J. C. Lattes, 1985), 74.

TABLE 7.3. The Plan's Investment Commitments for Telecommunications

Plan	Years	Total Commitment	Annual Commitments
II	1954–57	1.25 Billion	0.31 Billion
III	1957–61	4.45 Billion[a]	0.72 Billion
IV	1962–65	4.50 Billion	1.12 Billion
V	1966–70	10.20 Billion	2.04 Billion
VI	1971–75	45.00 Billion	11.30 Billion
VII	1976–80	110.00 Billion	22.00 Billion

Source: Libois, Genèse et Croissance.
Note: Amounts in French francs.
[a]Commitment for this plan includes both the Telco and the Postal Service.

telecommunications infrastructure. PTT revenues rose from 10.9 billion francs in 1973 to 61.9 billion in 1983; total lines in service climbed from 5.66 million in 1973 to 22 million in 1984. France rose from one of the lowest telephone density countries in the OECD to the sixth-ranked country in 1986, behind the United States, Sweden, Switzerland, Canada, and Germany.[15] Also by 1989, 70 percent of the French public telecommunications network was operating on digital central switches, making it the most digital network in the world.[16]

The sudden interest in an improved telecommunications network had little to do with disgruntled consumers or with the availability of new switching technologies. Network modernization caught the fancy of French politicians because it promised to create significant demand for French-designed and manufactured switching equipment. With a serious trade deficit, declining levels of capital investment, and high unemployment, the government looked to investment in the telecommunications infrastructure as one strategy for dealing with these problems. Not only did the sector hold a lot of promise for French manufacturers, it was an industry in which the state continued to exercise considerable control over entry, unlike other sectors such as computers, civil aviation, and semiconductors, where the government's industrial policies were much less successful.

To argue that certain forms of government ownership impose significant levels of political constraints on management does not *necessarily* imply that all such pressure detracts from economic performance and inhibits development. The French modernization program is an example of political priorities promoting accelerated economic development.

15. Darmon, *Grand Dérangement*, 76.
16. "French Telecommunications System: World's Most Highly Digitalised Network," *Financial Times* (London), 19 July 1989.

Institutional Status and Political Constraints

The performance of French telephony throughout the past century has been tied to its political fortunes. As a government agency, the telco's management was seriously restricted by the political priorities of successive governments that were uninterested in funding capital expenditures. Once the government took an interest in the sector, the goals and implementation of capital expenditure projects were shaped by political concerns. This section briefly summarizes how the telco's institutional status sensitized it to the government's political priorities.

Immediately after its nationalization, the *Société des téléphones* was merged, like the telegraph, with the postal monopoly.[17] The telco was given virtually no administrative or organizational identity and was assigned to a department that had no political resources to compete for scarce budgetary authorizations. It was not until 1941 that the government recognized the distinction between the post and telecommunications by separating them into two different *direction generale*, although they remain until this day united in a single ministry. The telecommunications department was called the *Direction générale de télécommunications* (DGT).

Along the public-private continuum identified in chapter 2, the French DGT ranks on the extreme public end. To this date, telecommunications is treated as a functional department within the administration, in contrast to other French utilities such as Elf-Aquitaine, *Electricité de France*, *Gaz de France*, and the *Société nationale de chemins de fer* (SNCF), which have distinctive commercial organizations.[18] On virtually all of the criteria discussed earlier—finances (tariffs and borrowing), personnel, and management discretion—the telecommunications *direction* has had very little independence of political pressures.

Finance

The DGT and its successor, France Télécom, have had virtually no independent control over their annual budgets. Throughout much of its history, the telco was required to balance its operating and capital budgets. Recently, the government shifted positions and now encourages aggressive borrowing by France Télécom in order to fund capital expenditures. Its budget is subject to a

---

17. Bennett, *Telephone Systems*, 139.

18. Jacques Darmon, "Télécommunications: Vers une Dérègulation à la Française," *Politique Industrielle* 3 (Spring 1986): 86. In addition to public ownership of the telco, during the Socialist government's tenure in the early 1980s about 80 percent of the entire industry—service and manufacturing—was under government ownership.

number of oversights: it must be approved by the Minister of Finance, by the Assembly, and it must conform to the priorities laid out in the French Plan.[19] Indifference on the part of these institutions translated into a scarcity of capital funds.

The government also exercises considerable discretion regarding tariffs and borrowing by the *Direction*. Very little flexibility is afforded the *Direction* in the setting of tariffs; changes in tariff structures are proposed by the Minister of the PTT and are then reviewed by the Ministers of the Economy and of Finance who make the final decision regarding their acceptability. This decision is then brought into force by a presidential decree.

Moreover, the government can unilaterally, without the approval of telco management, raise or lower telecommunications rates. The Mitterrand government, for example, raised the basic unit rate for telephone service from 65.5 centimes to 75.0 centimes in August 1984. This initiative was taken with no regard for the opposition of DGT management.[20]

Until 1970, the telco was not permitted to borrow funds—it was entirely dependent upon self-financing.[21] Since 1970, the government has authorized the DGT to borrow funds on outside markets. The vehicle for executing this borrowing on national and international markets is the *Caisse Nationale des Télécommunications* (CNT).[22]

In the early 1970s the government also permitted the establishment of five *Sociétés de Financement* (Finextel, Codetel, Agritel, Creditel, and Francetel) that are leasing agents that borrow on the open market and purchase hardware which they then lease to consumers on a lease–buy back arrangement.[23] By opening up these new avenues of finance, the government permitted important increases in capital expenditures without severe tariff increases. Nonetheless, the government continues to control expenditures of these funds through its oversight of the capital and operating budgets of the telco and, therefore, these allocations remain tied to the government's priorities for competing areas such as health, culture, and defense.[24]

---

19. Robert R. Bruce, Jeffrey P. Cunard, and Mark D. Director, *From Telecommunications to Electronic Services: A Global Spectrum of Definitions, Boundary Lines, and Structures* (London: Butterworth, 1986), 532; Logica, *Communications in Europe—The Changing Environment* (London: Logica, 1983); Libois, *Genèse et Croissance*.

20. Bruce, Cunard, and Director, *Telecommunications*, 508.

21. Geneviève Bonnetblanc, *Les Télécommunications Françaises: Quel Statut Pour Quelle Enterprise?* (Paris: La Documentation Française, 1985), 154.

22. Bruce, Cunard, and Director, *Telecommunications*, 511.

23. Bonnetblanc, *Télécommunications Françaises*, 152–71.

24. Darmon, *Grand Dérangement*, 176.

Personnel

The French telco, like most bureaus in the French administration, is guided by a strict set of regulations regarding civil service employment. Restrictions on who can be hired, compensation packages, and promotions is heavily influenced by both the professional corps (the *Corps des ingénieurs*, the *Corps des administrations*, and the *Corps de l'inspection*) and by the civil service administration. These two bodies control hiring for particular positions and the numbers recruited annually from each corps. Civil service regulations and traditions simply do not permit the level of flexibility necessary for a fast-changing industry like telecommunications. These restrictive personnel policies place the DGT at a distinct disadvantage to the private sector, which is seeking the same skilled engineering and programming personnel but has considerably greater flexibility in hiring and compensation.

Management Discretion

Through virtually its entire history, telco management has had no autonomy from government policymakers and elected officials. As a result, investment programs and purchasing decisions are shaped by political priorities. Some efforts have recently been made to reduce this constraint by initiating long-term management agreements between the DGT and the Council of Ministers.[25] In return for a commitment to certain medium-term objectives, such as modernization of the telephone network, these agreements granted the telco more autonomy in day-to-day management.

In practice, telco management still has little autonomy. French authorities maintain tight control over management for two major reasons: the entity is one of the largest French firms, and its decisions affect a key industrial sector. The DGT had revenues of 72 billion francs in 1984, placing it among the top ten enterprises in France, and it employs a total of 165,000 people, about 0.8 percent of the total French labor force.[26] Telecommunications is also one of the key high-technology manufacturing sectors in France, employing in the neighborhood of 75,000 people. In addition to meeting most of the domestic demand (in 1983, imports accounted for no more than 7 percent of telecommunications equipment sales), the industry represents one of the country's most important manufacturing exports: telecommunications exports increased, in constant francs, 15.7 percent between 1973 and 1983 and, in

25. Bruce, Cunard, and Director, *Telecommunications*, 532.

26. Ministere des PTT, Direction Générale de Télécommunications, *Rapport d'activité 1983* (Paris: Direction Générale de Télécommunications, 1984).

1983, 25 percent of total telecommunications equipment production was exported, compared to 15 percent in 1979.[27]

Recognizing the importance of the telecommunications sector for the French economy, the government has sought to shape the telco's investment and purchasing decisions. A case in point is the government's *rattrapage* plan of the 1970s, which financed the rapid modernization of the French telephone network. An important political consideration behind the effort was the numerous jobs created within both the telco and the manufacturing sector that supplied the switching hardware, cable, telephone units, etc. During the height of this project in 1977, estimates of employment in the telecommunications manufacturing sector range between about 62,000[28] and 94,000 jobs.[29] Similar industrial policy considerations have led the government to pressure DGT management into offering new products (such as the *télécopieur de grande diffusion*, the Minitel, and the ill-fated Plan Cable), primarily with an eye to future exports.

Post-Infrastructural Challenge: Ownership and Competition

In the 1970s, as the French were successfully completing their *rattrapage* in basic telecommunications service, the industry entered a period of accelerated technological change; growth became much more demand, as opposed to supply, driven. Hence, the costs to French society of maintaining a highly politicized government monopoly began to mount, putting pressure on government authorities to reduce entry barriers and reorganize the nationalized telco. These changes raised two principal concerns: (1) returns to the State's investment in the telecommunications infrastructure, and (2) the international competitiveness of French industry.

Having invested considerable resources to modernize the French telecommunications infrastructure, the government was intent on maximizing its revenues by encouraging use of the public network. Technological advances posed two challenges in this regard:

1. to identify policies that would promote the introduction of these new innovative communications services, thereby ensuring high volumes of network usage;
2. to address the competitive threat of resale of network capacity over leased-lines or satellite links that threatened telco revenues.

---

27. Darmon, "Télécommunications," 84.
28. Albert Glowinski, *Télécommunications: Objectif 2000* (Paris: Dunod, 1980), 65.
29. Darmon, "Télécommunications," 88.

Technological and market transformations also threatened the continued international competitiveness of the French telecommunications equipment manufacturers and service providers. The days of protected markets, static consumer demand, and universal, as opposed to narrow, market segments had come to an end.[30] Unfortunately, these were the conditions under which France's state capitalism proved most effective, and these changes posed a very serious threat to its effectiveness.

More generally, the international competitiveness of French firms was at stake. As telecommunications assumes an increasingly important role in the operation of modern businesses, the price, range, and quality of these services have become an important competitive advantage for firms. Traditional telecommunications policies imposed costs on French society because they stifled innovation and competitive pricing, thereby making the country less attractive for certain kinds of business activities and likely inhibiting economic growth.

Both challenges—to maintain growth in network usage and to promote international competitiveness—required that the French telecommunications industry produce increasingly innovative and cost-competitive services and products. The next two sections suggest how political constraints and high entry barriers inhibited these ambitions.

Political Constraints

The negative consequences of management by political, in contrast to market, priorities mounted as the French telecommunications industry became much more demand driven.[31] Two areas have been particularly affected: the introduction of new products and services and pricing.

Products and Services

During the 1970s, the government assumed a more prominent role in shaping overall industrial policy for the telecommunications industry. Decisions regarding product or service introductions were evaluated in terms of their export opportunities for French firms and the new jobs they would create, as opposed to whether they addressed significant consumer demands.

---

30. Bruno Aurelle, *Les Télécommunications* (Paris: Editions la Découverte, 1986).

31. Darmon makes this point in his analysis of the problems besetting the French telecommunications sector. It is echoed by Coustel, who enumerated a variety of political constraints imposed on the DGT: participate in countercyclical economic policies, control the equipment manufacturing industry, maintain a strong research capability, implement price controls, contribute in a tailormade way to public spending, social redistribution, and borrowing on foreign markets (see Darmon, "Télécommunications," 37; and Jean Pierre Coustel, "Telecommunications Services in France," *Telecommunications Policy* 10 [September 1986]: 229–43).

Although these initiatives were conceived in order to promote the competitiveness of French telecommunications equipment manufacturers, they had a perverse impact on their performance.[32] First, the fortunes of manufacturers became directly tied to government funding decisions, which were often episodic, resulting in dramatic swings in production requirements. Second, responsibility for research and development is heavily controlled by the telco, which conducts feasibility tests for new products and then divides responsibility for development among manufacturers, CNET, and the universities. As a result, the manufacturers never developed much of an autonomous research and development capability, leaving these decisions in the hands of government officials.

This does not mean that all the telco's initiatives failed—some, in fact, succeeded quite impressively. On balance, however, investment and marketing decisions shaped by the vagaries of the government's political agenda are likely to undermine the performance of the telco. Two projects initiated in the 1970s illustrate the extent to which political demand shaped product introductions: Minitel and the *télécopieur de grande diffusion*.

One of the more-or-less successful initiatives is the Minitel videotext service introduced in 1978. Its introduction addressed two industrial policy goals: raise the penetration of French electronics in foreign markets and increase the use of the Transpac, the telco's recently completed high-speed data network. As part of the Minitel service, telephone subscribers were provided with a free terminal allowing them to access two separate data banks: one containing the telephone numbers of all French PTT subscribers, the other including a variety of informational services (such as newspapers, travel information, etc.). The service utilizes the Transpac data network, thereby addressing the goal of increased usage. In addition, the terminals are provided by French manufacturers, Thompson and Matra. The government hoped that initial orders for terminals would provide these companies with sufficient economies of scale, permitting them to conquer international markets for similar video terminals, thereby creating more jobs in the sector.

Minitel is clearly the most successful videotext service in the world.[33] The government estimates that, including the cost savings associated with producing telephone books, Minitel earned 620 million francs in 1985. The usage statistics are impressive: France Telecom will exceed its goal of 5 million Minitels and will have 6 million units installed by 1990; in 1987, 1.1 million new Minitels were installed, a 51 percent increase in one year; calls increased from 104.0 million in 1985 to 513.8 million in 1987; hours of usage increased from 11.7 million in 1985 to 52.4 million in 1987; Minitel traffic

---

32. This discussion is based on Darmon, "Telecommunications," 167.

33. Nadine Epstein, "Et Voila! Le Minitel," *New York Times*, 9 March 1986.

represented 53 percent of annual volume billed on Transpac; and there are 8,000 information services offered by Minitel.

While the service has gained widespread acceptance in France, its commercial success is questionable. First, the terminals have not generated the export benefits that the government had initially envisioned. Second, the program continues to lose money according to recent reports by the *Cours des Comptes*: France Télécom invested 8.3 billion francs by the end of 1987, but had recouped only 2.9 billion. By 1995, the *Cours des Comptes* projects a cumulative deficit of 4.1 billion francs.[34]

Prior to Minitel, the DGT proposed the development of a facsimile machine costing in the neighborhood of 1,000 francs that would be available to all telephone subscribers. Once again, the primary motivation was the government's industrial policy. It hoped to promote the fortunes of French electronics firms by generating a domestic market for this new technology. Four companies were provided development capital for the *télécopieur de grande diffusion* (TGD): Cit Alcatel, Thomson-CSF, Matra, and Sagem. It soon became clear that the technology simply did not exist to manufacture a facsimile machine for such a low price; the price was raised, first to 2,500 francs and then to 10,000 francs. At this price there was not much of a consumer market in France (or anywhere else in the world) and the telco decided to abandon the project.

On the other hand, there was a professional market for a much more sophisticated facsimile machine than the one promoted by the DGT. In fact, the DGT did the French manufacturers a considerable disservice: it encouraged them to build a low-end facsimile machine for a market that did not exist and left them with a machine that could not be competitively sold in a market that did exist.[35]

In both these cases, the government's industrial policy goals shaped decisions regarding product offerings by the telco. The Minitel case suggests that political pressures do not necessarily result in economic failure. *On balance*, however, in an economic sector where demand for services and products is increasingly specialized and changes frequently, firms burdened by political constraints perform less well when compared to those that are guided primarily by market forces. In other words, we are more likely to see the mistakes illustrated by the case of the TGD, as opposed to the successes of the Minitel project.

---

34. France Télécom argues, on the other hand, that once Minitel-related receipts from its Transpac subsidiary are included, the return is about 9 percent on investment. Moreover, they argue that this does not include benefits generated for French industry (such as hardware and software sales and advertising).

35. Darmon, *Grand Dérangement*, 105.

Pricing

Where political constraints are high, tariffs tend to reflect political priorities, as opposed to the demand for services and the costs to supply them. One of the primary political objectives served by tariffs is the cross-subsidization of one class of consumers by other classes of consumers. The French telco, more so than the telcos of most other developed countries, has heavily subsidized its local residential consumers with revenues from long-distance services and business subscribers. In 1966, revenues from local services accounted for only 16 percent of the French telco's total revenues—the lowest percentage of all major European countries.[36] Table 6.3 in the previous chapter provided comparative tariffs for France, Germany, the United Kingdom, and the United States for 1986 and 1987. Local tariffs in France were similar to those in the other countries. On the other hand, domestic long-distance rates in the United Kingdom were more than 60 percent lower than in France, and international long-distance was less than half the cost in 1986 (the gap began to narrow in 1987). Through much of the 1980s, compared to average European tariffs, the cost of leasing dedicated business lines has been falling in the United Kingdom while rising in France.

Darmon estimated that, in order to eliminate the distortions caused by cross-subsidies between various groups, the basic connect tariff for residential users would have to be increased by 140 percent, local, time-sensitive tariffs by 23 percent, and long-distance charges *reduced* by 58 percent.[37] The government moved somewhat in this direction with its 1984 increase of 25 percent in local tariffs—the strategy appears to be one of gradually increasing local tariffs in order to eliminate pricing distortions. Similarly, competition has forced the French telco to reduce its rates for international long-distance calls. Between 1984 and 1986, tariffs on long-distance calls to North America were substantially reduced on four different occasions—in February 1985 alone, tariffs declined 21 percent.[38]

As long as political pressures remain significant, pricing decisions will be much less responsive to market conditions and more sensitive to a political agenda (such as increased revenues or cross-subsidies). In the infrastructural period of telecommunications development when demand was relatively inelastic, this had few practical implications, but during the post-infrastructural period when demand is considerably more elastic, such inattention to market signals can have very negative implications for the introduction of innovative services and industry growth.

---

36. C. Pautrat and B. Hurez, "Place de la Tarification dans la Stratégie des Télécommunications," *Le Bulletin de l'Idate* 9 (February 1986).

37. Darmon, "Télécommunications," 58.

38. Richard Clavaud, "Fin d'un Monopole," *L'Expansion*, April 1986.

Technological advances and changes in consumer demand posed a serious political dilemma for the French government: the political benefits from its control of the national telco could only be maintained at the expense of declining competitiveness of French industry and the introduction of fewer innovative communications services.

Government-Enforced Entry Barriers

As well as reducing political constraints, entry barriers play an important role in directing management's attention to market demands. The French experience in the post-infrastructural period offers some support for the contention that lack of competition reduces sensitivity to market demand and inhibits performance. Two areas are particularly illustrative: value-added network services (VANs) and the adoption of facsimile machines.

As shown earlier, VANs cater to rather specialized consumer demands that are in constant flux—in contrast to the universal services historically provided by telcos. In the United States, for example, thousands of different VANs serve a wide range of end users.[39] The argument in favor of minimal entry barriers to the VANs industry is that competition will promote the aggressive marketing, innovation, and diversity that drive this market.

The French have been reluctant to dismantle entry barriers, with the result that the VANs and information services industries have developed slower than in countries with competition. Although France has a much more modern telephone network and telephone penetration rates are higher, it falls behind the United Kingdom in the VANs and information services markets. In 1985, the European VANs market was valued at approximately $0.5 billion: the United Kingdom accounted for half of the market and France for approximately 25 percent.[40] The explanation centers on the high entry barriers confronting independent suppliers in France, compared to the less stringent regulatory obstacles facing British entrepreneurs.[41]

The adoption of facsimile machines follows a similar path. Although this technology has been available since the 1920s, it did not enjoy widespread distribution until the late 1970s. With the intention of promoting domestic

---

39. For examples of value-added network services and for a discussion of their global proliferation see Robert R. Bruce, Jeffrey P. Cunard, and Mark D. Director, *The Telecom Mosaic: Assembling the New International Structure* (London: Butterworth, 1988), chaps. 2 and 3. Also see the listing of such services in U.S. Department of Commerce, National Telecommunications and Information Administration, *NTIA Telecom 2000 Charting the Course for a New Century* (Washington, D.C.: U.S. Department of Commerce, 1988), chaps. 9 and 10.

40. Robert Priddle, *VANs and their International Implications: New Frontiers for Merging Voice and Data* (San Jose, Calif.: Dataquest, 1987), 1–2.

41. Danny Green, "New Public Services Sales Set to Rise Fast," *Financial Times* (London) 12 December 1986.

manufacturers of this equipment, the French government has maintained strict entry barriers to the industry. It has employed two effective strategies. First, as the major distributor of facsimile equipment in France, France Telecom is able to regulate entry by simply refusing to purchase and distribute certain equipment. Second, through its authority over the certification of equipment, France Telecom is able to exclude manufacturers from access to the French market. Through most of the 1970s and 1980s, the telco has effectively excluded all but one French manufacturer—Thomson—from the facsimile market. Up until the late 1980s, the Thomfax product manufactured by the Alcatel/Thomson group accounted for over 85 percent of the market. It has been the principal facsimile product of the major distributors in France: DGT, Thomson, Telic Alcatel, and 3M Corporation.[42]

In contrast to the French approach, the British eliminated virtually all entry barriers to the facsimile market.[43] Equipment certification has not been employed in a discriminatory manner. British Telecom has not used its near-monopoly position to keep out certain manufacturers. In fact, BT did not begin distributing facsimile equipment until 1987, after facsimile penetration had already reached significant levels.

The entry barriers erected by the French have seriously inhibited the growth of the facsimile market. Prices remain significantly higher than those in the United Kingdom, there is a much narrower range of models in France, and French distribution and marketing are more limited. Dataquest estimates that in 1987, 45,000 facsimile machines were sold in France (11 percent of total sales in Europe), compared to 100,000 in the United Kingdom (accounting for 25 percent of total sales in Europe).[44] Because of its stringent entry barriers, the penetration of facsimile equipment in France has lagged behind the United Kingdom, the United States, and Japan, where competition has been encouraged.

The Political Debate

Recent changes in the telecommunications industry have dramatized the costs associated with entry barriers and political constraints, but the criticism of these regulatory policies has a long history in French political debate.

As early as 1920, critics argued that the telco should be privatized in order to reduce the negative impact of political pressures. Laffont, the under-

---

42. Dataquest, *European Telecommunications Industry*, vol. 1 (San Jose, Calif.: Dataquest, 1986), 1.

43. Dataquest, *European Telecommunications*, 2.

44. Dataquest, "Fax Market Surges Ahead: Japan Leads the Pack," *Dataquest Research Newsletter* 1 (1988): 4.

secretary of state for the Post and Telegraph, argued that the state was simply incapable of managing the industrial and commercial enterprise required for the provision of telephone service.[45]

The French Assembly, while agreeing with Laffont's assessment of the telco's performance, did not share his enthusiasm for privatization. Shortcomings in the management of the telco were addressed with a separate budget that allowed more autonomy in planning and executing investment programs. A financial reform provided for refundable advances (essentially loans) that could be used to finance the modernization of the telephone network. All in all, however, this did not reduce political control over the telco.

With the depression and World War II, the issue of telephone service dropped from the public agenda, not to be raised again until the 1960s. Giscard d'Estaing, then minister of finance, proposed in his *Loi de Finance* of 1968 that the DGT be separated from the Post and that it be granted public enterprise status, similar to that of *Electricité de France*. This, he argued, would encourage a more entrepreneurial and commercial management style, thereby improving the availability and quality of telephone service.[46]

A number of proposed organizational reforms followed. M. Galley, minister of the PTT, argued in 1969 that it was not reasonable to expect a government department to meet the commercial, marketing, and financial demands of managing a telco.[47] An interministerial committee was established in 1971 to consider the problem. It recommended that the post and telecommunications be maintained in one entity but that it be accorded the same public enterprise status that characterizes the U.S. Postal Service or the British Post. No action was ever taken on this recommendation.

In 1973, the Assembly established another commission, the *Commission parliamentaire de controle de gestion du service publique de téléphone*, which considered various reforms that would improve the management of telephone service provision. The majority of the commission concluded that piecemeal modifications to the DGT's statute would provide insufficient autonomy, preferring a major organizational change that would transform the DGT into a government corporation (like *Electricité de France*).[48] The government considered these recommendations too radical and "risky," opting, instead, for a massive infusion of investment funds (110 billion francs) to modernize the telecommunications infrastructure.

The Mitterrand government also recognized this dilemma and, in 1982, the new PTT minister, Mexandeau, announced a change of policy emphasis.

---

45. Paul Laffont, *L'illustration Economique et Financière*, numéro spécial, 1922.
46. Libois, *Genèse et Croissance*, 241.
47. Libois, *Genèse et Croissance*, 241.
48. Libois, *Genèse et Croissance*, 243.

The government, Mexandeau argued, should no longer concern itself with the promotion of particular products and services but should focus on the expansion and improvement of the telecommunications network, leaving to the private sector the responsibility to develop and market new products and services.[49] The post-Giscard years of French politics have been marked by an ascendancy of liberalism.[50] During the 1986 Legislative elections, organizational reform for the DTG was frequently debated. Jacques Chirac, leader of the *Rassemblement pour la république* (RPR) and subsequently prime minister, indicated that he would favor the privatization of the telephone service provider and, during the government's two year tenure, the PTT minister, M. Longuet, proved to be an ardent proponent of liberalization of the industry.[51]

The liberalization debate has continued under the Socialist minister Quilès, named in 1988. In an effort to develop a set of reforms for the PTT, Quilès appointed Huber Prévot to organize a national debate on the subject and to prepare a report summarizing his findings. The final report supported a number of liberal reforms, including increasing the managerial autonomy of France Telecom and providing the ministry with its own budget.[52]

This extended political debate over the industry has recently culminated in a uniquely French policy response: state-guided liberalization.

The Politics of Liberalization

The French case is testimony to the power of the state to dominate the liberalization process, virtually excluding the participation of other major interests. Unlike the United Kingdom and the United States, where interest groups are a driving force behind policy changes, or Germany, where corporatist institutions play an important role, in France, ministry officials have virtually monopolized the policy-making process. Manufacturers, consumers, end users, and labor unions have relatively little input into the policy process.

Responsibility for overseeing the telecommunications industry has become increasingly concentrated in the hands of the telco (France Télécom). Essentially an operational institution, it has also assumed considerable policy-making authority. Once the modernization of the telephone network became a

49. Logica, *Communications in Europe*, 158.

50. Suzanne Berger, "Liberalism Reborn," in *Contemporary France: A Review of Interdisciplinary Studies*, ed. Joyon Howorth and George Ross (London: Frances Pinter, 1987).

51. Gerard Longuet, "La Bataille Mondiale des Télécoms," *Politique Internationale* 34 (1986): 193–202.

52. Hubert Prévot, *Rapport de Synthese: A l'issue du débat public sur l'avenir du service public de la Poste et des Télécommunications* (Paris: Minister des Postes, des Telecommunications et de l'Espace, 1989).

high government priority, the telco's power within the French administration rose. Between 1973 and 1982, the agency witnessed extraordinary increases in its budget, giving it the power to stand up even to the venerable finance ministry. During the 1980s, its budget allocations began growing more slowly and the agency was forced to underwrite subsidies to the *filière électronique* that includes the space, computer, and semiconductor industries. These activities sapped the telco's finances, forcing it into greater and greater debt. Its political power has also been somewhat eroded. Its opposition to the merger of Alcatel and Thompson was ignored; it was forced to significantly modify the Plan Cable in the face of opposition from local communities; and, in the early 1980s, it faced increasing threats to its monopoly over many activities.

Nonetheless, France Télécom still dominates the telecommunications policy-making process. This industry, like many others in France, is very much "administered" by the government: major corporations still take their cues from their respective *tutelles* in the administration.[53] Telecommunications, in particular, is highly regulated and subsidized by the government. Only very recently did France Télécom surrender its regulatory authority over equipment connected to the telecommunications network. The agency remains the most important client for French equipment manufacturers. According to Darmon, the state purchases 75 percent of the switching equipment and 90 percent of the transmission equipment produced by domestic manufacturers.[54] In 1983, 41 percent of all telecommunications equipment manufactured in France was purchased by the DGT. Added to this dependency is the fact that industry research and development is, in large part, underwritten by France Télécom.[55] In return, the agency sets rates of return on research and development expenditures at what many consider a very low 8 percent, and it requires that firms submit all projects to France Télécom for approval.[56] It comes as no surprise, then, that French firms are very reluctant to criticize the telco.[57] They simply cannot afford to challenge an agency that literally controls their corporate fate. Consequently, there are no powerful pressures for liberalization from the telecommunications equipment industry. Even though they might privately favor competition or the end of the monopoly on all

---

53. The political/industrial policy responsibilities of the DGT and its successor, France Telecom, are described in Darmon, "Télécommunications," Aurelle, *Telecommunications*, 94–95; Coustel, "Telecommunications Services in France"; and Libois, *Genèse et Croissance*.

54. Darmon, *Grand Dérangement*, 153.

55. The Chirac government removed some of the responsibility of the DGT to subsidize the equipment manufacturers in 1986, but the telco remains active in providing research subsidies.

56. Darmon, *Grand Dérangement*, 154.

57. Darmon, *Grand Dérangement*, 165 and 206.

services, French industry has been too dependent on the state to take serious issue with its major policies.

The French State Challenged by Liberalization

With respect to liberalization of the telecommunications sector, France presents a contrast to the United Kingdom and Germany. Unlike the pluralist environment of the United Kingdom, pressure for the reduction of entry barriers or for the privatization of the telco in France has been relatively ineffective. At the same time, in contrast to German corporatism, there has been little effective opposition to liberalization.

In the French case, the state provides both the impetus for liberalization and represents a formidable barrier to its adoption. On the one hand, state planners recognize the economic imperative of lowering entry barriers in order to promote innovation and growth, but, on the other hand, they have been extremely reluctant to relinquish their control over the industry.[58] A tension has developed between a strong, interventionist state with significant powers to intervene in the market and the policy imperative of a more liberal economic regime that requires it to relinquish its authority over the economy.[59]

Irrelevance of Interest Group Pressures?

Liberalization in the French statist economy proceeds in spite of the absence of strong procompetitive pressures from industry or consumers. In an economy where the state dominates economic activity, most of the natural constituents for liberalized policies are too dependent upon the state to seriously challenge government-enforced entry barriers or public ownership. At the same time, of course, interest groups are a relatively ineffective opposition to procompetitive policies.

The major proponents of liberalized telecommunications policies in the United States and, to a lesser degree, in the United Kingdom have been large business consumers (the computer services companies such as IBM and Geisco), communications companies (particularly television companies), and large financial services firms (such as banks and insurance companies). In France, this natural, proliberalization constituency has been effectively silenced because of its dependence on, or close ties to, the French administra-

---

58. Berger notes that the new liberalism that has emerged in France in fact seems to retain an important role for state action in the economy, although the exact nature of its role is not well articulated in major writings. See Berger, "Liberalism Reborn," 100.

59. Michael Loriaux, "States and Markets: French Financial Interventionism in the Seventies," *Comparative Politics* 20 (January 1988): 175–83.

tion.[60] First, many of these major consumers are publicly owned and directly accountable to the government. Examples include Bull Computers, Thomson-CSF, two of the major television networks, many of the major national banks, and insurance companies. Second, even those that are not government-owned are frequently heavily dependent upon government contracts or assistance. Their dependence on the state makes it very difficult for these entities to publicly or privately challenge the appropriateness of the government monopoly or entry barriers to the industry.

Another natural constituency favoring reduced barriers to competition are firms seeking entry into the industry. In the United States, for example, MCI Communications was a major advocate of reduced barriers to the long-distance telephone industry because of its desire to compete with AT&T. Certainly, France has its share of young entrepreneurial firms seeking to enter new markets. But even these firms tend to receive funding from governmental authorities, or from institutions very sensitive to the priorities of the state (the Credit National, for example). It is unlikely that an entity with the specific aim of challenging the state's monopoly in the telecommunications industry would easily find funding for its efforts. As a result, "[t]oday in France, there are no ambitious and resolute entrepreneurs, impatient to openly advocate deregulation."[61]

Strong procompetitive pressures challenging government-enforced entry barriers are unlikely to emerge in an economy where the state plays such an important role as a shareholder in many of the major corporations, as the banker for much of the capital investment, and as the *tutelle* for most of the important industrial sectors.

At the same time, this ineffectiveness undermines any opposition to policies liberalizing entry to the telecommunications sector. Earlier, I identified two constituencies likely to oppose initiatives reducing entry barriers: organized labor and equipment manufacturers. Both of these groups exercise little influence over French policies concerning privatization or competition.

In the Fifth Republic, labor's role in the policy-making process has been minimal.[62] One of the primary reasons is the sharp divisions within the labor movement. Moreover, the union movement in France represents a small percentage of the active work force, compared to other industrialized nations.[63] Finally, throughout most of the Fifth Republic, French politics has been dominated by the Right, which has shown little enthusiasm for including labor

---

60. Coustel, "Télécommunications Services"; Darmon, "Télécommunications."

61. Darmon, "Télécommunications," 93.

62. Frank Wilson's examination of interest group politics in Fifth Republic France notes that, even under the Socialist government, labor's influence over policy was weak; see Frank Wilson, *Interest Group Politics in France* (Cambridge: Cambridge University Press, 1987), chap. 10.

63. Wilson, *Interest Group Politics,* 72.

in the policy-making process. Under Giscard, the technocrats that dominated policy-making were particularly scornful of labor participation.

Unlike Germany, where labor has been a very active participant in the corporatist structure overseeing the Bundespost operation and in the debate regarding liberalization, organized labor in France has been conspicuously absent from the process. A rather striking illustration of organized labor's insignificance is the fact that the *Association des Ingénieurs des Télécommunications*—the elite corps that comprises much of the DGT's senior management—was denied any representation on the *Commission Nationale des Communications et Libertiés* (CNCL). The only telecommunications representation was an industrialist.[64] The fact that the government did not even see fit to include a member of this very elite employee organization testifies to the irrelevance of labor representation in the policy-making process.

Established telecommunications equipment manufacturers are typically strong allies in the fight against reducing entry barriers because increased competition can jeopardize the favorable treatment they receive from the national telco and can threaten their share of protected markets. But in France, like labor, manufacturers' ability to block initiatives by the government is limited. The major French telecommunications firms—Alcatel, Thomson, and Matra—are corporate eunuchs, so dependent upon the administration for direction, subsidies, and markets, there is little likelihood of them exercising any independent influence on the government's policy decisions. As Darmon points out in a chapter entitled "Master and Slave," the French telecommunications industry has been conditioned to look to the State for direction concerning research, product developments, labor policies, investment, mergers, and acquisitions. Once the State decides on a policy initiative, the norm is for French telecommunication firms to fall in line—rarely do they publicly challenge the government.[65]

Competitive Threats to French Telecommunications

Why then, with such minimal pressure for change, did the French move forward with liberalization? The answer lies with the continued central role of the state in the French economy. More so than other nations, the French state actively shapes industrial policies and corporate strategies in an effort to promote the adjustment of the French economy to external pressures.[66] To a

---

64. International Telecommunications Institute, *French Study* (London: International Telecommunications Institute, 1986), 31.

65. Darmon, *Grand Dérangement*, chap. 8.

66. John Zysman, "The French State in the International Economy," in *Between Power and Plenty: Foreign Economic Policies of Advanced Industrial States*, ed. Peter Katzenstein (Madison, Wis.: University of Wisconsin Press, 1978).

large extent, it is the absence of effective institutional counterbalances to government power that accounts for the state's success. Pressures from internal sources—such as business or labor—continue to be much less important determinants of French industrial policy than are the government's perception of international threats to the French economy. The state moved toward liberalization because the bureaucracy recognized that its *dirigiste* and protectionist policies were becoming less effective and threatened to reverse the considerable advances that had been achieved in the French telecommunications industry. Loriaux describes a similar dilemma in the case of the French financial sector, traditionally dominated by very effective *dirigiste* policies, where international pressures forced the state to adopt liberal reforms.[67]

For a number of years the French government has been able to insulate the telecommunications market from foreign pressures and exploit these barriers to the advantage of domestic manufacturers. During the *rattrapage* of the 1970s and 1980s, the State has had unquestioned authority over the technologies, products, and services supplied. Moreover, during this period they exercised this authority with an explicit goal: strengthening the international competitiveness of French telecommunications firms. But as the industry changed, becoming increasingly demand, as opposed to supply, driven, the French government's ability to maintain entry barriers rapidly weakened.[68]

As I pointed out earlier, the post-infrastructural period of telecommunications development is characterized by technological developments that have made it increasingly difficult for countries to maintain entry barriers. The French are no exception. Within the country, France Télécom's monopoly over voice and data transmission has been threatened by the use of private networks. Although there are restrictions on the use of private networks— prohibitions of resale of capacity and interconnection to the public network— observers have noted that they are frequently violated, thereby shifting long-distance traffic off the public network.[69]

France Télécom's international traffic has also suffered from competitive forces. With deregulation in the United States, traffic between the United States and Europe has become increasingly competitive. Not only are there a number of American carriers competing for traffic, but some of the European telcos have adopted very aggressive pricing strategies in the hope of attracting international traffic. Rather than pay steep rates between France and North

---

67. Loriaux, "States and Markets."

68. N. Curien and M. Gensollen discuss the increased importance of demand in the telecommunications industry ("Determining Demand for New Telecommunications Services," in *Trends of Change in Telecommunications Policy*, Organization for Economic Cooperation and Development [Paris: OECD, 1987], 134–43. Jean Pierre Coustel outlines the pressures this posed for the DGT in France ("Télécommunications Services," 239).

69. Coustel, "Télécommunications Services," 234.

America, French firms have been routing their North American traffic through other European countries (particularly the United Kingdom and the Netherlands) where trans-Atlantic rates are much lower.

Another important concern is the impact of high tariffs and poorly developed telecommunications services on businesses located in France. Firms located in France do not have access to the range of telecommunications options and tariffs found in more liberal regulatory environments, thereby putting them at a competitive disadvantage with their international competition. For example, large, multinational firms expect negotiated pricing contracts with service providers. But, as the Prévot Report points out, France Télécom has very little flexibility in such negotiations because of its status as a government agency. The result is that multinational firms voted with their feet, locating in European countries where telcos offer more competitive pricing and services.

International competition and technological developments put the French state under considerable pressure to modify their insular policies. The government responded not with an enthusiastic embrace of liberalism, but by adopting initiatives that minimized the control they relinquished over the industry while, at the same time, trying to maximize the economic benefits of limited liberalization.

State-Guided Liberalization

In adopting liberal policies the French state has not abandoned statist institutions. The state has adopted liberal policies because of pressures from international markets and the realities of technological change. We can characterize this as state-guided liberalization—or *libéralisme de l'état*—where the state tolerates only the degree of liberalization it considers necessary to promote the international competitiveness of its industry.

Liberalization is not a concession by the state to the demands of political interests, but rather a defensive response by state planners to economic and technological pressures outside their control. The policy's tenure is entirely at the discretion of the state. As long as liberalization serves the industrial policy goals of the state, it will continue in effect. In an economy where few interests can effectively challenge the state, it is very difficult to institutionalize support for liberal policies and, therefore, minimize the chances of "deliberalization." What the state giveth, it can easily taketh away.

In France, liberalization has not proceeded along the "interest pressure" model that characterized its adoption in the United States and United Kingdom. While recognizing the benefits of competition, the French state has been reluctant to relinquish control over entry into the important telecommunications sector. Virtually none of the liberal competition policies implemented by the state eliminate government-enforced entry barriers. Rather, they represent state-sponsored competition: the elimination of entry barriers for selected, government-approved firms.

Similarly, these liberalization policies do not abandon public ownership for the widely claimed benefits of privatization. Rather, the French have sought out strategies, short of privatization, that promote a more efficient and demand-sensitive telco that remains under the direct control of the government.

Strategies for Reducing Political Constraints

Both the Right and Left in France have been very hesitant about the privatization of the French telco because of its overwhelming importance in an industry considered to be of critical importance to the nation's international competitiveness. Its monopoly over the public network and its importance as a consumer of high-technology equipment and software gives the entity a very powerful role in shaping the fortunes of the French communications and computing industries. Nonetheless, policymakers were faced with the need to increase the entity's autonomy from political oversight in order to enhance economic performance. They settled on a strategy of modifications to the telco organization designed to reduce political constraints.

France Télécom: A Government Corporation

Short of privatization, modifying the status of a telco from a government agency to a government corporation is likely to reduce political constraints. In an attempt to improve the performance and international competitiveness of France Télécom, authorities have moved in this direction. The model proposed by both the Left and the Right is that of an *établissement public industriel et commercial* (EPIC), very much along the lines of the organization of Elf-Aquitaine, the successful French government-owned multinational oil company.[70]

First, the telco would no longer be restrained in terms of the services or products it could develop and market. As a government agency, France Télécom is under considerable explicit and implicit constraints regarding the types of activities in which it can engage. Politically, it is difficult for government agencies to compete in markets with private entities. On the other hand, it is more acceptable for government-owned corporations, particularly those in

---

70. See Pascal Salin, "Privatiser, dérèglementer et s'ouvrir à la concerrence étrangère," *Le Monde des Télécoms* (May 1987), 17–18; Darmon, *Grand Dérangement*; Gerard Longuet, "Bataille Mondiale," 193–202.

which the government is not the sole shareholder, to enter competitive markets.

Second, as a government corporation, the telco would be freer to acquire and divest itself of subsidiaries. This would allow the French telco to rapidly enter new markets through acquisitions and joint ventures. It would also enable them to expand into international markets through the acquisition of foreign entities. France Télécom views the recent expansion efforts of its major international competitors with some envy.[71] British Telecom, for example, has become an important player in the global telecommunications service industry with its equity participation in the U.S. cellular radio venture operated by McCaw Communications and its acquisition of Tymnet, the U.S.-based VAN provider. Such expansion through acquisitions and joint ventures would face fewer political obstacles if France Télécom were granted the status of a government corporation.[72]

Personnel policies constitute a third issue. Policymakers are concerned that France Télécom will not be able to effectively survive competition, either domestic or international, unless it can radically modify its management system and improve the performance of its work force. By redefining the entity as a government corporation, its employees would no longer be civil servants, providing management with much more flexibility in hiring and firing and in designing incentives for superior performance.[73]

Divest Regulatory Responsibilities

Policymakers have begun divesting France Télécom of its regulatory responsibilities, recognizing that this presents conflict of interest problems when France Télécom makes regulatory decisions about firms with which it competes, and that it distorts the telco's role as an operational, as opposed to a political, entity. In May 1989, the government created within the PTT ministry, the *Direction de la Réglementation Générale*, a separate department that is responsible for regulatory matters concerning the telecommunications and

---

71. See the statement to this effect by a senior manager of France Telecom: Jean-Jacques Damlamian, "New Strategies for New Challenges," *1992 Single Market Communications Review* 2 (1990): 49–50.

72. For example, the French Telecom subsidiary, Transpac, has been considering acquiring a minority interest in Telefonos de Mexico. See Anne-Marie Roussel, "Transpac Seeks Purchase in Mexico," *Communications Week International* 32 (11 December 1989): 2. France Telecom, in fact, has already entered into a number of selective international ventures, including equity participation in U.S. telecommunications firms. See Jonathan Aronson and Peter F. Cowhey, *When Countries Talk* (Cambridge, Mass.: Balinger Publishing, 1988), 226.

73. Prevot, *Rapport de Synthese*, 61–62.

communications industries. Nonetheless, regulatory oversight remains within the same ministry and many critics have raised serious reservations about its independence from the influence of France Télécom.[74]

Independent Subsidiaries

Unlike the United Kingdom and Germany, France has a long and extensive history of government ownership, giving rise to a certain creativity on the part of management in identifying strategies for reducing political constraints. Faced with the need to promote innovative new services designed for an increasingly demanding and fragmented consumer base, the management of France Télécom has turned these responsibilities over to independent subsidiaries, somewhat more insulated from the political constraints imposed on a government agency.[75] In fact, virtually all of the successful new services introduced by the telco in the 1970s and 1980s were implemented by independent subsidiaries.

Transpac was one of the earliest independent subsidiaries, established with the explicit goal of managing France's packet switching network (which they proudly claim is the largest of its kind in the world).[76] It was created because the public packet switched network faced stiff competition from dedicated leased-lines and from other international telcos. Moreover, its success depended upon aggressive marketing and responsive service to very demanding business users.

Accordingly, Transpac was established as a partially owned subsidiary of the telco: 67 percent was controlled by the telco, 28 percent by large users, and 5 percent by Transpac employees. This afforded management the independence from governmental constraints necessary to effectively develop attractive products and compete with established data network providers. As Bonnetblanc points out, the attractions of independence from political constraints is more efficient management, the ability to attribute costs, the transparency of accounts, and the promotion of user input into management and product design.[77]

A second prominent subsidiary of France Télécom is France Cable et

---

74. The agency's responsibilities would include management of frequencies for radio-telephone, representation of France on the international level, terminal equipment licensing, and enforcement, including policing various telecom service providers and implementing regulations.

75. Robert R. Bruce, Jeffrey P. Cunard, and Mark D. Director, *The Telecom Mosaic* (London: Butterworth, 1988), 94.

76. A packet switched network provides high-speed transmission facilities for businesses that transmit large volumes of data, voice, or video signals.

77. Bonnetblanc, *Télécommunications Françaises*.

Radio (FCR). The subsidiary was established primarily as a reseller of enhanced services to businesses.[78] These services included "Transfix" (a data transfer service on specialized lines that includes the former Transmic service), Transcom (a 64 Kbit/second data transfer service on the standard switched telephone network), and Transdyn (a high-speed data transfer service that includes Telecom-1). FCR has also been active in the marketing of telecommunications services in foreign market services (for example, it is the owner of a U.S. international common carrier).[79]

Both Transpac and FCR are now grouped under a holding company, *Compagnie générale des communications* (COGECOM), that ensures that the entities operate at arm's length from France Télécom. COGECOM has grown in recent years and now includes among its holdings firms that specialize in public and private networks, computer communication, engineering, data processing/communication, and the sale of terminals, cable television, satellite, mobile radio, and electronic message services.

The French state—whether under the direction of the Right or Left—is clearly unwilling to significantly undermine its authority over the telecommunications industry by privatizing France Télécom. At the same time, the government recognizes that the future competitiveness of the French telecommunications industry demands a sizeable degree of autonomy for telco management. French policymakers adopted a politically "efficient" solution to this dilemma: maintain government ownership and, therefore, ultimate control over the industry, but enact institutional changes that minimize the impact of political constraints on business decisions.

Competition: A Last Resort

A second important policy option confronting French policymakers is the issue of entry barriers. Reducing them has been widely advocated as a strategy for improving the performance of the telecommunications industry by forcing telcos to price competitively, providing a yardstick against which the public can evaluate the efficiency of public enterprises, promoting the introduction of innovative, new services, and reducing cross-subsidies. Unlike the United States and the United Kingdom, the French have been much less enthusiastic about promoting competition although, as the following discussion indicates, French authorities have not been able to ignore the need for reducing entry barriers.

As is the case in most developed countries, competition is more the exception than the rule in the French telecommunications industry. Entry

---

78. Bruce, Cunard, and Director, *Telecommunications*, 521.
79. Bruce, Cunard, and Director, *Telecommunications*, 520.

barriers are steepest in network and basic services. Both local and long-distance telephone service are a strict monopoly of the national telco and are likely to continue under this regulatory status for the foreseeable future. Similarly, governments of both the Left and Right are very reluctant to license competing telecommunications networks (as the United Kingdom did when it permitted Mercury to offer competing network services). Nonetheless, even here there have been some recent exceptions: authorities have licensed a consortium to provide a cellular mobile radio network that will compete with the one to be operated by France Télécom, and the telco's monopoly over the ownership of cable networks has been relaxed.

French governments have also been reluctant to abandon entry barriers to the leasing, programming, and reselling of telecommunications capacity. Resale of leased telephone capacity is seen as a serious threat to the integrity of the national telecommunications network and, therefore, has been discouraged. In addition, the government continues to impose significant restrictions on firms entering the VANs sector. With respect to customer premises equipment, the French government has allowed limited competition among French manufacturers, but has made it very difficult for foreign manufacturers to enter the market.

Yet beginning with the Socialist government elected in 1982, the state initiated limited measures promoting some competition in the industry as a means to improve efficiency, innovation, and the range of offerings available to consumers (both business and residential). The Plan Cable introduced in 1982 was a revolutionary step because it offered a unique opportunity for private firms to provide communication services over a dedicated network. That same year, Socialist minister Mexandeau revamped the Minitel videotext services, focusing more on business consumers and encouraging the participation of private value-added service providers that would compete among themselves to encourage Minitel subscribers to access their online data bank services.[80] During this period, the Mitterrand government also opened up competition in the television and radio industry that had been monopolized by government-owned media outlets. But these hesitant steps were only a precursor to the period of considerable liberalization that was initiated once the Socialists were replaced by Chirac's government in 1986.

Elected on a platform advocating greater liberalization of the economy, Chirac's government accelerated the dismantling of entry barriers to France's telecommunications markets. In the field of cable television, the Communications Law of 1986 removed many restrictions on the number of cable systems in which private entities could invest; it also allowed private firms to compete

---

80. B. Miege, P. Pajon, and J. M. Salaun, *L'industrialisation de l'audiovisuel* (Paris: Editions Aubiers, 1986), 27.

with France Télécom for the rights to construct and operate cable networks. The following year, the government provided for competition in the field of cellular radio, value-added services, and paging.[81]

In January 1988, the government issued a *projet de loi*, "La concurrence dans les telecommunications," that proposed a number of far-reaching liberalization measures, including the licensing of alternative network providers, the dismantling of entry barriers to the value-added services industry, the separation of the operational and regulatory responsibilities of France Télécom, and the establishment of separate subsidiaries for France Télécom's competitive activities (in order to prevent anticompetitive cross-subsidies).[82] With the defeat of Chirac's government in 1988, these legislative plans were abandoned.

The recently elected Socialist government of M. Rocard has indicated that they will proceed more slowly with respect to liberalization.[83] Nonetheless, liberalization has advanced.[84] The government has relaxed restrictions on the development of "teleports" that provide advanced national and international network services to multinational firms that have heavy communications needs. Up until recently, they were prohibited because they represented a competitive threat to France Télécom. The Prévot Report commissioned by the Socialist minister, Quilès, has recommended major changes in the organization of France Télécom and in telecommunications regulations. Moreover, the prime minister has indicated that he is sympathetic to such reforms in the PTT.

None of these government initiatives represent the kind of regulatory *boulversement* that took place in the United States or in the United Kingdom. Just as the French have taken a very measured approach to privatization, they have also moved very slowly in dismantling entry barriers. The goal has been to minimize the entry barrier concessions while maintaining a high degree of control over the market. Three of the most prominent liberalization sectors illustrate this policy of state-guided liberalization: customer premises equipment, value-added network services (VANs), and cable television.

Customer Premises Equipment

As an example of procompetitive policies, French officials are quick to point to the customer premises equipment market, which has been open to competi-

---

81. The Minister's decision to promote competition in the cellular radio sector is described in *Le Monde*, 29 January 1987.

82. Ministère des Postes et Télécommunications, *Juris PTT*, no. 11.

83. Paul Betts, "French Caution over Liberalising Telecoms," *Financial Times* (London), 20 July 1988, 3.

84. Henri Bessières, "PTT: La Réforme Introuvable," *Télécoms Magazine* 27 (September 1989), 68–72.

tion since 1920, long predating the introduction of competition to the U.S. market. This liberal policy is somewhat illusory; the French government has, through its equipment certification procedures, virtually excluded foreign firms from the market. As a result, in 1988 three French firms dominated the market: Alcatel (and its various subsidiaries), SAT, and Jeumont Schneider (recently acquired by the German firm Bosch). Under increasing international pressure to reduce entry barriers, the French government has permitted some foreign competition, but only on a negotiated basis (the most recent example is the entry of Northern Telecom into the French market). Entry barriers are slowly being removed, but only in a very selective manner, with competition restricted to those entrants approved by government authorities.

Value-Added Networks

Liberalization of the VANs market represents an even greater threat to State control because the industry is presently monopolized by France Télécom. Nonetheless, recognizing the necessity of liberalization as a means to promote the development of these services, the State has adopted a strategy of minimizing the reduction in its influence over the industry while at the same time maximizing the benefits of liberalization. The major features of the strategy fit the pattern of state-guided liberalization:

1. maintain state ownership while making institutional modifications to reduce the negative impact of political constraints, and
2. introduce very restricted competition that makes entry contingent upon government authorization.

Unlike the universal services that telcos have traditionally provided, value-added services are typically custom designed for very narrowly defined user groups. This poses a problem for the traditional telco organization that is accustomed to very broadly consumed, universal services. The competitive solution allows private firms to lease telecommunications network capacity, provide a value-added service such as data banks or electronic mail, and market both the communications and service as a package to end users. In France, a complete elimination of entry barriers represents too much of a threat to telco revenues and government control over the industry. In the state-dominated model adopted in France, state entities—as opposed to private firms—take the lead role in designing major value-added services and regulating entry.

State-guided liberalization preserves public ownership but encourages institutional changes that promote responsiveness to economic, as opposed to political, pressures. With this goal in mind, France Télécom has created a number of independent subsidiaries specifically responsible for developing

and marketing value-added services. They have also encouraged these subsidiaries to develop applications in partnership with private firms, often with
companies that are likely consumers of these services.[85] The telco subsidiaries
largely responsible for marketing VANs include FCR, which markets user-
defined networks, Telesystems, which establishes and markets information
networks and electronic mail systems, Teletel, which promotes the Minitel
service, and Transpac, which provides packet switching services.

The distinctly statist approach to the liberalization of value-added services is well illustrated in the approach adopted by France Télécom for the
promotion of videotext and Integrated Services Digital Network (ISDN) services. In both cases, the state has reserved its right as primary service providers and has allowed only limited entry by competing private firms.

Videotext is a service that provides consumers with interactive access to
data bases through a terminal—located in the residence—that is connected by
telephone lines to computers that house the information. French authorities
decided that the introduction of such a videotext service would further two
important industrial policy goals: absorb the transmission capacity created
when the Transpac packet switching network was created, and generate demand for French-manufactured computer terminals. From a simple electronic
telephone directory, Minitel expanded into a full-fledged videotext service
offering a variety of information services. Although the administration of the
terminal connection and transmission facilities is the responsibility of Teletel,
a France Télécom subsidiary, the actual services (such as hotel reservations,
inquiries regarding entertainment, and stock quotations) are provided by private entities. With 4.7 million terminals in 1989, the service has reached
remarkable levels of penetration in France.

Minitel's success can be attributed to two main factors. First, the government minimized political constraints by placing responsibility for Minitel in
the hands of an independent France Télécom subsidiary, Teletel. Second, the
government correctly recognized that Minitel's chance of success would improve if private firms were given complete freedom to design and market
services for consumers. In effect, the government maintained its complete
control over transmission, but promoted competition among the actual service
providers.

By 1990, France Télécom expected that most of France will have access
to its new ISDN (or RNIS as it is labeled in France). To promote the use of the
network and thereby amortize a very significant investment, the government
telco has adopted a strategy similar to the successful one employed by Teletel:

---

85. For example, FCR and Agence France Presse are involved in a joint venture, Polycom,
that will provide satellite-based data broadcast services throughout Europe (see Bruce, Cunard,
and Director, *Telecom Mosaic*, 290).

place responsibility for these services in the hands of independent France Télécom subsidiaries and encourage the participation of private firms in developing applications.

As a result, a number of France Télécom subsidiaries are entering into joint ventures with private firms to develop and exploit specific ISDN application services. These subsidiaries are assuming a considerable portion of the initial development costs with the expectation of benefiting from future profits generated by the joint ventures, transmission charges, and consulting revenues.[86] Recent examples of these collaborative ventures include the following.

- Service SA, Sarde (a subsidiary of the government research facility, CNET), and France Télécom will develop a service that allows the transmission of photo images.
- France Télécom, the Union de crédit bancaire, and the Fédération nationale des agents immobiliers et mandataires will jointly fund a project aimed at providing real estate agents with the capability of accessing a bank of "real estate images"—images of the exterior and interior of properties for sale.

France Télécom has entered into similar agreements with some of the major computer manufacturing and programming companies, including Cap Gemini Sogeti, the state-owned Bull group, Electronic Data Systems (a subsidiary of General Motors), AT&T, and Digital Equipment.

The state is pursuing a number of objectives with its ISDN policy. First, it hopes to promote the development and use of the public ISDN network, as opposed to private leased-lines. This maximizes the state's revenue stream and ensures continued control over entry into the industry.[87] It is unlikely, for example, that foreign entities could dominate the ISDN services industry with France Télécom acting as the final arbiter over service offerings. Second, with France Télécom taking an important interest in each of these projects, the state will continue—although somewhat indirectly—to have control over the value-added services industry. Once again, we see a delicate balance between encouraging private competition in the VANs industry while, at the same time, maintaining state control over the sector.

While the state has been actively encouraging private firms to enter the

---

86. Odile Conseil, "RNIS: France Télécom à la rescousse des usagés," *Télécos Magazine* 16 (July/August 1988): 15.

87. Aronson and Cowhey (*When Countries Talk*, 184) describe the attempts by European PTTs to introduce ISDN in such a manner so as to prevent serious erosion of their control over value-added services as "benign mercantilism."

VANs industry in partnership with the government telco, it has been decidedly ambivalent about dismantling entry barriers to stand-alone private service providers. Under pressure from its international trading partners (the United States in particular), the French government has adopted a policy that, on its face, opens up entry into the VANs industry. In reality, the regulations imposed on VANs by this policy effectively limit the number of likely entrants to the industry.

First, they impose a distinction between "horizontal" VANs— those serving end users in dissimilar industries—and "vertical" VANs—those providing service to firms in a similar industry such as airlines or banks. In both cases, VANs that are transporting data at high rates—which is likely to include most commercial entities—will require ministerial authorization.

Second, the policy requires VANs to provide an Open Systems Interconnection (OSI) offering to end users. This is a technical requirement that makes little economic sense, given that the OSI standard will not exist in any usable form until well into the 1990s.[88] The government has also imposed very stringent restrictions on billing for VAN services. Transportation and service costs must be billed separately, and transportation billings cannot exceed 15 percent of France Télécom's revenues.

The VAN regulations reflect the government's mini-max strategy: minimize control over the industry while maximizing the benefits of competition. While expressing a desire to promote innovative and competitive VANs, the government insists on maintaining control over the amount of basic transmission services provided by these VANs (it cannot be allowed to become too significant because it can reduce revenues by bypassing the public network), over the technology adopted (always championing the interest of French manufacturers), and over the companies permitted to enter the market (ministerial authorization gives the government the opportunity to discourage foreign firms, for example).

Cable Television

Like most governments, the French authorities consider cable television a local natural monopoly.[89] But in a major break with tradition, the government has pursued a liberal policy, permitting private entities to provide cable television service. Recognizing that its success would depend upon the fit between consumer tastes and the programming offered, the authorities hoped to

---

88. Northern Business Information, *Telecom Market Letter* 8, no. 20 (1987): 12.

89. For an excellent review of the issues concerning the monopoly status of cable television, see Ithiel de Sola Pool, *Technologies of Freedom* (Cambridge, Mass.: Harvard University Press, 1983), chap. 7.

capitalize on the entrepreneurship of the private sector in the design and marketing of innovative programming for the mass public. At the same time, however, the government wanted to control the basic network and police the programming made available to subscribers.

The initiation of the "Plan Cable" in France was not the result of demands by either consumers or potential suppliers of the service. Rather, French authorities saw cable as a means to promote the development of a fiber optics industry (cable and switches).[90] The international market for fiber optics cable and equipment was expected to experience high growth rates in the 1980s, and state planners hoped that government promotion of fiber optics cable systems would provide French manufacturers with an initial protected market.

Although France Télécom was prepared to give private entities the responsibility for generating programming and aggressively marketing the service, they were decidedly unenthusiastic about relinquishing their control over the actual network facilities.[91] A transmission technology, after all, is very similar to an application network, with the advantage that it has a wider bandwidth, allowing it to carry larger volumes of information (video and large volumes of data, for example). As new interactive applications were developed, the DGT expected that local cable networks would serve as important *télédistribution* media—providing, for example, video and data services for business consumers. The state was not prepared to tolerate private ownership of a medium that could eventually compete with the local telephone network.

Both of these political priorities—protecting the government monopoly over basic transmission services and promoting French manufacturers of fiber optics equipment—led the government to adopt a policy of state-guided liberalization once again. As is characteristic of this strategy, the state promotes policies that minimize any loss of control over the industry but, at the same time, maximize the possible benefits from the involvement of private entities.

The difficult question for French authorities concerned how much political control would have to be sacrificed in order to adequately promote private investment in the development and marketing of cable television services. French authorities began with a policy that maintained much of the control over cable television in the hands of France Télécom and local authorities, minimizing the role of the private sector.[92] From this starting position, state

90. See *Telephony*, 8 August 1988; Bruce, Cunard, and Director, *Telecom Mosaic*, 301; Darmon, *Grand Dérangement*, 33; Miege, *L'industrialisation de l'audiovisuel*, 30; Betts, "French Caution," 18.

91. Paul Betts, "Cable Television: Why France is taking such a bold gamble," *Financial Times* (London), 15 May 1984, 18; Jean-Francois Lacan, "Télévision par Cable à Rennes: Inauguration du Premier Réseau en Fibre Optique," *Le Monde*, 9 January 1987.

92. Betts, "Cable Television," 18.

officials were forced to make increasingly larger concessions to the private sector, because the construction of cable systems and the marketing of their services progressed at a snail's pace throughout the 1980s. By 1988, after six years of authorization, there were only 570,500 residences that could access cable service and only a total of 29,900 subscribers—a penetration rate of only 5.2 percent. Germany, on the other hand, authorized cable some time later than France, but by 1988 served 9.8 million residences and had 3.8 million subscribers—a penetration rate of 38.5 percent.[93]

The initial policy promulgated by the Mitterrand government in November 1982 gave primacy to the government's political agenda. First, the DGT would own and build all cable systems in the country. The systems would be leased to cable operating companies for a fee of 42 francs per subscriber. These operating companies would take the form of *sociétés d'économie mixte* (SEMs) and local authorities would own a minimum of 33 percent of their equity. Moreover, private investors would be restricted to participation in a single SEM. With regard to ownership, this proposal ensured that the state— either through the DGT's interest in the network or the local government's participation in the service provider—would maintain a preeminent role.

Second, Plan Cable insisted that the systems adopt fiber optics cabling, a new technology based on the transmission of light waves over microglass fibers. The plan made a modest concession, allowing coaxial cable—a traditional technology based on the transmission of electrical signals over copper wiring—to be used in some circumstances for the first two years of the plan, until French manufacturers could gear up for the production of fiber optics equipment. Nonetheless, it was clear that industrial policy goals would outweigh any considerations of how the high cost of fiber optics might affect consumer demand for cable services (coaxial was generally about one-third the cost of fiber optics cable).

Third, Plan Cable imposed significant restrictions on programming. Concerned with the health of the French television and cinema production industries, the government prescribed stringent regulations regarding the importation of foreign material and the amount of resources cable operators would be required to devote to local programming.[94]

In order to succeed, the government's cable plan needed to strike the correct balance between state control and sufficient concessions to private investors and local governments. Initial results left little doubt that such a balance was not obtained: the first contract with the DGT for the development of a cable system was not signed until 1985, three years after the policy was

---

93. Philippe Pelaprat, "France: Mobilisation pour sauver le cable," *Télécoms Magazine* 14 (March/April 1988): 35.

94. Lacan, "Comment la DGT à réussi à casser le plan cable," 20.

announced.[95] This system, located in Rennes, did not become operational until March 1987.[96]

Part of the explanation for this failure is the government's political agenda—promote the French fiber optics industry and develop and control a potentially important wide-band fiber optics network—which was completely antithetical to the commercial viability of cable television service. These political constraints were so stringent as to discourage both the private sector and local governments from participating in the industry.

The state's indecision regarding the actual "rules of the game" also seriously dampened the interest of private business and local governments. For much of the period between 1982 and 1986, authorities were extremely vague about how the cable operators would be regulated. The terms under which the DGT would finance the construction of the local cable network were not clearly spelled out, the role of the *Haute Autorité*—the government body regulating communications—over the cable operator was not decided upon until May 1984, and the regulations concerning foreign programming were not decreed until January 1985.[97] This reflected a profound uncertainty on the part of officials about exactly how they should balance their political agenda with the need to ensure commercial viability of the service.

It eventually became clear to government authorities that further concessions would have to be made in order to attract private capital to the French cable industry. As part of the Chirac government's law liberalizing the communications industry, many of the restrictions on cable television operators were dropped. Local governments now had the choice of awarding a cable service concession—*opérateur commercial*—to a private firm or consortium; alternatively they could create an SEM in which they would assume an ownership interest. They were also given the option of contracting with a private entity that would assume responsibility for both the construction and maintenance of the cable network and the operation of the service itself—*cablo-opérateur*—following the model that is presently employed in the United States. In addition, the government removed the restriction on the number of cable systems in which private firms could invest. Because of the important economies associated with managing multiple cable systems, French investors became much more interested. Three firms have been particularly active: *Compagnie générale des eaux*, *Compagnie lyonnaise des eaux*, and the *Caisse des dépôts et consignations*.[98]

95. Regine Chaniac, "1982–1985: 3 Plans cable à l'épreuve," *Le Bulletin de l'IDATE: L'Europe des communications*, 21 November 1985, 229.

96. Lacan, "Television par cable."

97. Miege, *L'industrialisation de l'audiovisuel*, 31; Lacan, "Comment la DGT," 20.

98. Pelaprat, "Mobilisation," 39.

But even with this important liberalization, the state retains considerable control over cable television. The majority of cable networks have been built and financed by France Télécom. Where they are not the technical operator, it is often another state entity such as the *Caisse des dépôts et consignations*. But even in the case of the commercial operators (or programmers), the state preserves an important element of control. First, the participation of local governments in many of the *société d'économie mixte* provides the central authorities with some potential leverage over their management. Second, France Télécom, through its Cogecom subsidiary, has assumed direct financial interest in a number of the cable franchises. Third, the state savings institution, the *Caisse des dépôts et consignations*, is one of the three major investors in cable systems. Finally, a number of other nationalized institutions have invested in cable systems, including the Crédit agricole, Elf-Aquitaine, and the Banque nationale de Paris.[99]

The history of cable television in France illustrates the problems associated with state-guided liberalization. The success of these policies is dependent upon the right balance between the government's political agenda and concessions to the private sector. If the state does not concede sufficient control to private entities, investment will not be forthcoming. In the case of the videotext service, for example, French authorities appear to have struck a successful balance between control and concessions. But with respect to cable television, the political agenda of the state has weighed so heavily in the policies adopted that the private sector—at least up until quite recently—has been singularly uninterested in providing financing for franchises.

The End of the Statist Economy?

In the summer of 1990, the French legislature passed into law most of the recommendations of the Prévot report. These changes will alter the political and legal status of France Télécom. As a result of the legislation, France Télécom and the Post Office will be split into separate organizations and given operating autonomy. Political constraints on each entity will be reduced, allowing France Télécom greater control over its budget and capital investments. Moreover, the telco's legal status will change, allowing it to enter into contracts with other private or government entities, either in France or abroad.

---

99. Pelaprat, "Mobilisation," 39. It should also be pointed out that the state also has a number of regulatory avenues through which it controls cable operators. For example, the *Direction de la reglementation generale* (DRG) recently extended its authority over the licensing of satellite receivers at the head-end of cable systems (the means by which cable systems receive their satellite-transmitted programming). See Gilles Lautrec and Christain Sevignacq, "Les PTE renforcent leur controle sur le cable," *Telecoms Magazine* 34 (1990): 12–13.

This does not signal the abandonment of this important instrument of statist policy-making. In fact, the government has pursued its policy of making minimal concession to pressures for liberalization while maintaining, to the degree possible, its influence over the industry. The government will continue to exercise considerable influence over France Télécom: privatization was clearly rejected as an option; the telco will be expected to respect a multiyear *contrat de plan* that will spell out its obligations regarding tariffs, investments, borrowing, and performance; acquisitions and tariffs changes will remain under the supervision of the state; the entity remains a part of the Ministère des Postes et Télécommunications; and employees of France Télécom will continue to have civil service status.[100] The senate committee that prepared a report on the proposed changes was highly critical of the reticence of the government toward liberalization of France Télécom, arguing that the reforms did not go far enough in freeing the entity to operate as a commercial entity.[101]

Nonetheless, these changes will allow France Télécom to respond to external pressures. Specifically, the European Commission has pressured countries to separate the regulatory responsibilities from the operational activities of the telco (although under the French legislation, both the regulatory agency and the telco are under the same ministry). Second, with its new legal status, France Télécom will be able to participate more actively in acquisitions and joint ventures with both domestic and foreign partners. The liberal changes accomplish both of these goals without totally sacrificing control over the telco.

The process by which this legislation was fashioned also raises questions about the preeminent role of the state in shaping public policy. In a marked departure with the statist style of interest mediation, the Prévot Commission actively sought out the input of organized labor and, to a lesser extent, telecommunications users. To some extent this was in anticipation of strong opposition from labor. As anticipated, labor was quite vocal in its opposition to many of the suggested changes—work stoppages were held by the major unions in protest of the legislation. In particular, labor strongly opposed any movement in the direction of privatization or the notion that France Télécom employees should lose their civil service status. On both counts, the enacted legislation reflected the concerns of labor: privatization was rejected and civil service status was maintained.

Certainly the style of policy-making in this instance suggested a marked deviation from the statist model of French government decision making.

---

100. "Le Project de Loi 'institutionnel,'" *Télécoms International* 34 (1990): 15.

101. Anne-Marie Roussel, "French Senators Want More Reform," *Communications International* 44 (18 June 1990): 13.

Whether the final outcome resulted from the input of these different interested parties is difficult to say. The package of government reforms was quite moderate, even in comparison to the recent liberalization in Germany. Whether this resulted from the demands of labor or from the desire of the government to maintain its control over the industry is difficult to determine. Some have argued that the government simply used labor pressures as an excuse for the European Commission that was expecting more radical liberalization initiatives.

The French government has far from abandoned its statist control over the telecommunications industry. Nonetheless, the policy developments in this sector of the economy illustrate the increasing difficulty that the French will have in maintaining statist institutions under mounting pressures from global competitive economic forces and the political constraints associated with European integration.

Before concluding this discussion of French telecommunications, I would like to briefly examine the Japanese case in the context of this discussion of France. The two countries have statist political institutions, but their policy developments have been somewhat different.

Japan: A Brief Addendum

Although Japan is not one of the central case studies in my discussion, the country's global economic importance requires that we at least briefly explore how developments in its telecommunications industry fit with the theories of performance and liberalization summarized above. Three aspects of the recent history of Japan's telecommunications service provider, Nippon Telegraph and Telephone (NTT), require explanation.

- How do we explain the success of Japanese efforts to increase telephone penetration after World War II?
- Why has the country been slow to develop new telecommunications service technologies?
- What is the explanation for Japanese liberalization and privatization initiatives?

Public Ownership Promoting Infrastructure Development

I have argued that government-owned entities can be very effective vehicles for channeling investment resources into the development of basic infrastructures, such as the telecommunications network. Moreover, public entities with lower levels of political constraints are likely to perform better than those that are subject to significant political oversight. In both respects, NTT nicely fits the theory.

Responsibility for providing telecommunications services was transferred from the Japanese Ministry of Communications, the Japanese PTT (Teishinsho), to the Nippon Telegraph and Telephone Company in 1952. While the ministry continued to oversee the telco's operations, it was organized as a "government enterprise" under the categorization scheme developed earlier.[102] Accordingly, the entity had considerable independence from political pressures. In fact, the entity has become the largest Japanese company and exercises considerable independent political and economic power in Japan.

This relative independence of political oversight has served the Japanese telecommunications industry well. Unlike the situation in France and the United Kingdom, where telco management fought a losing battle to retain control over investment funds, NTT management was able to invest its revenues into rebuilding the Japanese telecommunications infrastructure throughout the 1950s and 1960s. The NTT turned in a very strong postwar performance record. As Nambu, Suzuki, and Honda point out, "NTT reached its goal of satisfying the unfilled demand for access and of building up the direct distance dialing system. . . ."[103] From 1952, when the NTT was formed, to 1970, penetration rates increased from 1.8 percent to 79 percent, giving Japan one of the highest penetration rates in the developed world.

Public Ownership and Demand-Driven Technology

Although often effective at building basic infrastructures, government-owned entities are likely to face serious problems in industries that are highly sensitive to consumer demands. This, I argue, characterizes the new telecommunications service industries that have emerged within the last three decades. Recent events in Japan seem to bear out this argument. Although Japanese telephone penetration is high, the telco has lagged seriously behind in its development of new telecommunications services. As Nambu, Suzuki, and Honda point out, " . . . the demand for data communications began to grow (although almost ten years behind the U.S. growth), spurring complaints about the inefficiency of public monopolies and government regulation."[104]

---

102. Tsuruhiko Nambu, Kazuyuki Suzuki, and Tetsushi Honda, "Deregulation in Japan," in *Changing the Rules: Technological Change, International Competition, and Regulation in Communications*, ed. Robert W. Crandall and Kenneth Flamm, 148 (Washington, D.C.: Brookings Institution, 1989).

103. Nambu, Suzuki, and Honda, "Deregulation," 148.

104. Nambu, Suzuki, and Honda, "Deregulation," 148.

Liberalization and Privatization

Japan, like France, has a statist style of interest mediation where the state dominates economic policy-making. As I argued in the case of France, this leads to state-guided liberalization, where the state enacts liberal policies that generate benefits from increased competition and corporate autonomy but enable policymakers to retain control over industrial policy. Like their counterparts in France, Japanese government officials recognized that liberalization of the industry was necessary in order to promote the developments of new telecommunications services (essential for the continued competitiveness of Japanese business).

NTT is an important vehicle of the distinctive Japanese statist industrial policy. Unlike other industries such as automobiles, computers, and consumer electronics, where the government's role has been relatively indirect, the telecommunications industry is one where, by virtue of state control of the telco, the government can directly shape the investment and research and development activities of major firms. NTT directly shaped the development of new telecommunications technologies through its own research and development activities. In effect, NTT underwrote the research and development costs for both services and equipment that were subsequently manufactured or offered by Japanese firms. This, of course, represented a direct and substantial subsidy to Japanese industry.

In addition, NTT was very selective regarding the Japanese firms favored in its procurement activities. Five major firms made up what is referred to as the "NTT family of contractors": Hitachi, NEC, Fujitsu, Sumitomo, and Oki. NTT awarded contracts to these firms, not on the basis of competitive bidding, but rather as the result of collective pricing agreements.[105] This ensured that prices for the products and services provided by these firms to NTT were considerably inflated, which in turn helped underwrite much more competitive pricing of these products in export markets.

Counterbalancing the desire to maintain its control over industrial policy in this sector were liberalization pressures from Japanese business and from the U.S. government. Increasing numbers of Japanese businesses felt that their international competitiveness was compromised by the lack of competition in the telecommunications service sector, and many larger firms saw profitable opportunities associated with the reduction of industry entry barriers.[106] In response to a mounting trade deficit with Japan, the U.S. govern-

---

105. Jon Woronoff, *Japan: The Coming Economic Crisis* (Tokyo: Lotus Press, 1980); Roya Akhavan-Majid, "Telecommunications Policymaking in Japan," *Telecommunications Policy* 14 (April 1990): 159–68.

106. Kas Kalba, "Opening Japan's Telecommunications Market," *Journal of Communication* 38 (Winter 1988): 96–106.

ment put increasing pressure on the Japanese government to liberalize the telecommunications equipment and service markets in the hope of promoting opportunities for U.S. exports.

The dilemma for the Japanese government was the desire to maintain control over an important industrial sector but, at the same time, recognizing the need to improve its performance through liberal policy initiatives. This conflict between the statist agenda of the Japanese bureaucracy and the pressures for liberal reforms was further complicated by interministerial battles over who would assume responsibility for overseeing the industry. Policies adopted to date have removed entry barriers in those sectors where competition is essential for innovation and growth (specifically for value-added network services), but have maintained strong state control over basic network services and over the manufacturing industry.

In 1985, two laws were passed by the Japanese Diet that helped the state maintain this delicate balance between liberal entry barriers and government control over industrial policy. First, the Telecommunications Business Law significantly reduced entry barriers to, and regulation over, the provision of telecommunications services (for example, it greatly facilitated the provision of value-added services and introduced a licensing procedure for companies wishing to own and operate their own telecommunications lines and equipment). These initiatives appear to have had their intended effect: the number of value-added services provided in Japan has increased rather dramatically, and long-distance rates, particularly private-line rates, have fallen considerably for certain markets. The beneficiaries of these initiatives have primarily been Japanese businesses dependent upon competitively priced communications and innovative service offerings. Also, the market liberalization has benefitted both domestic and foreign firms wishing to enter either the VAN or common carrier business. Compared to the French, the Japanese were willing to relinquish more authority over new telecommunications services.

On the other hand, the Japanese were much more cautious about undermining NTT's role in the basic service sector and in promoting the country's successful telecommunications equipment industry. Recognizing the need to improve the efficiency of the telco, the government introduced the Nippon Telegraph and Telephone Corporation Law that made NTT a semiprivate institution with some of its shares held by the Japanese public. But this was far from relinquishing control over the entity. The privatization left the bulk of NTT shares in the hands of the government, and the Ministry of Post and Telecommunications (MPT) continued to exercise some oversight over the entity's top personnel, budgeting, and investment. One reason for this hesitant privatization is the concern of some elements in the government that they continue to exercise influence over the telecommunications industry.

Japan has now evolved into a dynamic, diversified, capitalist economy where the economic choices for business and government have become considerably more complex than they were when the country experienced rapid rates of growth in the 1960s. Nowhere is this uncertainty regarding the complexity of choices and its implications for statist economic policies more evident than in the case of telecommunications. Should the government maintain its control over the industry and thereby continue to influence technological and industrial developments? Or should it opt for a more independent, decentralized, and competitive industry? This uncertainty regarding the appropriate industrial model has resulted in an uncharacteristic degree of conflict, both within the government and among different interested parties in Japan.

Statist governments are interested in control over the telco because this provides considerable influence over developments in the telecommunications sector of the economy. There is some evidence in the Japanese case that the telco's economic weight is declining rather substantially and, therefore, the importance of state control may be waning in the eyes of Japanese bureaucrats. For example, NTT purchases accounted for 44 percent of telecommunications equipment production in Japan in 1976. By 1985, this share had dropped to 26 percent.[107] NTT's share of purchases will continue to decline as the network matures and exports, businesses, and residents account for a greater share of telecommunications equipment production.

At the same time, observers, including some government commissions, have noted that the partial privatization of NTT has not generated the expected management efficiencies and price declines because the entity continues to exercise a virtual monopoly over the provision of services and equipment sales in Japan. Furthermore, there has been a significant rift within the Japanese government that centers around who will exercise primary control over the industry. The Ministry of International Trade and Industry (MITI) would like to see the regulatory role of the MPT reduced, but opposes immediate divestiture of NTT into smaller regional units. On the other hand, the once reticent MPT has come out in favor of divestiture, recognizing that a more heterogeneous telecommunications industry would promote the regulatory responsibilities of the MPT.[108] In fact, the principal factors shaping liberalization initiatives in the Japanese case were not so much the conflict between government authority and market forces, but over which of the two major government ministries would have control over telecommunications industrial policy—an industrial sector considered to be preeminent for the industrial future of the country.

---

107. Kalba, "Opening Japan's Telecommunications Market," 103.

108. Michael Galbraith, "Divesture, Japanese Style," *Telephony*, 28 March 1990, 52–62; "MITI Adds Divestiture Opinion," *Communications Week*, 12 February 1990, 12.

This rift within the bureaucracy and the uncertainty about the benefits of keeping NTT together as one entity illustrates the degree to which statist institutions and norms are being challenged in Japan. With the rapid growth in the Japanese economy and its greater importance in global economic and political developments, the viability of statist institutions is being dramatically undermined.

Although both France and Japan have statist political institutions, they experienced certain distinct differences in their development of the telecommunications service industry. Most important, the Japanese government seemed to intervene with a much lighter hand than was the case in France. We see this in the early postwar period when the government established NTT as a government corporation with a comparatively limited amount of political oversight (certainly relative to the situation in France). As a result, the Japanese telecommunications infrastructure attained higher rates of penetration growth than France throughout the 1950s and 1960s.

Second, Japan's ability to maintain statist institutions has been much more circumscribed than is the case with France because of (1) the exposure of the Japanese economy to global political and economic pressures, and (2) Japanese business is more independent of government than is the case in France. Because of the size and export orientation of the Japanese economy, the Japanese government was under much more pressure from foreign and domestic firms, and foreign governments (the U.S. government in particular), to reduce its hold over the telecommunications industry through liberalized entry barriers. In addition, the Japanese government does not exercise the same level of control over business as the French do. As a result, there is a much higher likelihood that Japanese businesses would pressure government officials for liberalization because of their interest in entering new telecommunications service markets (this in fact is what happened with respect to the VANs market).

Conclusion

Any simple link between public ownership and economic performance is clearly debunked by this analysis of the French telecommunications industry. For almost a century—between the time the telephone was introduced in France in 1877 through 1970—the country suffered a comparatively poor level of service provision. This chapter has sought to develop an explanation for this relatively poor performance. The hypothesis that links poor performance with government ownership is unconvincing for two reasons. First, French telecommunications service was in private hands during the early period of development and its performance was decidedly mediocre compared to that of the publicly owned telcos in neighboring Germany and Switzerland.

Second, the dramatic improvement in French telephony that occurred in the 1970s was entirely engineered by a government agency. There was no need to privatize the entity in order to dramatically improve its performance.

Political constraints appear to provide a much better explanation for the French telco's performance. First, as I have argued throughout the book, greater exposure to political pressure is associated with lower levels of economic performance. The historical account in this chapter clearly makes the point that political pressures have, for the most part, inhibited performance. While political pressures are likely to detract from economic performance *on balance*, they can have very positive impacts. Outcomes depend upon the nature of the government's political agenda and whether the state happens to guess correctly or not about investment priorities. There are examples developed in this chapter where government initiatives have produced impressive results. Nonetheless, the government's overall political agenda and its prognoses have proven to be poor guides for the French telco's investment priorities. Somewhat in contrast, the post–World War II Japanese government opted for a form of state ownership that permitted less political oversight of the telco management. Accordingly, the postwar performance of the Japanese telco has been quite impressive.

The success of government interventions will vary according to industry characteristics. Government-directed modernization programs, such as those that dramatically improved French telephony, can be very effective in supply-driven industries, particularly where the good is of a universal nature like the telephone. But in demand-driven industries, where services and products are more tailored to narrowly defined market niches (such as French cable television), the absence of competition and the presence of political constraints can seriously inhibit performance.

Finally, the French case is a striking illustration of how political institutions shape liberalization policies. Unlike the political setting characterized by the interest pressure model of Becker, the policy-making process in France is dominated by statist institutions. This has two important implications for the liberalization and privatization processes. First, there will be relatively little effective pressure for liberalization from private interests—either producers or consumers. The catalyst for such policy initiatives will lie with the technocrats that manage the state's economic policies. Second, liberalization initiatives are not likely to face any effective opposition because of the relative powerlessness of private interests vis-à-vis the state.

The result is what the French refer to as *libéralisme de l'état*. Unlike the pluralist environments of the United States or the United Kingdom, the state dominates the process of liberalization. As a result, liberalization policies reflect a distinct mini-max strategy: Government officials initiate policies that minimize any erosion of their control over the economy while maximizing their economic benefits at the same time. Practically, this means that the government has been very reluctant to privatize government assets, preferring to reorganize the telco and its subsidiaries in order to reduce political pressures. And although the government recognizes the need to reduce entry barriers, they have done so only reluctantly and usually with a number of provisions that continue to restrict the extent of competition.[109] In contrast, the ability of the Japanese government to maintain statist control over the liberalization process has been considerably more circumscribed by the exposure of the Japanese economy to global pressures and the somewhat more independent nature of Japanese business interests.

---

109. This reluctance to give up control over government-owned entities has been very well illustrated of late with the battle over the *noyaux durs*. Although the Chirac government proceeded with a number of privatizations during the two years of its power, they were careful to put a controlling block of shares into the hands of parties (either private or public) who could be counted on to promote the interests of the government. Since the Socialists have taken power, however, there has been some pressure to move these controlling interests out of the hands of Chirac partisans into the hands of individuals and institutions more sympathetic to the Left.

CHAPTER 8

The United Kingdom: Pluralism and Change

British telephony shares a century of rather undistinguished performance with its French and German equivalents. Once again, political constraints, not ownership per se, account for the poor performance of the British telco under both private ownership (prior to 1912) and public stewardship (until 1984). The United Kingdom's response to pressures for change in telecommunications policy differed considerably from its continental neighbors. Both France and Germany resisted liberalization and privatization of telephony, while the British enthusiastically embraced both policies.

This chapter illustrates the link between political constraints and economic performance, and the role political institutions played in promoting the eventual liberalization of the industry. Three major developmental themes are analyzed: the failure of private ownership, seventy years of public mismanagement, and liberalization in the 1980s.

The British Telco's Track Record

As was shown earlier (fig. 6.2), the pre–World War II performance of British telephony ranked far behind that of Sweden, somewhat higher than Germany and France. Unlike many of its European counterparts, Britain's telecommunications network was relatively intact after World War II. But this advantage was short lived. Throughout the 1960s and 1970s, the British telecommunications infrastructure experienced lackluster growth.[1] In 1965, the United Kingdom ranked twelfth among twenty-one OECD countries, with 112 telephone lines per thousand population. This figure had risen to 331 per thousand population and its rank climbed to tenth by 1980. By contrast, Germany moved from sixteenth to ninth and Japan from seventeenth to eleventh in this same period. The United Kingdom's penetration was rather paultry compared to top-ranking Sweden with 580 telephone lines per thousand population.

Figures 8.1 and 8.2 provide an even more critical picture of British

---

1. Steven Rattner, "Britain to Sell 51% of Its Telecom Phone Company," *New York Times*, 20 July 1982.

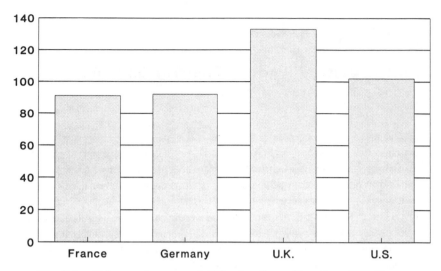

Fig. 8.1. Telco employees per 1,000 subscribers. (Data from ITU, *Yearbook of Common Carrier Telecommunications Statistics* [Geneva: ITU, 1989].)

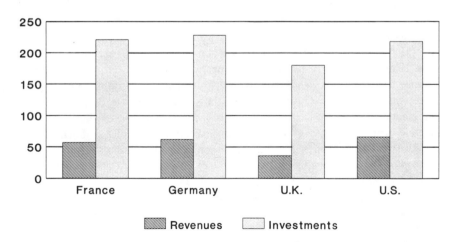

Fig. 8.2. Revenues per 1,000 telco employees and total gross investments per line. (Data from ITU, *Yearbook of Common Carrier Telecommunications Statistics* [Geneva: ITU, 1989].)

telecommunications. They compare the performance of British Telecom with its counterparts in the United States, France, and Germany. On all three indicators British Telecom lags behind. In terms of employees per 10,000 subscriber lines, a measure of the productivity of its labor force, BT's costs surpassed those of AT&T by 25 percent and were 55 percent above those of the West German Bundespost. Measuring labor productivity as revenues per employee, BT earned almost 90 percent less per employee than AT&T, although only marginally less than the French PTT. One explanation for this serious handicap is BT's low levels of capital investment; they invested approximately 35 percent less per subscriber line than their three counterparts.

Failure of Private Ownership

In its early years, the British government entrusted the development of telephony to private firms. Ultimately, this experiment failed because the British government, intent on protecting its telecommunications revenues, made private investment in the industry increasingly risky and, therefore, unattractive.

By the late nineteenth century, it became clear to postal authorities that the telephone represented a menace to its telegraph revenues. Authorities envisioned small service providers competing among themselves within local communities. It soon became apparent, however, that competition at the local level was inefficient. A drive to rationalize the industry ensued. The vehicle for this rationalization was the Telephone Company, which became the United Telephone Company in 1879 when it merged with its principal competitor, the Edison Telephone Company.[2] With this amalgamation, the private telco more aggressively began building its intercity telephone lines, which posed even more of a threat for government telegraph revenues.

For the next three decades the Post Office conducted a successful campaign designed to protect its telecommunications revenues, thereby undermining efforts by the private telcos.[3] First, an 1880 ruling of the High Court, requested by the government, ruled that the telephone fell within the Post Office's monopoly over "electric telegraphs" established in the Acts of 1863 and 1868.[4] Still unwilling to assume the responsibility for developing telephony, the Post Office granted United Telephone licenses to offer telephone

---

2. Much of this discussion of the early history of British telephony is based on the excellent account by Douglas Pitt, *The Telecommunications Function of the British Post Office: A Case Study of Bureaucratic Adaptation* (Westmead, U.K.: Saxon House, 1980).

3. Herbert Laws Webb, *The Development of the Telephone in Europe* (London: Electrical Press, 1910), 26.

4. Pitt, *Telecommunications Function*, 27.

service for a thirty-one-year period and required that the company pay a 10 percent royalty on gross receipts.

Second, they imposed severe restrictions on private, intercity telephone service. Initially, the Post Office opposed private intercity trunk lines because of their threat to telegraph revenues. Nonetheless, under determined telco pressure, the government and the private companies negotiated a Trunk Wire Agreement that included restrictions on the number of subscribers having access to intercity communications. This restriction was removed in 1884 after strong opposition from the British press. Once again, however, the government imposed a 10 percent royalty on gross revenues from intercity traffic.[5]

Third, the Post Office vigorously opposed efforts by the private firms to consolidate their disparate operations. The private firms, convinced that the government would introduce competition into their franchise areas after the expiration of the telephone patent in 1881 (which it did through the Telegraph Act of 1888), saw consolidation as a means of improving their bargaining leverage with the government. In spite of the opposition of the Post Office, the United, Lancashire, and Cheshire Companies successfully amalgamated into the National Telephone Company (NTC).

Nationalization of the telcos became almost certain after the government took over NTC's trunk facilities in 1896. As a result, the NTC was reluctant to invest in new distribution technologies and network expansion.[6] Public criticism of NTC's local service grew, playing into the hands of those in the Post Office who supported nationalization.

Political pressures on the private telcos accelerated in the early part of the twentieth century. The Post Office imposed an accord on telco licensees giving the government the option to buy their plant and equipment in 1905. It included a clause that restricted compensation at the minimum possible price for the plant; it did not allow the telcos to claim compensation for goodwill; and it only allowed telcos to be compensated for a working plant. These conditions strongly discouraged the construction of plants with a large margin of spare capacity.[7]

Like the French situation, vague government intentions and a serious threat of nationalization discouraged investors from assuming the risk of funding capital expansion. As Pitt points out, "The impending takeover had the effect of inducing complacency in the NTC Directorate which from 1908 onwards, had placed a moratorium on plant development."[8]

---

5. Pitt, *Telecommunications Function*, 29.
6. Pitt, *Telecommunications Function*, 32.
7. Webb, *Development of the Telephone*, 41.
8. Pitt, *Telecommunications Function*, 54.

A Select Committee, appointed in 1905 to consider whether the Post Office should take over the NTC, recommended nationalization, setting a purchase date for 31 December 1911. Nationalization proceeded in the United Kingdom, as it did in most other European nations, as a means of protecting government revenues from their telegraph monopoly. It gave the government the option of either slowing down the introduction of telephony, thus maintaining telegraph revenues, or encouraging its growth, generating a new source of revenues. An expanding private telephone industry also threatened the importance of the Post Office as a service provider and policymaker.[9] In fact, if private telephony was too successful, the department would eventually shrink in size. Absorbing telephony into the Post Office would strengthen the department and ensure an expanding employee base. Other factors typically associated with nationalization, such as ideology or the economic inefficiencies of natural monopoly, played a minor role in the government's decision.

The Interwar Years

As in France and Germany, the period between the two World Wars dramatized the extent to which political considerations seriously inhibited the expansion of public telephony. During this period, British governments faced the same overwhelming need to reduce government expenditures as did the German and French governments. The implications were essentially the same for all three countries: minimize the telco's expenditures and maximize its contribution to the government's overall budget.

There was, nonetheless, greater pressure on British decision makers to modify the state telephone monopoly from four major sources: user groups, the personnel responsible for telephony within the Post Office, members of Parliament, and the political parties. Considerable resistance to change was offered by the postal unions. The debate essentially concerned two issues:

- Critics saw a need to separate the telco from the postal activities of the Post Office in order to promote a more aggressive marketing of telephone service. Throughout the Post Office hierarchy, right down to the regional and provincial units, telephony personnel were subordinated to the well-entrenched postal authorities.
- Critics opposed the Treasury's tight control over the telco's capital expenditures program, the revenues it extracted from the telco operations, and its micromanagement of departmental affairs.

---

9. See W. Niskanan, *Bureaucracy and Representative Government* (Chicago: Aldine-Atherton, 1971), for a discussion of the incentives for government departments to expand their range of responsibilities and their number of employees.

Early pressure for change came from business users. As a result of demands from Chambers of Commerce, representing large business users of telephone equipment, a Select Committee was established in 1920 "to enquire into all aspects of the telephone service."[10] The committee concluded that the Post Office was restricting, rather than encouraging, the development of telephony, citing their particularly poor job of promoting the new technology in rural areas. They also noted the negative impact the parsimonious Treasury imposed on the telco's efforts to engage in long-term planning.[11] These recommendations went unheeded. With the rising inflation of the post–World War I era, the Treasury, heeding the admonishments of the Public Accounts Committee, seriously restricted all but the most necessary capital expenditures. Telephony did not fall in this latter category. The absence of any serious response from the Post Office or the government to these recommendations was the catalyst for organizing political support for change. In 1924, users formed the Telephone Development Association with the "purpose of stimulating greater public interest in the telephone as a communications medium."[12] They wanted telephony pursued as a business, rather than a capital-starved department of the Post Office.

Added to these organizational efforts was the vocal criticism of the Liberal party. Their 1929 election platform included a strong recommendation for increased capital spending by the telco and more aggressive marketing of its service—this, of course, fit well with the Keynesian policies they were promoting as a solution to economic stagnation. They suggested that the entity adopt a more businesslike organization, along the lines of the BBC and Central Electricity Generating Board.

The Treasury was skeptical of any radical breaks with tradition. They refused to countenance any change in the organization of the national telco, and, as a result, the technological innovation and diffusion of telephony suffered. For example, as a result of the Treasury's fiscal and administrative conservatism, it insisted that each addition of an exchange to the rural system required a prior guarantee that its revenues would cover its costs.[13] The Treasury would not accept the argument that increases in rural subscribership would raise the attractiveness of the system, thereby generating revenues from increased overall demand. It was also reluctant to endorse large capital expenditures: during the period of inflation right after World War I, the telco had to fund investment from declining real resources; during the subsequent period

---

10. Pitt, *Telecommunications Function*, 45.
11. Pitt, *Telecommunications Function*, 46.
12. Pitt, *Telecommunications Function*, 47.
13. Pitt, *Telecommunications Function*, 53.

of declining prices it was forced to cut telephone prices, thereby further reducing its ability to fund capital expansion.[14]

Those working in the postal section of the Post Office, well placed at all levels of the Post Office administration, were equally determined opponents to change. The most senior decision makers in the Post Office Secretariat were all postal officials and opposed any changes that would enhance the power of telephone personnel. Their reticence was supported by key regional- and provincial-level cadres and by rank and file members of the postal hierarchies.

This intransigence led to further pressures for change. In 1932, 320 MPs supporting the National Government signed a Memorial advocating:

1. the end of Treasury micromanagement and support for a self-funding reserve that would reduce Treasury oversight of their capital expenditures;
2. the adoption of a utility-type organization for the telco that would encourage a more business-oriented approach to the marketing of telephony.

The "Memorialists" were supported by a joint committee representing the principal industrial, commercial, and trading interests of the United Kingdom. These groups won strong editorial support from the newspapers, especially the *Times*.[15]

In response, the government appointed the Bridgeman Inquiry, whose recommendations were very similar to those of the Memorialists:

1. reduce Treasury control over capital expenditures and day-to-day administration by setting a fixed annual payment (10.75 million pounds) that would be paid by the Post Office to the Treasury;
2. enhance the autonomy of the telecommunications personnel in the Post Office by eliminating the dominant Secretariat, replacing it with a governing board on which telephone personnel would be represented, and creating similar governing boards at the provincial levels.

But even these relatively modest proposals were eventually defeated. Post Office officials were able to exploit the divisions among the different interest groups in order to protect their turf and thwart any attempts to change the status quo. The Memorialists were a coalition of MPs from the right,

---

14. Pitt, *Telecommunications Function*, 54–55.
15. Pitt, *Telecommunications Function*, 71.

center, and left of the political spectrum, and, although all denounced the inefficiencies of the Post Office, they could not agree on measures to improve the situation. In addition, unions within the Post Office were strongly divided on the matter: postal unions, championing the notion of public service, were decidedly against any change in status quo. The Union of Postal Workers (UPW) was particularly antagonistic to the Bridgeman recommendations regarding regional reforms, because they would seriously undermine their control over telephone personnel. On the other hand, the union representing telephone engineers adopted just the opposite stance, arguing that the proposals for reorganization were not radical enough. The Institute of Professional Civil Servants supported reforms, arguing that technical grades should have more access to top positions and that the telephone and telegraph service should be separated from the Post Office, but continue under state ownership.

The Postwar Period

Following World War II, political constraints continued to inhibit development of telephony, but, unlike France and Germany, the United Kingdom ultimately adopted radical changes in the telco's organization and industry regulations. Three political constraints burdened telco management in the postwar period: the continuing pressure to reduce government expenditures, the priority given to export promotion, and the stop-and-go nature of economic policy-making.

Although demand increased dramatically for telephone service following World War II, capital expenditure authorizations, necessary to serve this expanding consumer base, were not forthcoming. For a thirty-year period following the war, British governments continually faced economic crises necessitating draconian efforts to reduce budget deficits. Because capital was scarce immediately following the war, expenditures were authorized for only the most important projects. In the early 1950s, the government faced a serious deterioration in the external balance of payments that prompted measures to cut back on the expenditures of government departments. Another major balance of payments crisis in 1957 meant further restrictions on capital expenditures. During the 1960s and 1970s, high inflation, a growing government deficit, and balance of payments problems produced further Treasury limits on capital expenditures.

British telephony suffered from these expenditure restrictions because the Post Office had neither the political constituency nor the bureaucratic presence that might have reduced their exposure. The result was a series of budgetary setbacks. At each successive economic crisis, the Treasury and the Capital Issues Committee held back capital spending by the Post Office as part of its austerity program.[16] Bealy indicates that levels of investment by the telco declined well into the 1960s—the investment programs of 1958–59 and 1959–60 were actually restricted to a level below that of 1957–58.[17] The National Plan developed by the Labour government of 1965 promised to double capital expenditures by the year 1970, but the balance of payments problems that emerged immediately after the announcement led the Treasury to quickly rescind these promises. Telephone development was inhibited not only by restrictions on capital expenditures but also by the uncertainty regarding funding. The stop-and-go nature of economic policy during the postwar period seriously undermined any long-term planning by telco management. It was not uncommon for government to authorize increases in capital funding for a project in one year and then, in the following year, prevent the telco from raising capital that would permit completion of the project. Pitt cites the example of Treasury authorizing certain expenditures (such as marketing staff) but disallowing funds for the necessary technical personnel to meet demand (e.g., engineers for installation).[18]

Because of a deteriorating balance of trade throughout much of the postwar period, government capital expenditures were channeled into activities that directly contributed to foreign earnings. The British telco was not spared these political pressures. One idea promoted by the Treasury involved directing capital expenditures to the expansion of intercity trunk lines because this would most directly help large businesses who, in turn, were most likely to be engaged in exportation. This reduced the telco's revenue because, at the time, local, as opposed to intercity service, was more profitable. Ironically, it also hurt the major British telecommunications equipment manufacturers— active in the export market—because it reduced their domestic market for customer telephone equipment, depriving them of economies that would have made them more competitive internationally.

Pressures for Change

There can be little doubt that the British telco was buffeted by political pressures throughout the postwar period, just as its counterparts in France and Germany were. On the other hand, the policy-making process in the United Kingdom promoted much more vigorous debate over the need to remove the telco from political oversight.

The Labour government of 1945 set an important political precedent

---

16. Pitt, *Telecommunications Function*, 106.
17. Pitt, *Telecommunications Function*, 110.
18. Pitt, *Telecommunications Function*, 105.

when it created a number of "public corporations." These nationalized entities were permitted very flexible management and were relatively free of parliamentary and Treasury oversight. Although many supported the reorganization of the Post Office as a public corporation, opponents prevented any change in the department's status. They effectively argued that the Post Office had been part of a central department for over three decades and it would be inappropriate to change now. Second, they insisted that the strategic defense importance of telecommunications—which had been dramatized during the war—made it imprudent to give the entity the status of an independent public corporation.[19]

Throughout this period there was considerable criticism of British telecommunications service and its mismanagement under the authority of the Post Office. In response, successive governments commissioned studies to defuse some of the criticism and, they hoped, identify a political solution to the problem. The White Paper of 1955 made the now familiar argument that the Post Office should be accorded quasi-independent status regarding its finances and in the general running of its affairs.[20] In return, the Post Office would be expected to balance its expenditures with revenues and to make an annual contribution to the Treasury of 5 million pounds. The White Paper also called for the development of a "planning climate" whereby expenditures would be evaluated for a three-year period.

Like every other reform, this one eventually fell victim to political realities. The balance of payments crisis of 1957 resulted in dramatic cutbacks in investment and put an end to the "planning climate." Other recommendations associated with greater operational and budgeting independence were never seriously implemented.

As a defensive measure, the Post Office reacted to external pressures and commissioned a number of internal studies, including the Lumley Committee inquiry of 1950 and the Wolverson Report of 1962. For the most part, these inquiries recommended only minor changes in the status quo. The Lumley Committee suggested a certain degree of internal reorganization, but this was quickly rejected by the powerful postal union.

Nonetheless, pressure for change continued to mount. The large business users, particularly in the financial and service areas, were increasingly critical of Post Office management. In addition, the unions representing telecommunications personnel within the Post Office continued their battle with the postal unions, demanding greater autonomy for the telecommunications operations.

In 1960, these pressures resulted in another White Paper and the subse-

---

19. Pitt, *Telecommunications Function*, 103.
20. Pitt, *Telecommunications Function*, 102.

quent Post Office Act of 1961. The act introduced some modest changes that were designed to give the postmaster general greater scope for running the department as a self-contained business.[21] The Post Office Trading Fund was recreated, providing a certain degree of financial independence, and the adoption of commercial accounts made it easier to judge the entity's commercial performance. Nonetheless, capital borrowing was restricted to 80 million pounds per annum and the Post Office was required to repay, over twenty-five years, 800 million pounds on accrued liabilities.[22] Overall, these measures amounted to very minor changes in the entity's independence from political pressures.

Another White Paper on Telephone Service was issued by the Labour Party in 1963. It contained a bold announcement of a massive five year plan of capital expenditures that, as noted above, were abandoned soon after because of a deteriorating balance-of-payments situation. The report also reflected the "managerialism" rhetoric of Prime Minister Wilson promising the country a major "organic revitalisation in the public sector."[23] This was reinforced by pressures from the Post Office Engineers Union (POEU), which lobbied Post Office Minister Benn to reduce Parliamentary and Treasury oversight of the department's affairs. Benn responded by appointing the accounting firm of McKinsey to conduct an inquiry into the functioning of the Post Office.

These criticisms of the telco's organizational status and its impact on telephony became even more urgent by the middle of the 1960s. Critics noted that Post Office planners continued to hold negative attitudes toward domestic subscribers and promoted telephony with halfhearted advertising and marketing campaigns. They also pointed to a wholly inadequate departmental forecasting capability, which meant poor allocation of rather scarce capital investment funds. Criticism was also brought to bear on the telco's failure to exploit its power as monopsonistic purchaser—"Bulk Supply" agreements that were not based on competitive bidding favored suppliers, not consumers.

In the latter half of the 1960s, political momentum was building for a major change in the organization of the Post Office. An Economic Development Council Committee was set up in 1965 to consider Post Office affairs and produced, once again, the usual structural critique. The POEU became an increasingly strong advocate for separation of the postal and telecommunication agencies, while the UPW fought successfully against any such separation, recognizing that their members would be the poor sister of any such arrangement. There was also a feeling among the UPW that the postal opera-

---

21. Pitt, *Telecommunications Function*, 139.
22. Pitt, *Telecommunications Function*, 141.
23. Pitt, *Telecommunications Function*, 143.

tion, without the telecommunications activities, would drift into decline, and, with it, the number of jobs for its members would decrease.[24] Although Benn was somewhat sympathetic to separation, Wilson made it quite clear that, given the close ties between the Labour party and the UPW, such an initiative was not politically feasible.[25]

The recommendations of the 1966 Select Committee on Nationalized Industries, while not particularly influential, raised considerable political controversy over the fate of the Post Office. Its recommendations followed those of most earlier reports that noted the need for organizational change. The POEU and UPW seriously opposed each other on the issue.

A White Paper that followed the Select Committee's recommendations endorsed an omnibus corporation that would be expected to meet expenditures with revenues but would be free of day-to-day scrutiny by Parliament and the Treasury. It also recommended maximum service separation within the organization. Conservative spokesmen argued for twin corporations, with some even advocating private participation, a move opposed by the Labour party.

The Post Office Act of 1969 implemented most of the White Paper recommendations: it changed the status of the Post Office from a government department to a public corporation; separated, at the regional level, post and telecommunications operations; and transferred responsibility for personnel from the Civil Service Commission to the Post Office.[26]

Public Ownership and Political Constraints

Throughout the history of the state-owned British telco political constraints impinged on three principal areas of decision making: finances, employment, and corporate strategy.

British Telco Financing

Before privatization, none of the traditional sources of capital funding—borrowing, the equity markets, and profits—provided the telco with adequate capital funds. Neither have government subsidies provided much funding.

Borrowing. As a government agency, the British telco's only source of borrowed funds was the government. Even after the 1981 liberalization, BT bonds sold to the public were considered public expenditures—private bor-

---

24. Michael E. Corby, *The Postal Business 1969–79: A Study in Public Sector Management* (London: Kegan Page, 1979), 99.

25. Pitt, *Telecommunications Function*, 151.

26. Corby, *Postal Business*, chap. 2.

rowing was out of the question.[27] During the late 1970s, the British treasury's cash limits on public sector borrowing impeded the telco's modernization program. For example, in 1981, BT was only allowed to borrow £380 million as part of its efforts to finance a £2 billion per year modernization.[28]

As a result of these restrictions, the British telco has had to rely almost exclusively on internally generated funds for financing capital investments. For example, in 1981, British Telecom had an internal funding ratio exceeding 100.0 percent, while the Bundespost financed only 42.8 percent of its capital funding from internal sources. Such dependence on internal funds seriously inhibited efforts to modernize telecommunications.

Tariffs. In principal, British Telecom was free to set its own rates without government approval. As a political reality, the British telco formulated tariffs in close consultation with the secretary of state. The evidence regarding the impact of government regulation on tariffs is mixed. Between 1968–69 and 1978–79 overall prices actually fell by 30 percent.[29] Because this was substantially less than the reduction in costs, gross margins improved from 44 percent in 1968–69 to 50 percent in 1978–79. Nonetheless, there have been periods of government-imposed price restraint. Between 1971–72 and 1974–75, government restrictions forced the telco's prices to fall more rapidly than costs, causing gross margins to shrink.[30]

On the other hand, political pressures forced the British telco to cross-subsidize certain classes of consumers. The 1981–82 BT Annual Report indicated that only three services contributed to profits: inland subscribers' calls (the profitable element here is trunk or domestic long distance), international telephone services, and international telegraph services. Services that were operated at a loss included local subscriber service, business rentals, residential rentals, apparatus rentals, call office receipts, private circuits, telegrams, telex, miscellaneous, and agency.[31] Although there was a strong economic case for eliminating these cross-subsidies, political pressures made such a move unlikely.

Government subsidies. The British telco has not benefited from significant government subsidies; rather it has been quite profitable. For the period 1977 through 1982, British Telecom's return on net assets was approximately 6 percent, although it varied with service.[32] In their analysis of the 1984 BT

27. "The Born-Again Technology," *Economist*, 22 August 1981, 17.

28. "British Telecom: Cold New World," *Economist*, 1 August 1981, 25.

29. The following discussion is based on Richard Pryke, *The Nationalised Industries: Policies and Performance Since 1968* (Oxford: Martin Robertson, 1981), 179–80.

30. Corby, *Postal Business*, 140.

31. Logica, *Communications in Europe: The Changing Environment* (London: Logica, 1983).

32. Logica, *Communications in Europe*, 36.

public offering, de Zoete and Bevan, London stockbrokers, highly recommended the issue, indicating that BT return on capital was greater than that of AT&T.[33]

British Telecom Labor Force

Political pressures affected two important aspects of managing the telco's labor force: employee tenure and salaries. One of the chief factors inhibiting the performance of the British telco was its inflated work force. Although the French and British telcos served approximately the same number of telephone lines (19.5 million) in 1982, the British Telecom had 50 percent more employees than the French telco. As public sector employees—prior to 1969, civil servants—the telco labor force had considerable job security.

The strength of the telco's labor unions also ensured generous wage settlements. Successive British governments—both Labour and Conservative—have yielded without much resistance to the wage demands of public sector employees. Even Prime Minister Thatcher has been reluctant to adopt an aggressive line with public sector employee unions.[34] In 1983, it was pointed out that BT engineers "had enjoyed job security and a place near the top of the manual worker earnings league for many years."[35] In an analysis of British Telecom's need to drastically increase telephone rates, the *Economist* lay the blame directly on the firm's inability to keep down its labor costs: "The monopoly's real problem is inefficiency, and mainly its inability to keep down its operating costs. July's wage settlement is estimated to cost approximately £100 million more than budgeted for."[36]

Labor costs for the British telco have risen substantially higher than for other manufacturing concerns. Between 1968 and 1978, the real staff costs per employee in the British manufacturing sector increased from a base of 100.0 to 128.9. By contrast, the index for the British telco increased from 100.0 to 139.1, a 10 point difference.

Corporate Decision Making

Political considerations also shaped the telco's purchasing decisions. The government entity was under government pressure to buy British products because of its policies promoting domestic equipment manufacturers. This has produced a very close relationship between the British telco and the three

33. *Financial Times*, 1 June 1984, 12.

34. *Economist*, 9 February 1980, 19–20; Joseph R. Monsen and Kenneth D. Walters, *Nationalized Companies: A Threat to American Business* (New York: McGraw Hill, 1983), 46.

35. *Financial Times*, 12 October 1983, 15.

36. "British Telecom: Fewer Eggs," *Economist*, 18 October 1980, 86.

large British telecommunications manufacturers, Plessey, GEC, and Standard Telephones and Cable (STC).

British Telecom's largest recent capital investment has been the upgrading of analog switching equipment to a digital format. Research and development costs for the new digital exchange—the System X—were jointly shared by British Telecom, Plessey, and GEC. Digital exchanges manufactured outside the United Kingdom were never seriously considered.

By forcing the telco to opt for a British exchange, the government slowed the modernization of the country's telecommunications network and added considerably to the cost of the effort.[37] At the time, there were a number of digital exchanges available from non-British manufacturers (such as Ericsson's AXE system) that would have served the same purpose at much less expense. But, so long as the British telco remained a state enterprise, preferential treatment of local manufacturers could be counted on.[38]

Accelerated Change: Competition and Privatization

With the election of Margaret Thatcher in 1979, British telecommunications policy took a dramatic liberal turn. The Thatcher government adopted two significant legislative initiatives that reduced political constraints and significantly lowered industry entry barriers. In 1981, the Post Office was split into two entities. One of these was British Telecom, created as a public corporation responsible for providing telecommunications services and equipment. A second legislative initiative, in 1984, resulted in the sale of 51 percent of BT's shares to the general public.

Hiving Off: The Telecommunications Bill of 1981

British Telecom was created in 1981 as part of the government's liberalization of the telecommunications industry. By separating the telco from the Post Office and giving it the status of a public corporation, the Thatcher officials felt that the firm would lose the bureaucratic mentality characteristic of government departments. BT's chairman expressed the intention "to change the ethos of this organization from that of a civil-service mentality to that of a market-oriented customer-oriented business."[39] This organizational change did not eliminate political constraints: for example, BT was still denied the

---

37. "The Born-Again Technology," *Economist*, 22 August 1981, 10.

38. *Financial Times*, 18 January 1984, 14; *Financial Times*, 20 April 1983, 10.

39. For a discussion of the efforts of British Telecom management to change the entity's corporate culture, see Kevin Morgan and Douglas Pitt, "Bureaucracy, Deregulation, and Technology: The 'Ramping' of British Telecom (BT) and AT&T," paper presented at the annual meeting of the American Political Science Association, Washington, D.C., 1988. See also "Communications: British Telecom Gets Aggressive," *Business Week*, 16 November 1981, 160.

right to borrow on the private market, tariffs continued to be manipulated for political purposes, and purchasing remained under government supervision.

Second, the bill's sponsor, Sir Keith Joseph, the minister of state for industry, included a number of procompetition measures designed to stimulate inventions and sales of telecommunications equipment in the United Kingdom, promote economic growth by providing consumers with a wider choice of equipment and services, and improve the performance of British Telecom. The British Telecommunications Bill ended the Post Office's monopoly over the provision of telecommunications equipment by permitting competitors to supply all but the first telephone at any location. Competing equipment manufacturers or retailers would now have access to the sizeable market for telephone sets and for the more sophisticated customer premise equipment such as Private Branch Exchanges (PBX) for offices.

Steps were also taken to liberalize the telecommunications service industry. The bill empowered the secretary of state for industry to license private undertakings to offer "Value-Added Network services to third parties over British Telecom's network, and to provide telecommunications services over privately created and operated transmission systems."[40] In 1982, the government issued a license to Mercury Communications to offer competing telecommunications services over an alternative network.

Even though far-reaching by European standards, these measures stopped short of complete liberalization of the industry. British Telecom retained the right to provide the first telephone on all customer premises. Moreover, the government insisted that post office engineers retain the sole authority for equipment installation and repair.[41] In order to protect local manufacturers, the bill prohibited foreign manufacturers of customer premise equipment from competing in the British market for three years. Finally, the bill provided for an equipment licensing procedure that seriously inhibited the entry of new competition. Two bodies were established to certify that equipment could be connected to the BT network. The British Standards Institution established general standards, while "the British-Electro-Technical Approvals Board (BAT) tests the actual devices for compliance with standards."[42] This cumbersome procedure significantly delayed the approval of new equipment.

The 1984 Telecommunications Act

The 1984 act under which 51 percent of BT was sold to the general public represented an effort to reduce political constraints and increase market pres-

---

40. Logica, *Communications in Europe*, 23.
41. "British Telecom: Yellow's the Colour," *Economist*, 14 February 1981, 57.
42. "When the Monopoly Has to Stop," *Economist*, 28 February 1982, 57.

sures on management. Government officials expected three chief benefits from privatization. First they thought such a move would encourage entrepreneurial, as opposed to bureaucratic, attitudes among BT management—no longer would they be part of the public service bureaucracy.[43] Second, such a move would subject management to the discipline of stockholders and the stock market, rather than to Whitehall. If management performed poorly, stock prices and dividends would decline, placing pressure on management to improve results. This would have the important subsidiary benefit of reducing the bargaining strength of labor. As a political entity, it was difficult for management to stand up to the wage demands of labor; as a publicly traded corporation, management would be obliged to hold firm in wage negotiations. Third, by placing BT in private hands, it would no longer be subject to the government's external financing limits.

Although privatization addressed the problem of political constraints on management, the government was then left with the issue of anticompetitive behavior by a private monopolist. British Telecom was privatized with much of its monopoly intact (unlike AT&T, which lost its local network activities as a result of the 1982 divestiture agreement). British Telecom and its employees lobbied hard to prevent changes in its structure and to minimize competitive threats to its market position. Their efforts proved very effective. The government, in an attempt to make the share offering as attractive as possible, avoided policies that might undermine the profitability of BT—the "light rein of regulation" as it was labeled. This, of course, meant that they were reluctant to dismantle the entity, to promote extensive competition, or to burden it with excessive regulation.

The government adopted a regulatory, as opposed to structural, approach to the prevention of anticompetitive behavior (in contrast to the Modified Final Judgement in the United States, wherein structural solutions dominated regulatory ones). A number of regulatory safeguards against anticompetitive behavior by BT were implemented. Most important, BT was granted a twenty-five-year license by the secretary of state that stipulated BT's public service obligations, indicated how it ought to set prices, and how it should organize subsidiaries. The license prohibited cross-subsidization of competitive with noncompetitive activities—for example, it required the establishment of a separate subsidiary for CPE manufacturing and marketing.

Government officials also imposed a price-capping formula on BT through the so-called RPI-X formula, which restricted price increases on basic services (including national long distance but excluding international calling) to the retail price index minus 3 percent. Finally, the bill created the Office of

---

43. See *Financial Times*, 27 September 1983, 16; Morgan and Pitt, "Bureaucracy, Deregulation, and Technology."

Telecommunications (Oftel), which is a nonministerial government department with a staff of approximately 120 responsible for regulating the industry.[44] Its duties are somewhat fuzzy and its discretion in taking initiatives is quite high. As a result, the procompetitiveness of the agency is very much dependent upon its director.

Compared to most other developed nations, the United Kingdom initiatives liberalizing telecommunications have been far-reaching, certainly much more so than the policies adopted in Germany and France. The interesting puzzle, addressed in the next section, is to explain the dramatic policy divergences between the United Kingdom and its European neighbors.

Political Institutions and Policy Change

Up until the latter part of the 1970s, British policies regarding telephony resembled those of the French and the Germans. By 1984, the United Kingdom had radically distinguished itself by separating British Telecom from the Post Office and selling a 51 percent interest in the company to private investors. How do we explain this dramatic dismantling of entry barriers, particularly in light of the reticence of the French and German governments? The British policy response differed because of the decidedly pluralist nature of its policy-making institutions. Pluralism had three important ramifications.

First, unlike France, interest groups in the United Kingdom are at the same time much less beholden to the state and more comfortable with the give and take of lobbying civil servants, ministers, and members of Parliament. By contrast, French interest groups tend to be either very dependent upon the state (as is the case of business) or uncomfortable with the give and take of the pluralist process (French unions are more at home with confrontational action). Furthermore, in the United Kingdom, interest group independence has not been seriously compromised by corporatist institutions.[45] In the corporatist environment of Germany, interest groups tend to be co-opted into semi-official decision-making arrangements where their freedom of action is seriously compromised by a process that demands consensual resolution of conflict.

Second, barriers to participation in the policy process are much lower in the United Kingdom than they are in France and Germany. This is the result of

---

44. For an excellent discussion of the regulatory structure imposed on the industry by the Telecommunications Act, see John Vickers and George Yarrow, *Privatization: An Economic Analysis* (Cambridge, Mass.: MIT Press, 1988), 208.

45. Andrew Shonfield, in *Modern Capitalism: The Changing Balance of Public and Private Power* (New York: Oxford University Press, 1965), provides an excellent documentation of the failure of the British to develop more of a consensual decision-making environment.

the number of relatively independent decision-making entities in the British policy-making process.

Finally, pluralist institutions in Britain permit policy outcomes that are built on the support of minimum winning political coalitions. This contrasts with Germany, for example, where corporatist institutions effectively prohibit minimum winning coalitions because they require coalitions of the whole (i.e., consensus) on many important policy issues. Because minimum winning coalitions are a feature of the British policy process, efforts to challenge established regulations have a greater chance of success. Groups are more likely to successfully challenge existing regulations because they will not have to contend with the veto power of established interests.

Costs of Entry Barriers and Government Ownership

As the costs to society of maintaining entry barriers mount, those bearing the burden of these restrictions have greater incentives to organize and press for change. In the United Kingdom, like most countries, those bearing the greatest burden were large business users. In 1982, 30 percent of the U.K. telecommunications market was accounted for by 300 major business users, and all business users represented 70 percent of that market.[46]

One of the most pressing concerns was the inability of the Post Office to offer acceptable high-speed data transmission services. As a result, businesses lobbied for competition in the provision of various network services (such as customized packet switching networks) and for value-added network services.[47]

The costs of poor telephone service represented a particularly serious problem for the powerful financial community in the City of London. By the latter part of the 1970s, telecommunications played an important role in the financial services industry—for those firms that wished to remain competitive at the global level, state-of-the-art communications capabilities were essential.[48] First, with technological advances, the ability to store, analyze, and transmit large volumes of data has become necessary in order to remain competitive in the financial services industry. Second, the market for British banking, securities, insurance, and publishing services is increasingly defined

---

46. S. C. Finch, "A User's Perspective," *Business Telecom Proceedings of the International Conference* (London: Online, 1983), 38.

47. See Jill Hills, *Deregulating Telecoms: Competition and Control in the United States, Japan, and Britain* (New York: Quorum Books, 1986), 90; and United Kingdom, *Report of the Post Office Review Committee* (The 'Carter Report'), Cmnd. 6850 (London: HMSO, 1977).

48. Bruce Williams ("Organizing for Information Technology," *Business Telecom Proceedings,* 149) illustrates the importance of telecommunications for different industry sectors. Telecommunications has a "dominant" role in banking, insurance, and data base services.

in global terms, putting a premium on the quality of communications and the ability to transmit and manage large volumes of voice and data traffic. Given these trends, it is not surprising that the financial community reacted with some concern to the poor quality and technical backwardness of British telephone service.

Dissatisfaction with the British telco was, of course, not confined to the financial community. For example, manufacturing firms (particularly the multinationals) were increasingly dependent on sophisticated communications networks to coordinate their various development, manufacturing, and distribution operations located throughout the country and the world. As the importance of telecommunications grew in the 1960s and 1970s, organizations of business user-groups multiplied and their memberships increased. Two of the most important of these groups were the Post Office Users' National Council (POUNC), established by the 1969 act, and the Telecommunications Managers Association (TMA).[49] In 1958, the TMA had only six members; by 1983, the organization's membership had climbed to over 400.[50]

Groups other than business were affected by these policies. The trade unions played a key role in shaping the final policies adopted. Although the unions strongly opposed privatization, once the DEP began drafting the Bill, their representatives strongly promoted a regulatory and competitive environment that would be favorable to BT.[51]

As we would expect, residential consumers, the interested party with the greatest number of members, were the least well organized. Just as in the United States, the impetus for liberalization did not originate with the average residential consumer—the collective action costs were simply too high. On the other hand, large business consumers could easily be galvanized to lobby for change because of their small numbers and the increasing costs imposed on them as a result of poor quality telephone service.

Pluralism and Pressures for Change

Those groups pressing for changes in British telecommunications policies had a variety of avenues for influencing decision makers. In contrast, major policy decisions in Germany are the reserve of a small group of representatives from the government, manufacturers, and unions; in France, state technocrats dominate such decision making.

Although the Thatcher government was certainly predisposed to liberalization of the telecommunications sector, before the 1978 election it was not

---

49. For a discussion of the PONUC, see Corby, *Postal Business*, 168.
50. Finch, "User's Perspective," 38.
51. Vickers and Yarrow, *Privatization*, 236.

an important political priority. After the election, interested parties convinced Thatcher of the urgency of privatization. The initial policy concept emerged from the City. Details of the legislation were the product of intense negotiations among a number of different interested parties. It is incorrect to view the policy as simply a radical initiative of the Thatcher government.[52] Liberalization and, to a lesser extent, privatization had been on the policy agenda long before the election of Thatcher. What concerns us here is the manner in which British political institutions facilitated (and hindered) efforts to put the issues of liberalization and privatization on the political agenda. In their attempt to influence the outcome of legislation, proponents and opponents of change focused their efforts on four principal institutions: the cabinet, Whitehall, Parliament, and, after its creation in 1981, Oftel.

The Cabinet

It is the cabinet, and particularly the prime minister, that is ultimately responsible for policy modifications. On any particular issue there is no established protocol regarding consultation. With respect to telecommunications, Prime Minister Wilson paid close attention to the views of the Post Office administrators and the UPW. Thatcher, on the other hand, appointed a small group of advisors from the business community who were responsible for identifying strategies for improving the effectiveness of government agencies, including the Post Office. Consultation is decidedly idiosyncratic and often involves a variety of nongovernmental inputs.

Much of this consultation with interested parties is conducted behind closed doors.[53] But the cabinet does, on issues of national importance, often appoint Royal Commissions that survey a wide range of opposing positions on an issue. The cabinet also prepares White Papers that serve as the basis for national debate prior to introducing legislation. As I indicated above, the government was under pressure throughout the postwar period to introduce policy changes that would improve the quality of the country's telephone service. In response to these pressures, the government did, on a number of

---

52. Some argue that Thatcher's liberalization and privatization initiatives violated the policy-making norms of the United Kingdom by circumventing the traditional "policy communities." See Jeremy Moon, J. J. Richardson, and Paul Smart, "The Privatisation of British Telecom: A Case Study of the Extended Process of Legislation," *European Journal of Political Research* 14 (1986): 339–55; Grant Jordan and J. J. Richardson, "The British Policy Style, or the Logic of Negotiation," in *Policy Styles in Western Europe,* ed. Jeremy Richardson (London: Allen and Unwin, 1982). I would simply add that the British political institutions make such circumvention more likely than in other systems, where pluralist traditions are much less well developed.

53. Douglas Ashford, *Policy and Politics in Britain: The Limits of Consensus* (Philadelphia: Temple University Press, 1981).

occasions, instruct commissions to recommend changes in the Post Office, based on the testimony of interest parties.

The most recent commission to examine the performance of the British telco was the Carter Committee, appointed by the secretary of state for industry in 1975. Pressure from users, particularly the Post Office Users' National Council, prompted the government to initiate this investigation. As Pitt points out, the committee's hearings and final report reflected "the pulls and pushes of the Post Office's own political system."[54] Included here were the often opposing views of government, unions, consumers, and management.

With the rising importance of telecommunications, the Thatcher cabinet increasingly relied on commission hearings and reports to guide its development of policy. This multiplied the opportunities for interested parties to participate in the policy-making process and reduced the likelihood that the government would adopt regulations that maintain or erect entry barriers. An example is the Communications Steering Group established in 1987 by the secretary of state for trade and industry to advise the cabinet on developments in the United Kingdom electronic communications industry over the next two decades and the policy options open to the government.[55] The Steering Group included extensive consultation with interested parties through both formal written submission and informal exchanges. An initial fifty written responses were received by the group followed by another thirty submissions in response to a discussion paper prepared by a consultant group.[56] Similar efforts were part of the *Peacock Committee on Broadcasting*, the *Independent Review of the Radio Spectrum*, the *Report on the Inquiry into Cable Expansion and Broadcasting Policy*, and the *Report of the Mobile Radio Committee*.[57]

To some extent, the Thatcher cabinet promoted the proliferation of these commissions and inquiries and encouraged very widespread participation of private interests. Promoting the participation of a diverse group of interests ensured that entry barriers to the industry would be kept low because many of the participants invariably are aspiring entrants into these industries.

---

54. Pitt, *Telecommunications Function*, 191.

55. The policy recommendations of the Steering Group are reported in United Kingdom, *Department of Trade and Industry Communications Steering Group Report: The Infrastructure for Tomorrow* (London: HMSO, 1988).

56. United Kingdom, *Steering Group Report*, 4.

57. United Kingdom, Home Department, *Peacock Committee on Broadcasting* (London: HMSO, 1986); United Kingdom, Home Office, *Terrestrial Land Mobile Services: Spectrum Requirements and Availability to the End of the Century Report of the Mobile Radio Committee* (London: HMSO, 1982); United Kingdom, Home Office, *Report of the Inquiry into Cable Expansion and Broadcasting Policy* (London: HMSO, 1982); United Kingdom, Home Office, *Report of the Mobile Radio Committee* (London: HMSO, 1982).

Whitehall

The British political system invests considerable power in the hands of the senior civil service.[58] Although Whitehall tends to be the focus of policy-making in Britain, it mediates and consults, rather than dominates. Manned by professional civil servants, it depends upon the input of interested parties in order to prepare and implement policies. Policy-making in Whitehall, therefore, is characterized by informal discussions between interested parties and civil servants. The two groups have a mutual interest in maintaining an open dialogue. Unlike France, the state and interest groups are mutually dependent.

As a result, much of the legislation in Britain is worked out through close collaboration between senior civil servants in the various ministries and representatives of interested parties. This does not mean, as it does in the German case, that major interested parties have any guarantee of being consulted. No interest group in the British system has any iron-clad assurance of being consulted in the policy-making process. Whitehall actively involved major business users (particularly firms from the financial sector) and management of the British telco in the preparation of legislation. They did not see fit to consult with labor nor with representatives of consumer groups.

With the election of a Conservative government in 1979, large business users increased their pressure for a reorganization of the Post Office and the liberalization of the telecommunications sector. One of the key issues put forward by the banks was the possibility of establishing a competitor to British Telecom for the provision of network services. In 1980, they initiated discussions with DTI senior officials that outlined the feasibility of such an undertaking, and this ultimately became a part of the 1981 bill.

Business users in general found that, with the change in government, the Department of Trade and Industry had become much more receptive to their demands. The head of the Telecommunications Managers Association noted that:

> This [consultation between the government departments and end users] is perhaps the area in which the business users had their greatest surprise. After years of knocking on doors we were astonished when a number of them suddenly flew open. We found ourselves being listened to by the Secretary of State, by Ministers, and by a most helpful and responsive team within the Department of Industry.[59]

---

58. Ashford, *Policy and Politics*.
59. Finch, "User's Perspective," 41.

Even before the passage of the 1981 bill, Treasury officials and merchant banks from the City explored the possibility of privatizing British Telecom. The banks, of course, had two objectives: one was the promotion of better telecommunications in the City; the other concerned the fees that they would receive for managing the underwriting task associated with the issuance of British Telecom equity to the public.

Whitehall played a dominant role in the design and passage of the final privatization bill in 1984. Initially, the notion of privatization was regarded as politically unpopular and unworkable. Nonetheless, a minority within the DTI were strong advocates of privatization and pushed hard to find innovative strategies for implementing a successful (both politically and economically) denationalization.[60] Officials from the DTI worked closely with British Telecom and private industry in the preparation of the legislation. The latter included mostly the major telecommunications manufacturing firms and the large business users.

British Telecom was the major influence on the final form of the legislation. They maintained very close links with DTI officials in order to avoid the type of breakup that was imposed on AT&T, to minimize the competitive threats that would face the company, and to ensure a favorable regulatory structure.[61] For the most part, their efforts paid off. Groups effectively excluded from the consultation process—primarily unions and consumer interests—were forced to look elsewhere for input into the final policy-making process.

Parliament

Parliament has had a more peripheral role than other institutions in shaping telecommunications policy. Nonetheless, dating back to the very early part of the twentieth century, Select Committees of Parliament have served as a forum in which criticism about the telco's performance was voiced. Recommendations of the 1966 Select Committee on the Nationalized Industries led to the Post Office Act of 1969, which introduced a number of organizational changes in the Post Office.

To some degree, British MPs are able to develop a base of support independent of the party leadership, allowing them to respond to lobbying efforts of smaller, particularistic interests.[62] In contrast, the elected repre-

---

60. See the account in J. Solomon, "Telecommunications Evolution in the UK," *Telecommunications Policy* 10 (September 1986): 186–92. He was actively involved in the government's preparation of the privatization legislation.

61. Vickers and Yarrow, *Privatization*, 210.

62. Bruce Cain, John Ferejohn, and Morris Fiorina, *The Personal Vote: Constituency Service and Electoral Independence* (Cambridge, Mass.: Harvard University Press, 1983).

sentatives in France and Germany are much less independent, and, as a result, lobbying interests are forced to create ties with the national parties, which is more difficult and costly. Legislative processes that discriminate against smaller interest groups are less receptive to the demands of groups challenging existing entry barriers. They are more likely to favor established interests that benefit from government-enforced entry barriers.[63]

During the most recent debate over the privatization of British Telecom, the back-bench MPs played an important role in minimizing the negative impact of the legislation on rural constituencies. Under pressure from this group of constituents and rural interests represented by Rural Voice, Conservative back-bench MPs and members of the House of Lords lobbied to prevent a reduction in the quality of service to rural subscribers and an increase in rates.[64]

Members of Parliament were also the object of intense lobbying by British Telecom management. Neumann describes the extensive and frequent briefing programs conducted by the company's Corporate Affairs Department in an effort to garner MP support.[65] Recognizing that MPs could shape the final privatization legislation, British Telecom had representatives present at all the debates in the Commons and in Standing Committees.[66]

Oftel

The 1984 telecommunications act created the Office of Telecommunications, headed by a director general of telecommunications (DGT). Oftel, at least under the direction of Professor Carsberg, has served as a strong independent advocate of competition in the telecommunications industry. As a result, challenges to uncompetitive behavior on the part of British Telecom often receive sympathetic treatment by Oftel. The agency's rulings in such matters as the British Telecom purchase of Mitel, the IBM and BT joint venture in the VANs market, and the interconnection agreement between Mercury and BT have all been critical of what was viewed as fundamentally uncompetitive behavior by BT.[67]

Oftel's mandate is somewhat vague. To issue policy directives, it needs

---

63. This argument is developed by Noll, "The Political and Institutional Context of Communications Policy," in *Marketplace for Telecommunications: Regulation and Deregulation in Industrialized Democracies*, ed. Marcellus Snow (New York: Longman, 1986), 55–57.

64. See Moon, Richardson, and Smart, "The Privatisation of British Telecom," 349.

65. Karl-Heinz Neumann, "Economic Policy Toward Telecommunications, Information, and the Media in West Germany," in *Marketplace for Telecommunications*, ed. Marcellus S. Snow (New York: Longman, 1986): 131–52.

66. Vickers and Yarrow, *Privatization*, 210.

67. See the analysis of these decisions in Vickers and Yarrow, *Privatization*, chap. 8.

the concurrence of other governmental bodies such as the secretary of state or the Monopoly and Mergers Commission. Therefore, to some extent, its ability to shape telecommunications policy is a function of the support it commands among interested groups, the cabinet and Whitehall. It is clear, however, that interest parties have come to view the agency as a means to prevent anticompetitive behavior on the part of BT and to promote (or prevent, for that matter) further dismantling of entry barriers to the industry. A case in point is the recent *Review of British Telecom's Tariff Charges* conducted by Oftel. Some criticized the agency for embarking on such an "uncalled-for investigation," to which the director replied:

> The system of regulation of telecommunications will work only if it is accepted as responsible by a sufficient proportion of the population. The representations I received—from Members of Parliament of all parties, from representative associations of consumers, from business people and from domestic customers—all indicated very great concern about the way in which the price control formula was working out. In the face of that concern, it would not have been reasonable for a regulator to refuse to investigate the situation.[68]

Oftel has, in effect, been added to the points of access for interested parties seeking to affect entry barriers to the telecommunications industry. In fact, many argue that Oftel—not the Thatcher government—is responsible for promoting competition in the U.K. telecommunications industry.[69]

Pluralism and Political Protectionism

After the 1979 Conservative electoral victory, there was a formidable political coalition favoring liberalization and, eventually, privatization: a government recently elected with a strong House of Commons majority and a powerful body of business consumers. Thatcher was able to enact legislation with the support of large business interests, ignoring the coalition of interests that opposed such measures, including the postal unions, some residential telephone subscribers, and the equipment suppliers. In fact, it is widely believed that the government pushed privatization of the telco (and other concerns for that matter) as part of their campaign against the growing power of unions in the British economy. The Thatcher government believed that union demands for increased wage and decision-making concessions were much more suc-

---

68. Bryan Carsberg, "Regulation of British Telecom: A Reply to Beesley, Laidlaw and Gist," *Telecommunications Policy* 11 (September 1987): 240.
    69. M. E. Beesley, B. H. Laidlaw, and P. Gist, "Prices and Competition on Voice Telephony in the U.K.," *Telecommunications Policy* 11 (September 1987): 230–36.

cessful in the public, as opposed to the private, sector. Privatization, therefore, would weaken the unions' bargaining power.[70]

There were no institutional provisions—as there are in Germany—that forced the government to negotiate a policy compromise that satisfies all major interested parties. This permitted successive Labour governments to ignore the service complaints of business users and it allowed Mrs. Thatcher to implement a set of radical policy changes despite strong protests by Labour and some elements of industry. In short, British political institutions facilitate liberalization of entry barriers because they permit initiatives based on minimum winning coalitions. Because there are always major losers associated with the reduction of entry barriers, political institutions that force consensus policy-making inhibit procompetitive policies.

Assessing the Impact of Privatization and Competition

Britain offers a rare opportunity to evaluate the implications of liberalization and privatization on the performance of the telecommunications industry. Unfortunately, the government initiated change on both variables simultaneously, making it difficult to separate the independent effect of either. An attempt to separate their impact is important because many question whether privatization has had any impact, independent of increased competition, on the performance of British Telecom.[71]

Three areas are examined below that shed some light on the controversy: BT's response to competition and privatization, the impact of liberalization on the customer premises equipment market, and liberalization's implications for the telecommunications services sector.

Three different sets of data are presented in order to evaluate the impact of the organizational changes on BT's performance: changes in BT's corporate strategy, public impressions of BT's performance, and quantitative measures of productivity.

Changes in BT's Corporate Strategy

Following the 1981 decision severing British Telecom's ties to the Post Office, management embarked upon a major restructuring of the corporation. Anticipating increased competition, the organizational changes were designed to provide management with better financial controls and to facilitate the marketing of BT products and services.

Under increasing pressure from competition, British Telecom became

---

70. Heldrun Arbomeit, "Privatisation in Great Britain," *Annals of Public and Cooperative Economy* 57 (1986): 153–79.

71. Vickers and Yarrow, *Privatization*.

more dependent upon profits to fund capital investments, necessary if it was to compete effectively. In response to these pressures, BT was divided into profit centers that could be more easily held accountable. Four main divisions were created: *Inland Division* is responsible for the provision of local and domestic long-distance service, *British Telecommunications Equipment* (BTE) handles the sales of customer premises equipment, both residential and business, *Major Systems* does all of the purchasing of main exchange and transmission equipment, and *British Telecom International* provides all of BT's international services.[72] The chairman's office is no longer the sole profit center; each division is now evaluated according to their respective contribution to BT's overall profitability. Each division now has the opportunity to shape its business plans to best exploit their particular market niches—British Telecom International, for example, has short- and long-term business plans that are very different from those of British Telecom Equipment.

Another significant organizational development was BT's decision to assemble a marketing force of about 1,000 sales people. Prior to liberalization, BT had no dedicated sales force—its technicians doubled as order takers.[73] This new group is responsible for marketing both customer premises equipment and value-added data services to consumers and businesses. At the same time, BT opened forty telephone concessions to display and sell BT telephone sets and other customer premises equipment.

All of these measures have been designed to turn a passive, fairly unresponsive government bureaucracy into a much more aggressive commercial provider of telecommunications services and equipment.

Public Perceptions of BT Service

Public opinion has not rated privatization a success. Residential consumers continue to rate BT service poorly, but it is not at all clear that this is a relevant measure of success.[74] Similar dissatisfaction was found following the liberalization of the long-distance carriers in the United States.[75] Two of the most serious problems associated with government monopolists are overstaffing and subsidized local telephone rates. Privatization and liberalization will force

---

72. *Financial Times*, 24 October 1983, 9.

73. "Communications: British Telecom Gets Aggressive," *Business Week*, 16 November 1981, 160.

74. A July 1987 report of the National Consumer Council presented the results of an opinion poll conducted in the United Kingdom. The poll indicated that Britons consider British Telecom to be the worst public service in the country and that its performance had significantly declined since it was privatized. See Carl Edgar Law, "Telecommunications in the UK since Liberalization," *Business Communications Review* (March-April 1988): 47.

75. See Alan Stone, *Wrong Number: The Breakup of AT&T* (New York: Basic Books, 1989).

carriers to reduce their labor forces and to price services closer to their actual costs. In the short run, both measures are certain to provoke displeasure on the part of residential consumers.

Business consumers, both from the private and the public sector, have also expressed frustration with the speed and effectiveness of network modernization. There is widespread feeling that BT has poorly managed the introduction of digital exchanges. The System X exchanges—which are the main component of the program—proved to be much more expensive and unwieldy than initially expected. To be fair, the decision to adopt the System X was made long before the privatization of BT, and the reasons for selecting this technology had much more to do with the government's industrial policy than the efficient introduction of digital switching into the United Kingdom.

The most damning criticism of BT is that it has neither improved its service nor noticeably reduced its tariffs to business consumers. A 1988 survey of telecommunications managers conducted by the Telecommunications Managers Association found that most respondents were dissatisfied with BT's service, more so than was the case in prior surveys.[76] There are also no indications that business users are paying significantly lower costs as a result of liberalization. It is estimated that business users have seen their telecommunications costs rise about 5 percent over the past ten years. Nevertheless, they do fare somewhat better than their European counterparts: French business users have seen their costs rise 11 percent over this ten-year period, while the Italians have faced a 64 percent increase.[77]

Liberalization of telecommunications in Britain has yet to generate important payoffs in the penetration of basic telephone service. In 1980, just prior to the initial telecommunications bill introduced by the Thatcher government, the United Kingdom had 331 main telephone lines per thousand inhabitants, compared to 295 in France and 334 in Germany. By 1984, the United Kingdom had 371 main lines per thousand inhabitants, compared to 402 in France and 403 in Germany.[78] Since the 1981 telecommunications bill, the United Kingdom has, in fact, fallen behind France and Germany in terms of telephone penetration. The introduction of competition has yet to reverse this relative deterioration of the British telephone network.

Comparative measures of productivity are an ideal yardstick for evaluating performance. The limited number of productivity comparisons undertaken have not been favorable to BT. The simplest measure of productivity is tele-

---

76. David Thomas, "Business 'Dissatisfied with BT Service,'" *Financial Times* (London), 18 March 1988, 7.

77. These figures are from Logica and were reported in John Lamb, "Bilan controverse de la privatisation de British Telecom," *Télécoms International* (October 1987): 14.

78. International Telecommunications Union, *Yearbook of Common Carrier Telecommunication Statistics* (Geneva: ITU, 1986).

TABLE 8.1.   Telephone Lines per Employee for Selected Countries

Country/System	Lines per Employee
Netherlands	200
Bell Canada	185
Italy	158
NTT (Japan)	151
Nynex (N.Y. State)	151
France	138
Spain	129
Germany	122
Sweden	110
British Telecom	94
Average	136

Source: Carl Edgar Law, "Telecommunications in the UK since Liberalisation," *Business Communications Review,* March–April, 1988, 51.

phone lines per telco employee. This is a weak measure for a variety of reasons: it ignores national cost differentials between capital and labor, the obligations of the telcos to provide certain social goods, government and union-imposed restrictions on hiring and firing, etc. Table 8.1 presents these data for selected developed countries. British Telecom ranks last among these ten countries. Even granting that there are difficulties in using this measure, BT's last place ranking is evidence of low productivity.

Efforts to measure productivity more carefully have produced similar, if somewhat less damning, results. Molyneux and Thompson have extended Prykes's 1981 study of the 1968–78 performance of the British telco to 1978 through 1985.[79] They reported a decline in BT performance after liberalization but, as Foreman-Peck and Manning point out, this is somewhat unfair, given Prykes's inflated estimates of productivity growth during the 1968–78 period.[80] Using much more refined measures of productivity, Foreman-Peck and Manning generate a comparison of BT's productivity with that of the telcos in Italy, Germany, Denmark, Spain, and Norway. Their comparative figures are presented in table 8.2. BT's performance is ranked below that of

---

79. R. Molyneux and D. Thompson, "Nationalised Industry Performance: Still Third-Rate?" *Fiscal Studies* 8 (1987): 48-82; Pryke, *Nationalized Industries.*

80. James Foreman-Peck and Dorothy Manning, "How Well is BT Performing? An International Comparison of Telecommunications Total Factor Productivity," *Fiscal Studies* (August 1988): 54–67.

TABLE 8.2.   International Telecommunications Productivity

	Labor Productivity Output Measures[a]			Total Factor Productivity Output Measures		
	Short-haul Equivalent	Long-haul Equivalent	Number of Calls	Short-haul Equivalent	Long-haul Equivalent	Number of Calls
Denmark (1985)	122	128	153	121	127	152
Germany (1985)	111	86	81	107	83	78
Italy (1986)[b]	96	57	101	80	47	84
Norway (1986)[b]	130	84	NA	185	119	NA
Spain (1986)	88	80	NA	92	84	NA
United Kingdom	100	100	100	100	100	100

Source: James Foreman-Peck and Dorothy Manning, "How Well is BT Performing? An International Comparison of Telecommunications Total Factor Productivity," *Fiscal Studies,* August 1988.

Notes: The table indices are the results of the Total Productivity Factor developed by Foreman-Peck and Manning. The higher the index number, the more productive the organization. Comparisons between pairs of organizations excluding BT cannot be made with these measures. NA = not available.

[a] Output measures consist of inland and international calls and "other" output. Inland calls are represented in each of the three different ways shown. The three measures (short-haul, long-haul, and number of calls) are alternatives.

[b] Capital account work has been excluded from the inputs.

Norway and Denmark, similar to that of Germany, and above that of Spain and Italy.

There is little question that BT's productivity has not significantly responded to the 1981 liberalization and the 1984 privatization. One explanation is that market structure and ownership simply do not matter. Another is that it is still too early to make a judgment on BT's response to liberalization and privatization. Most of the productivity measures are sensitive to two important inputs: labor and capital. Up until 1984, BT had little control over either of these factors. The telco did not have the flexibility to reduce its work force because public corporations are subject to political pressures regarding employment. Second, even during the early part of the Thatcher government—before privatization—the Treasury continued to ration capital spending.

Political constraints created an entity that underinvested, was overmanned, subsidized residential subscribers, and was not responsive to consumers. By 1985, most of these constraints were significantly reduced. To the extent permitted by the new regulatory regime, BT invested heavily, reduced their labor force, and cut tariffs in the areas most threatened by competition (business services, leased-lines, and long distance, for example). In the short run, all of these measures created dissatisfaction on the part of employees, consumers, and even shareholders.

Telephone Equipment

The government's liberalization of the telephone equipment market was designed to encourage entrepreneurs to develop and market new communications products, to widen the range of products, and to sharpen the performance of BT. In the short run, the policy succeeded primarily in addressing the latter two goals.

BT's Response

British Telecom responded to this area of liberalization by first expanding the range of telephone handsets available to subscribers.[81] In response to the liberalization of the small PBX market—Private Branch Exchanges with less than 100 extensions—BT widened the range of products available to include, for example, a popular PBX manufactured by Mitel. Establishing ties with foreign suppliers in Japan, the United States, and Canada permitted BT to expand its product offerings quickly.[82] It also formed a new subsidiary, Merlin, to develop a small but sophisticated digital exchange.[83]

Recognizing that liberalization would bring in new competitors, BT moved swiftly to commit customers to new products.[84] Because this equipment has an expected life of at least eight years, BT was able to tie up a good proportion of the market, leaving fewer opportunities for new entrants into the market.[85]

In 1983, BT started supplying larger PBXs to businesses—an activity left to the manufacturers prior to that time. This move, in addition to its aggressive marketing of smaller PBX systems, resulted in an actual growth in BT's share of the PBX market since liberalization. Table 8.3 presents the value of PBX sales for the years 1978 through 1984, distinguishing between PBXs sold by BT versus those sold directly to the customer. In 1986, five years after liberalization of the supply of telephone handsets and three years after the liberalization of the smaller PBX market, the *Financial Times* reported that BT had "retained a surprisingly large share of the equipment

---

81. Logica, *Communications in Europe*, 78.

82. *Business Week*, 16 November 1981, 160.

83. *Financial Times* (London), 20 April 1983, 10.

84. A similar strategy was undertaken by AT&T in the face of a liberalized U.S. customer premises equipment market. See Raymond M. Duch, "The Effects of the AT&T Consent Decree on the Telephone Equipment Market," paper presented at the Fourth Annual Research Conference of the Association for Public Policy Analysis and Management, Minneapolis, Minn., 1982.

85. Jason Crisp, "BT Responds Quickly to Fend Off Its Rivals," *Financial Times* (London), 6 January 1986, S6.

TABLE 8.3. PBX Sales in the United Kingdom

	1978	1979	1980	1981	1982	1983
U.K.-manufactured PBX sales by BT	6.3	18.2	33.2	81.1	86.8	90.2
U.K.-manufactured PBX direct to customers	26.6	26.4	48.6	56.0	64.7	59.9
Total U.K.-manufactured PBX sales	32.9	44.6	81.8	137.1	151.5	150.1

Source: Scott, Goff, Layton.

market from telephone handsets to large and powerful private exchanges (PABXs)."

Rather interestingly, the very political structure that facilitated the challenge to BT's equipment monopoly also aided the company's efforts to prevent serious erosion of its share of the equipment market. Management exploited the political process to keep foreign suppliers out and to impede the approval of competing equipment.

Competition did not flourish in the initial period following liberalization because BT and the major British equipment manufacturers, Plessey, GEC, Standard Telephones and Cable, and Thorn, convinced the government to exclude foreign competitors from the market for three years. The British manufacturers did not enthusiastically support liberalization of the equipment market because they had benefitted from BT's preferential purchases of their products for many years. Aggressive competition in the customer equipment market might reduce BT's market share, thereby seriously jeopardizing manufacturers' revenues from their lucrative contracts with British Telecom.[86]

Second, BT and British equipment manufacturers were able to convince DTI officials of the importance of maintaining very high standards for equipment connected to the BT network (to the point of dictating the acceptable sound pressure level to be present at the earpiece of a telephone instrument). By setting very high standards, the government made type approval for foreign equipment difficult. This continued to be a complaint by foreign equipment manufacturers until 1988.[87]

Finally, British Telecom maintained an important advantage in the equip-

86. *Financial Times* (London), 20 April 1983.

87. See Christopher R. Thomas, "Vendors, Users Grapple with Liberalization in the UK," *Telephony*, 23 September 1985, 48-50; Guy de Jonquieres, "UK Telephone Sales: Mickey Mouse Moves In," *Financial Times*, 28 December 1983, 9.

ment market: the company's size, its reputation, and subscriber fears that they would not receive fair treatment from BT if they installed non-BT equipment.[88]

Prices Fall and Choice Increases

Even though BT was able to retain, if not increase, its share of the customer equipment market, a flood of new products entered the United Kingdom, expanding the choices available to end users and significantly reducing prices.[89] In 1986, the *Financial Times* noted that:

> Since liberalisation, there has been a flood of equipment trying to get into the British market. So far the approval authorities have given the go-ahead to about 50 new makes of private exchange, about 40 smaller private exchanges known as key systems, about 400 types of telephone and about 20 ranges of cordless phones.
>
> Before liberalisation, by contrast, about 10 manufacturers supplied a limited range of private exchanges to the UK market.[90]

Prices have responded accordingly, dropping considerably in the period following liberalization.

The short-term benefits of liberalization have not included the development of many new products by British industry or the entry of many small entrepreneurial firms. While the world market for customer premises equipment had become increasingly competitive—in terms of price, features, and technology—the major British manufacturers, such as GEC and Plessey, accustomed to a guaranteed home market, had become quite uncompetitive in international markets. As a result, when British entry barriers were lowered, their products proved increasingly unattractive to British consumers. As a symptom, Law estimates that British companies have seen their share of the U.K. Telecom equipment market drop from 20 percent in its heyday to 4 percent today.[91]

Liberalization of customer premises equipment had two major impacts. First, British Telecom fought hard to maintain its share of the industry. This is hardly unexpected. But, in order to retain as much of its market share as

---

88. D. J. Thompson, "Privatisation in the UK," *European Economic Review* 31 (1987): 368–74.

89. Thomas, "Vendors, Users Grapple with Liberalization."

90. David Thomas, "The UK Equipment Suppliers Show Variety on Offer," *Financial Times* (London), 1 December 1986, S5.

91. Law, "Telecommunications in the UK."

possible, the company was forced to improve marketing, reduce its costs, lower prices, and increase the range of products it sold—exactly the goals of liberalization. Second, the British equipment market was flooded with competitors and prices dropped dramatically.

Telecommunications Services

Thatcher's efforts to liberalize the telecommunications services industry had two important features. First, her government passed legislation in 1981 and 1984 promoting competition in services by licensing a competing service provider, Mercury Ltd., and permitting the establishment of competing VAN services. More important, though, the government created a constituency for further service liberalization and established institutional channels (most significantly, Oftel) through which these demands could be accommodated. These efforts to induce competition have not always been successful. But, where effective competition has emerged, Britain has benefitted from a proliferation of services and falling prices. While British Telecom has not lost significant market share to competitors, the introduction of competition has provoked an aggressive response from the company.

Mercury's Competing Network

Mercury's initial plans called for the provision of domestic and international leased circuits to businesses. These would be high-speed digital circuits that could be used for the transmission of data, voice, facsimile, video, electronic mail, information services, and value-added services.[92] This was a market in which BT had come under increasing criticism because of poor quality transmissions and the long wait for leased circuits. Evidence regarding the impact of competition in the leased circuit business is mixed. Immediately after the legislation was passed, British Telecom made significant efforts to improve its service, but, more recently, complaints have risen regarding service quality and pricing. One explanation might be the limited area in which Mercury offers competing leased-line coverage.

When Mercury initially received its license, British Telecom responded very aggressively to the threat of competition in the leased-circuit market. As the *Financial Times* pointed out,

> Before Mercury was set up, business customers complained bitterly about the lack of high speed data communications from BT, the restricted

---

92. Logica, *Communications in Europe.*

range of apparatus that could be used on the network and the inordinate delays in providing private circuits. But in the last three years, BT has been responding to the threat of competition with an alacrity no one dreamed it possessed.[93]

Before Mercury had the chance to sign on its first customer, BT took preemptive action, cutting trunk charges on busy routes and significantly expanding the availability of digital links for business.[94] BT also adopted other measures to undercut Mercury's efforts to win market share. They established a National Network Unit in 1982 that was specifically designed to compete with Mercury and adopted a host of new services aimed at improving its competitiveness in business communications.[95]

Mercury initially thought that large businesses in the London financial district would be its primary market. Businesses in the City had been particularly critical of BT services and, therefore, were considered a receptive market. BT countered by significantly upgrading service in the area and announcing plans for a London Overlay Network consisting of high-speed digital fiber optic links. As early as October 1981, BT committed $30 million to this project.

These initial efforts by BT ensured that competition in this market segment would be introduced at a relatively sluggish pace. BT effectively slowed down Mercury's expansion plans by taking some of the attraction out of their leased-line offerings. Reduced revenues have contributed to Mercury's slow-paced extension of its leased-line service. By 1988, Mercury's offerings in this area remained quite limited, serving only a small number of areas and business.[96] By 1987, the company accounted for less than 1 percent of total telecommunications service revenues in the United Kingdom.[97] Without much competition, BT has behaved as one would expect: prices on leased circuits have risen considerably (60 percent in 1988), the waiting period has increased, and service has been spotty.[98]

---

93. Jason Crisp, "Mercury," *Financial Times* (London), 14 January 1985, 5.

94. *Financial Times* (London), 24 October 1983, 9.

95. Included among these improvements were the following:
   1. the expansion of the Kilostream digital private circuit service (these are circuits that can carry voice, data, and text simultaneously);
   2. expansion of the packet switched service, including an increase in the number of exchanges from 12 to 20 in 1983;
   3. modernization of the telex network;
   4. provision of private network packages, including local area networks for corporate customers;
   5. discounts of up to 15 percent for large users of international leased circuits.
See Logica, *Communications in Europe*, 41.

96. Hugo Dixon, "BT: Clearing the Line on Prices," *Financial Times* (London), 28 June 1988.

97. Lamb, "Bilan controverse," 16.

98. David Thomas, "Oftel Challenges 60% Rise in BT Private Circuit Tariffs," *Financial Times*, 29 January 1988.

The meager payoffs of liberalization have prompted a number of criticisms. First, some argue that the concept of effective competition among a duopoly such as BT and Mercury is unlikely. Collusion, they argue, will inevitably occur, resulting in monopolistic practices. These critics suggest either reducing the entry barriers to competition (i.e., licensing other network service providers) or increasing the regulatory oversight over the companies (in particular, subject their tariffs to the same restrictions that are imposed on residential rates). A second group of critics recognize that it will take some time for the second carrier to invest in the necessary physical plant to enable it to compete effectively with BT. They propose some regulation of business tariffs until the market becomes effectively competitive.

Finally, there are those who argue that increased regulation is not necessary with regard to leased-line tariffs. The only action they recommend is the reduction in entry barriers. If British Telecom faces levels of demand that it cannot accommodate and if they persist in raising tariffs, the solution is to reduce entry barriers. Either the tariffs are uneconomically high, in which case there will be entry, or they are competitive, in which case they will not attract new competitors.

The problem, most seem to agree, is not the viability of competition, but the lack of it. This might be a technical problem (it takes time for competitors to build the necessary infrastructure), in which case it will solve itself in the near future. Alternatively, it might be a regulatory problem— effective competition can only be assured if more than one competing carrier is licensed.

Value-Added Networks and Resale of Leased-Line Circuits

A value-added network is one that allows information to be interchanged directly between users of the service, but not without first being stored by the service provider for the purpose of subsequent retrieval, forwarding, or processing such that the delivered messages have been clearly altered as to format, protocol, or content.[99] Until 1981, all these services were a monopoly of British Telecom. By liberalizing the licensing of competing VANs, the government hoped to greatly expand the service offerings in the United Kingdom and promote the development of a VANs industry in the country. Although the licensing regulations adopted were unnecessarily complex and restrictive, they did promote the development of a relatively strong VANs industry.

As a result of this liberalization, the United Kingdom is the largest European market for VANs. As I pointed out earlier, VANs generated $919 million in revenues in the United Kingdom, compared to $666 million in

---

99. Logica, *Communications in Europe*, 43-44.

France and only $428 million in West Germany.[100] By 1985, there were over 600 services licensed in the United Kingdom (although only a small number generated sizeable revenues).

The government's VANs regulations established fairly strict and complex regulations in order to ensure that VANs operators did not simply lease telecommunications lines and then resell them to businesses. Government officials believed that this would seriously reduce BT and Mercury revenues. Since 1984, potential new entrants to the VANs industry have pressured the government to modify the licensing regulations. In 1987, responding to these pressures, the government significantly simplified and further opened up the VANs market. In addition to simplifying the licensing procedure, the new regulations permit limited resale of capacity for data transmission.[101]

Unconstrained by regulatory ambiguities, British Telecom has responded aggressively to the threat of competing VAN service providers with the introduction of a wide range of value-added services. In the early 1970s, they pioneered videotext with the introduction of Prestel, allowing subscribers with Prestel terminals to access central data bases over the telephone network. Responding to potential VAN competition, BT recently introduced an electronic mail box service provided by their subsidiary, Telecom Gold, Ltd.; a credit card verification service offered by another subsidiary, Telecom Silver, Ltd.; and Hotline, a computer-based news and business information service. British Telecom also dominates the market for audio and video conferences and radio paging. In a step widely criticized for its monopolistic goals and eventually prohibited by the government, British Telecom attempted to launch a managed data network service in partnership with IBM. The Office of Telecommunications and potential competitors predicted that such a formidable partnership would result in their monopolization of this part of the VAN market.[102]

The successful experiment with liberalized VAN regulations put added pressure on the government to permit the resale of leased-line capacity.[103] The resale of leased-line circuits has been widely rejected in Europe because it threatens telco revenues. It is attractive to businesses, including VAN licensees, because resale allows them to design private networks that make optimal economic use of leased capacity. Oftel served as an important conduit

100. These figures are from Frost & Sullivan Ltd., as reported in John Blau, "Germany Lags in VANS," *Communications Week International,* 4 June 1990, 10.

101. David Thomas, "Government Moves to Extend Freeing of Telecom Services," *Financial Times* (London), 18 March 1988, 5.

102. Jason Crisp, "Value-Added Network Services," *Financial Times* (London), 14 January 1985, 4.

103. See Julian Patterson, "New Rules Applied to an Old Game," *Communications Week International,* 29 May 1989, S10.

for demands that resale be liberalized because of its leading role in rewriting the Network Code of Practice that establishes regulations for those licensed to provide network services. The government established Oftel with the understanding that it would solicit a wide range of industry and user opinion. As I argued earlier, such inclusive policy consultations bias the outcome in favor of reducing industry entry barriers. This was precisely the outcome; Oftel officials reported that a majority of the responses to the agency's consultative document favored liberalization.[104] In 1989, Lord Young announced the elimination of restrictions on resale, the last major barrier to competition in the British telecommunications industry.

Competing Mobile Telephone Networks

Certainly one of the greatest successes of liberalization has been the proliferation of mobile telephone subscribers as a result of the government's 1984 decision to license competing private service providers. As a result, there are about eleven mobile telephones per thousand population in Britain compared to two in France and Germany.[105] More recently, the government once again took the European lead and licensed two other mobile communication technologies: personal communicator networks (PCNs) and telepoint. In both cases, there will be multiple private licensees competing for subscribers. One of the interesting implications of this proliferation of mobile communications networks in the United Kingdom is that they have the potential of offering local telephone service that competes directly with BT.[106]

Cable Television: An Alternative Carrier

Another constituency for further liberalization and a potential competitor to British Telecom is the cable television industry. Cable licenses have been awarded throughout the United Kingdom to private firms, many of them partially owned by U.S. communications interests. Unlike the situation in the United States, these cable licensees are urged to provide telecommunications services by U.K. regulations. The principal restriction is that they can only provide these services in their license area. Cable interests have begun a campaign to convince the government and regulatory officials that they should be permitted to cooperate with other licensees in other areas in order to broaden their telecommunications service. When the duopoly review is conducted in November 1990, this proposal will likely receive favorable con-

---

104. Patterson, "New Rules," S10.
105. "Telephones that Get Up and Go," *Economist*, 16 September 1989, 71.
106. "Telephones that Get Up and Go."

sideration. If cable interests are permitted to provide national telecommunications service over their networks, this will represent a further competitive threat to British Telecom.

Explaining the Results of Liberalization and Privatization

The liberal policy initiatives adopted by the British government have not had the unqualified successes that proponents of competition and privatization might have expected. There are two reasons for this, one economic the other political.

First, markets take some time to adjust to major changes in regulations. In some cases, such as the market for leased circuits, effective competition will take time to develop because of the costs of building the necessary physical plant.

More important, liberalization policies have not always had their expected effect because they were designed to accommodate a number of different interested parties affected by the reduction of entry barriers. While the Thatcher government ignored certain powerful interests (such as labor and consumers), compromises were made on behalf of other interested parties. As a result, the liberalization measures that were adopted reflected contradictory objectives. On the one hand, the policies promoted competition but, at the same time, they were designed to minimize their negative impact on certain constituents.

Thatcher's government was careful to protect the interests of residential subscribers and British manufacturing firms. The preeminent social goal pursued by the government in designing more liberal policies for the industry was maintaining universal telephone service. Because BT is the only provider of local telephone service, the government was concerned that the goal of universal service not be compromised.

BT also plays an important role in the government's industrial policy. The world market for telecommunications services and products is considered a prime growth industry, one in which the United Kingdom would like to regain lost market share. Thatcher's government was quite sensitive to the important role that BT, one of the United Kingdom's largest corporations, can play in the global telecommunications industry. In order to nurture the competitive potential of British Telecom in global markets, the government has been reluctant to adopt procompetitive measures that might weaken the company. For example, the option of divesting BT of its local or long-distance responsibilities was rejected because it threatened the company's global stature.

Industrial policy considerations have also led the government to restrict foreign participation in the British telecommunications industry. The goal was to encourage the development of a strong, indigenous telecommunications sector by shielding it from international competition. This obviously conflicted with the government's stated desire to see competition and product options flourish in the United Kingdom. British consumers and businesses would have a much wider selection of competing services and products if foreign competitors were given free access to the U.K. markets.

Finally, the government's fiscal goals have also conflicted with the desire for more competition. The planned privatization of British Telecom served an important fiscal goal: the funds generated by the sale would be used to reduce government debt. Prior to the public sale of BT stock in 1985, the government was reluctant to subject British Telecom to excessive competitive pressures because it wanted to enhance BT's value to investors. Any initiatives that might have been perceived by the investment community as encroaching upon BT's revenue potential would have lowered the value of its stock.

Conclusion

One reading of the data presented here suggests the total irrelevance of ownership and market structure for the performance of the British telco: it performed poorly as a private monopolist in the pre–World War I era, as a public monopolist in the sixty years that followed its nationalization in 1912, and as a private entity facing competition in the post-1984 period. The explanation is political. During the early period of private ownership, the threat of nationalization by the government discouraged capital investment and expansion. Government ownership imposed considerable political constraints on the telco that undermined efforts to invest in capital improvements. Finally, the Thatcher government's legislation privatizing and liberalizing the industry incorporated a number of political compromises that, at least in the short term, have weakened some of the economic benefits of the initiatives.

The recent British experience also provides an important insight into the political factors that facilitate privatization and the lowering of industry entry barriers. Pluralist institutions in Britain have favored the development of strong demand for change, and they have afforded government the flexibility to implement far-reaching changes based on the support of minimum winning coalitions. This contrasts with the French and German cases where statist and corporatist institutions inhibited demand for, and implementation of, such policy changes.

CHAPTER 9

Conclusion

The Institutional Factor

This book has analyzed the century-long history of telecommunications policy and tested a number of hypotheses regarding the impact of institutional variables on public policy. The findings take issue with both the conventional explanations for the poor performance of government-owned entities and the cross-national differences in economic policies (liberalization of entry barriers and privatization).

When scholars ask the question, "Does politics matter?", they typically are concerned with the impact of ideology, partisan differences, or elections on policy decisions.[1] I have argued and, I hope, convincingly demonstrated that these variables do not adequately account for cross-national differences in telecommunications policies.

The literature evaluating state, as opposed to private, ownership takes a narrow economic perspective, assuming that political effects are dichotomous: significant under government ownership and minimal for private firms.[2] In the case of telecommunications services, it is argued that state ownership can seriously undermine capital investment (either encouraging too much, too little, or simply inappropriate allocations). The absence of a profit

1. See Richard Rose, *Do Parties Make a Difference,* 2d ed. (Catham: Catham House, 1984); Francis G. Castle, *The Impact of Parties: Politics and Policies in Democratic Capitalist States* (Beverly Hills, Calif.: Sage Publications, 1982); James E. Alt and K. Alec Chrystal, *Political Economics* (Brighton, Sussex: Wheat Sheaf Books, 1983); Douglas A. Hibbs, *The Political Economy of Industrial Democracies* (Cambridge, Mass.: Harvard University Press, 1987); and James Alt, "Political Parties, World Demand, and Unemployment: Domestic and International Sources of Economic Activity," *American Political Science Review* 79, no. 4 (1985): 1016–40.

2. See L. De Alessi, "An Economic Analysis of Government Ownership and Regulation: Theory and the Evidence from the Electric Power Industry," *Public Choice* 19 (1974): 1–42; Richard Zeckhauser and Murray Horn, "The Control and Performance of State-Owned Enterprises," paper presented at the conference on Privatization in Britain and North America sponsored by the Bradley Policy Research Center, University of Rochester, Washington, D.C., 1987; and Richard Schmalensee, *The Control of Natural Monopolies* (Lexington, Mass.: Lexington Books, 1979), chap. 6.

constraint is associated with inattention to consumer demands and the development of unprofitable services and products. The evidence reported here suggests that such a view does not comport with reality. There are many exceptions to this generalization: state-owned firms that have performed well and privately owned firms that have registered mediocre performance levels. An adequate explanation of these differences requires a reconceptualization of the political effect.

I have argued for the primacy of institutional variables as an explanation for policy outcomes (the success or failure of government ownership) and for changes in economic policies (specifically, liberalization and privatization). Differences in the performance of national telcos are not accounted for by ownership per se, but rather by institutional factors that determine the extent of political control over management. Greater degrees of political control—which is very different than ownership—have traditionally detracted from the economic performance of public enterprises.

Similarly, governments have embraced liberalization and privatization policies with varying degrees of enthusiasm because the demands for such policies fare better in some institutional settings than in others. Policies liberalizing entry barriers or privatizing state-owned enterprises are more readily adopted in nations with pluralist, as opposed to statist or corporatist, institutions.

Government Versus Private Ownership

A principal goal of this book is to understand why government ownership seems to work in some cases but does not in others. The explanation is "institutional design." Much of the literature suggests that private firms outperform state-owned entities because of the incentive structures facing management. Private managers are rewarded for making a profit, while public managers are encouraged to pursue a variety of other political and social objectives. But government can design public institutions that minimize the negative impact of political constraints on the performance of publicly owned entities. In essence, it can create institutional settings that afford management more flexibility to pursue efficiency goals. With the appropriate design, management will value economic efficiency and can be sheltered from interests promoting a political or social agenda. Any model explaining the performance differences between private and government-owned firms without taking into account these institutional differences among publicly owned firms is misspecified.

The impact of these institutional differences varies according to the political and economic context. The role of the state in the economy affects the importance of private versus public ownership. Whether a firm is state- or privately owned matters considerably less in a state-dominated economy, like France, than in a "minimalist" state like the United States. Given that political constraints are relatively constant regardless of ownership in France, a better predictor of performance is the institutional link between management and the state. For example, the French government has promoted the formation of a "sympathetic" core of shareholders in French firms privatized by Prime Minister Chirac (*les noyaux durs*) that will ensure that management respects the interests of the French state.[3] Is the management of these firms any more or less free of political control than those directing the relatively autonomous public enterprises like Elf-Aquitaine? I would expect that management in both types of firms face significant political constraints. In a statist economy, the distinction between public and private is often uninformative. A better predictor of behavior and performance is the degree of political control over management.

Where *political* risks are significant, ownership is not a very good predictor of performance because the political constraints on private management seriously discourage investment. Political control over public management is much more benign. This is particularly the case in industries that require substantial capital expenditures. The early history of both the French and British telecommunications industries is testimony to the negative impact of uncertainty regarding governmental policy intentions on development. Private telcos would not commit capital when their concessions faced probable termination and possible nationalization. In contrast, the German telco, which was state operated from its inception, outperformed all of its private counterparts in Europe during the early period of the technology's introduction.

The economic context is also a relevant consideration. An institutional design that might be well adapted to a natural monopoly requiring very significant capital investments and facing very inelastic demand would likely be inappropriate for an industry characterized by highly differentiated consumer demands that are constantly changing. We see this in the evolution of the telecommunications industry from its infrastructural (capital intensive and relatively inelastic demand) to its post-infrastructural (capital costs declining and the elasticity of demand rising) periods. Performance will be less affected by political constraints in the infrastructural, as opposed to the post-infrastructural, period.

Although the popular press and political debates have painted public and private ownership in black and white terms, the evidence presented here indicates that its impact is considerably more complex. A failure to accurately characterize the relationship between government ownership and performance

---

3. Marie Bonnet, "Les grandes manoeuvres autour des privatisées," *La Tribune de l'Expansion*, 28 July 1988, 1.

can seriously distort estimates of the benefits likely to result from privatization.[4] In order to evaluate these benefits, it is important to understand the extent to which existing structures have institutionalized political constraints over management. Where this is significant, privatization is likely to net important performance gains. If such constraints are minimal, the benefits will be small or, possibly, nonexistent.

Entry Barriers

The assumption that lower entry barriers improve the performance of state-owned entities receives strong support in this research, raising the possibility that levels of competition, as opposed to political constraints or ownership, actually account for variations in the performance of state-owned entities. Some reject the argument that government ownership contributes to poor economic performance, insisting that levels of competition account for most variation in performance between privately owned, as opposed to state-owned, enterprises. Simply turning *government* monopolies into *private* monopolies, they argue, will have little impact on economic efficiency.[5] My evidence in this respect suggests that, at a minimum, there is an independent effect from the political constraints variable. Certainly, the regression analysis of historical data supports the political constraints hypothesis. On the other hand, the case studies suggest that competition might have a stronger impact on performance than political constraints.

The case of British Telecom is certainly the most puzzling. In the activities where the company retained a monopoly after privatization—primarily residential telephone service, including most long-distance service—BT continues to turn in a disappointing performance. Accordingly, some have concluded that privatizing a public monopoly is unlikely to generate much improved economic performance. However, such a verdict may be premature. British Telecom was only privatized in 1984 and remains burdened by earlier mistakes, including the commitment to purchase System-X public exchanges that cost BT dearly and slowed their efforts to digitize the telephone network. And while BT has shed a large number of its employees, it will take many years to socialize its work force in the norms of private enterprise.

---

4. This, of course, assumes that the decision to privatize is motivated by economic efficiency goals. As we have seen in the case of Thatcher's privatization initiatives, the motivating factors have been other political considerations, such as reducing the government's borrowing requirements.

5. George Yarrow and John Vickers, "Privatization in Britain," paper presented at the conference on Privatization in Britain and North America, Bradley Policy Research Center, Washington, D.C., 1987, 50.

An even more fundamental problem was the British government's decision to maintain both competitive and monopolistic activities in one entity.[6] Cross-subsidization of competitive activities with revenues from monopoly services is virtually a certainty in these situations because of the costs to regulatory authorities of ferreting out all of such occurrences. The combination of both privatizing British Telecom and introducing competition put increased pressure on management to cut prices and invest heavily in competitive activities. Revenues to support these activities could easily be generated in the sectors where entry barriers remained prohibitively high. BT management has behaved as expected: neglecting activities where entry barriers are high and focusing its attention and resources on those areas threatened by competition.

France Télécom raises just the opposite issue. Without privatization, the entity's performance has improved significantly in the last decade. Some might argue that the French case illustrates the importance of market structure, as opposed to ownership, in explaining economic performance. This is illusory. First, the French have not significantly lowered entry barriers to the industry. Rather, they have permitted some limited, state-guided liberalization, competition that remains under the control of the French state. Second, while the French have not privatized their telco, they have reduced the extent of political control over management by liberalizing access to the credit markets and permitting the entity to establish fairly autonomous subsidiaries.

Why do Policies Diverge?

Although faced with similar technological and economic changes in the telecommunications industry, the three cases, France, the United Kingdom, and Germany, each responded with very different policies. I attribute the differences to the distinctive political institutions in each of these countries. The United Kingdom, dominated by pluralist institutions, is the most receptive to both privatization and liberalization initiatives. On the other hand, France, with its statist traditions, is less fertile ground for these policy initiatives, and Germany, characterized as corporatist, is most reluctant to adopt such measures.

In the case of telecommunications policy, there is a tendency to assume a trend in the developed world toward more liberal regulation and private ownership. Such a model resembles similar cross-national characterizations of government social expenditures, health policy, and financial deregulation, for

---

6. John Vickers and George Yarrow, *Privatization: An Economic Analysis* (Cambridge, Mass.: MIT Press, 1988), 211–12.

example.[7] This is an essentially apolitical explanation for policy change because it assumes an underlying economic, social, or diffusion model that minimizes political differences among nation-states.

At least in the case of telecommunications, such a model is clearly inappropriate. The policy responses of the French, German, and U.K. governments have varied considerably. Moreover, the case studies presented here indicate that these variations can be linked to distinctive political processes in each of the countries. Faced with a relatively pluralist environment in the United Kingdom, special interests, dominated by large users in the City financial district, and a very sympathetic Conservative government designed and implemented a dramatic liberalization and privatization of the British telecommunications industry. Much less constrained by organized interests, the French government has had the luxury of moving ahead with liberalization when it believed such a policy would advance the interests of the state's industrial policy (and otherwise ignoring pressures). Moreover, when it decided to move cautiously in the direction of liberalization, the state faced little threat from interest groups opposing these policies. In Germany, the corporatist decision-making institutions seriously retarded any government efforts to liberalize the telecommunications industry. These institutions make it very difficult for new entrants into the industry to have any input into the decision-making process while, at the same time, they give strong veto power to established groups that have the most to lose from liberalization.

Obviously, there is no single determinant of policy differences among nations. There is considerable evidence indicating the explanatory power of other variables, such as ideology, culture, and economic structures. Nevertheless, the findings reported here make a strong case for adding political institutions and policy processes to the factors accounting for cross-national differences in policies regulating the economy.

I now examine, in a somewhat more speculative vein, the implications of these findings.

Institutional Change and the Global Economy

The global economy is rapidly changing and, with it, the challenges facing most major corporations. These changes can be summarized as follows:

- national economies are increasingly open, that is, subject to rising levels of foreign competition;

---

7. See Alt and Chrystal, *Political Economics*; Hugh Heclo, *Modern Social Policies in Britain and Sweden* (London: Macmillan, 1974); Frederick Pryor, *Public Expenditures in Communist and Capitalist Nations* (London: Allen and Unwin, 1968).

- capital is becoming increasingly mobile so that it is rapidly moved around the world;
- the product cycles for most new goods and services are shrinking;
- production decisions (which include, for example, marketing, administration, research, and manufacturing) to a greater and greater extent must be organized on a global scale.[8]

One implication of these changes is that the margin of error on corporate investment decisions is narrowing. Because of shorter product cycles, firms that make incorrect decisions regarding research and development and product introductions will quickly find themselves out of the business or carrying significant losses. The disappearance of U.S. firms from the dynamic random access memory chip market is an excellent case in point. An important element of success in these markets is innovation and the ability to adjust to rapid technological and market changes.[9] Political constraints represent a significant handicap to managements trying to compete in these industries because they inhibit this innovation and adjustment to change.

Another implication of these global changes is the growing importance of liberal markets (specifically those with low entry barriers). In a global economic system where national economies are increasingly subject to foreign competition, government-enforced entry barriers are costly for both local firms and consumers. They tend to drive up the costs of providing goods and services, either as intermediary goods to businesses (e.g., telecommunications services) or final products to consumers (e.g., banking or brokerage services). Second, they undermine the international competitiveness of local firms. National firms that have been fostered on protected markets are at an important disadvantage in international markets that are increasingly competitive. Michael Porter, for example, argues that one of the key elements that contributes to the competitive success of modern firms is the competitiveness of their home markets.[10] As trade barriers fall (for example, within the EC, North America, the ASEAN countries), pressures to promote greater liberalization will increase.

The likelihood that these liberal changes will be implemented is a function of political variables. Figure 9.1 illustrates the political environments that corporations face in the developed market economies. High political entry barriers are characteristic of corporatist regimes (the first row of cells), while

---

8. For an excellent summary of the changes confronting managers of international businesses, see Christopher A. Bartlett and Sumantra Ghoshal, *Managing Across Borders: The Transnational Solution* (Boston: Harvard Business School Press, 1989).

9. Michael E. Porter, *The Competitive Advantage of Nations* (New York: Free Press, 1990).

10. Porter, *Competitive Advantage*.

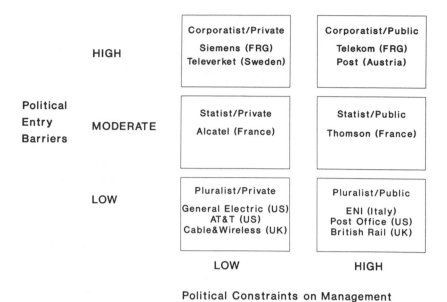

Fig. 9.1.   Political environments facing corporations

pluralist systems (the bottom row of cells) have significantly lower restrictions. Corporatist political institutions are more likely to inhibit liberalization, while pluralist structures promote such initiatives. Statist institutions fall between these two extremes.

The six cells in figure 9.1 represent different political environments confronting the managers of national firms. Strictly focusing on economic performance (the efficient allocation of resources and profitability), the firms in the upper right-hand cell are likely to rank lowest, while those in the lower left-hand quadrant will outperform the others.[11] As the global economy becomes more open and increasingly competitive, the corporate survivors will be firms facing limited political constraints on management and situated in political environments supportive of liberalization.[12] As Freeman points out, this may not bode well for the goals of intragenerational transfers of wealth

---

11. It is important to emphasize that the dependent variable in this analysis is strictly economic performance. There are, of course, a number of other performance measures that one might want to explore, such as the goals of income redistribution or improved quality of life (such as a cleaner environment).

12. This is also one of the conclusions developed by Michael Porter in *Competitive Advantage*.

that he demonstrates are favored by the corporatist/private or corporatist/public firms in figure 9.1.[13]

As economies become increasingly open and subject to international competition, political institutions are pressured to change. Corporatist institutions, for example, are under growing stress in Austria and Germany, where the social consensus that has guided policy-making for the past forty years is showing clear signs of breaking down.[14] In France, statist institutions are slowly assuming greater pluralist characteristics: the courts have assumed more independent authority over evaluating the constitutionality of legislation, and semi-independent regulatory bodies have been created to oversee such newly liberalized economic sectors as finance, the equities market, telecommunications, and audiovisual communications.

Similarly, there is a movement within many countries to reduce the political constraints that impinge on the management of national firms. In some countries, such as the United Kingdom, Canada, and France, this has taken the form of outright privatization, while in other countries, such as Germany and Austria, governments have adopted organizational changes short of privatization designed to accomplish similar goals (telecommunications reforms in Germany are a case in point).

The evidence of change toward more pluralist and private political institutions does not suggest a homogenization of the developed world's political institutions. Nor do these trends undermine the basic conclusions presented earlier. Economies such as those of Germany and Austria, and to a lesser extent Sweden, France, and Italy, have a preponderance of firms that face some combination of corporatist statist and public constraints that are likely to seriously inhibit their ability to adjust to rapid changes occurring in the global economy.

In Germany, Siemens provides an excellent example of corporate strategy heavily influenced by corporatist political institutions. Because of the firm's close working relationship with employee representatives and the government, benefits are generous and it has a larger work force than most of its global competitors.[15] But as compensation for these costs, the firm has a virtually protected monopoly for many of its products sold in Germany. This includes, for example, most of its telecommunications equipment products, large computers, large medical equipment, and power generators. As I pointed out earlier, liberalization of the German market will proceed slowly

---

13. John Freeman, *Democracy and Markets: The Politics of Mixed Economies* (Ithaca, N.Y.: Cornell University Press, 1989).

14. See Freeman, *Democracy and Markets.*

15. For discussions of Siemens's corporate strategy, see Thomas F. O'Boyle, "Siemens Hurls Itself Into Telecom Fray," *Wall Street Journal,* 22 March 1989, A10; David Goodhart, "Radicals and Conservatives in a Cultural Revolution," *Financial Times,* 3 March 1989, 13.

because of the veto power of the corporatist coalition. It is in the interest of most coalition members to maintain the status quo.

Siemens has undoubtedly benefited from this corporatist entente—the firm's profits and accumulated earnings are outstanding. Nonetheless, the firm is ill-prepared for the competitive pressures that it will face in other international markets, where it must compete if it is to continue profitably manufacturing many of its products.[16] Raised in this very protective corporatist environment, the firm lacks the competitive edge to survive in extremely open economies.[17] The areas in which the firm is likely to face the most serious problems are in markets where product cycles are short, demand is very much consumer driven, and price competition is intense. Not all of the firm's activities fall in this category. Certainly consumer electronics would fall in this category, but large manufactured goods, such as generators and transportation equipment, are probably not as seriously affected.

These broad conclusions are based on two very distinctive sets of findings. First, they assume that government constraints result in poor management decisions and liberalized markets enhance the international competitiveness of national firms. Although reasonably well supported by the evidence reported here from the telecommunications industry, there is considerable evidence challenging this conclusion. To some extent, I believe that divergent findings are a result of the distinction that I draw between demand- versus supply-driven industries. Success in the former category is dependent upon management's ability to handle short product cycles, narrowly defined consumer niches, extremely cost-sensitive manufacturing, and intense international competition. In supply-driven markets, consumer demands are less volatile, profit margins per unit are much higher, long-term customer loyalties are important, and international competition is less intense (particularly in industries that are heavily dependent upon government purchasing). This explains, for example, Germany's superior economic performance over the past decade.[18] Much of its success has come in traditional industries that I would characterize as supply, as opposed to demand, driven. The country has been less successful in the more demand-driven industries such as consumer electronics, personal computers, and communications equipment.[19]

---

16. Bartlett and Ghoshal, *Managing Across Borders*.

17. For example, the company's efforts to gain a footing in the U.S. telecommunications market has not been very successful. See O'Boyle, "Siemens," and Goodhart, "Radicals and Conservatives."

18. Peter Katzenstein provides very persuasive documentation of the successes of German political and economic institutions during the last decade in *Industry and Politics in West Germany: The Growth of the Semisovereign State* (Philadelphia: Temple University Press, 1987).

19. Bruce R. Scott, "National Strategies: Key to International Competition," in *U.S. Competitiveness in the World Economy*, ed. Bruce R. Scott and George C. Lodge (Boston: Harvard Business School Press, 1985).

A second finding is that pluralist institutions promote the liberalization of markets while corporatist structures tend to inhibit such policy initiatives. This proposition is entirely independent of my conclusions regarding the implications of liberal markets for economic performance. Moreover, I believe the proposition is consistent with other empirical studies in this area. Although Katzenstein, for example, concludes that Germany's corporatist (or parapublic) institutions have promoted rather impressive economic results, he also characterizes the last decade as one of "institutional stability." He points out that "the Big Change" (*die Wende*) that had been promoted in the early years of the Kohl government never materialized but rather gave way to incremental changes and experimentation within the context of Germany's traditional institutions.[20] While Katzenstein explains the failure of liberalization in terms of institutional stability, I characterize the explanation in terms of barriers to political entry and change.

The Future of European Telecommunications

The European Community is in a stage of institution building. Each of the models discussed here offer very different conceptions of how these institutions should be shaped. None of them is likely to be the exclusive inspiration for community policies. Nonetheless, the political challenges associated with refashioning European governmental and economic institutions greatly favor the emergence, in the next decade, of pluralist, as opposed to corporatist or statist, structures. This conclusion is strongly supported by recent changes in European telecommunications policy.

Many have expressed the fear that greater European integration will result in the emergence of institutions with a distinctly statist and corporatist hue.[21] Corporatist and statist tendencies certainly have considerable weight, both in the Council of Ministers (Germany and France) and within the European Commission. Nonetheless, the constraints of international economic pressures, the dynamics of the institution-building process, and the political forces within the community are clearly moving the community toward a distinctive pluralist/private model, at least for the telecommunications industry.

An important factor favoring pluralist institutional development is the overwhelming international pressure on Europe to enact radical changes to its telecommunications industry. Global economic pressures have focused the community's attention on two primary goals. First, there is a recognition that communications is of increasing importance in most industrial and service

---

20. Katzenstein, *Industry and Politics*, 328.
21. This is certainly the tenor of the criticisms that Prime Minister Margaret Thatcher has leveled against the European Community.

sectors of the economy, and that steps must be taken to improve the quality and reduce the cost of intra-European telecommunications.[22] Unless this is accomplished, European firms will remain at a serious disadvantage compared to their U.S. and Japanese competitors. Second, by reducing intra-European trade barriers, the EC hopes to improve the scale economies for European firms that manufacture telecommunications equipment and provide communications services. This would put European telecommunications firms on a more equal footing with their Japanese and U.S. competitors.

Neither of these goals necessarily dictate a pluralist, statist, or corporatist solution. They require that the European countries move toward common standards in both equipment and service offerings, but this could, in principal, be accomplished under any of the models outlined above. Pluralist/private solutions to these challenges appear to have gained the upper hand because of the political dynamics of the institution-building process.

A corporatist model could be imposed on those European institutions where European interests have very centralized organizations and are willing to participate in consensual decision-making forums. Similarly, the statist model could only succeed if the European Commission were able to command the degree of authority that is exercised by the French state, for example. Neither of these situations is probable because of the important role of the United Kingdom in the European Community. The country's pluralist structures (antagonism between labor and industry and the passive role of the state bureaucracy) are inconsistent with corporatist or statist approaches. On the other hand, because pluralism accommodates diversity by its very nature, this institutional model is most likely to be adopted.

A corporatist approach to the reorganization and deregulation of telecommunications in Europe, whereby governments (national and European) would work closely with industry and labor to refashion the European telecommunications industry, cannot succeed given the absence of such traditions in the United Kingdom. Much more so than in other European countries, the U.K. industry is private and competitive: telephone service is provided by competing private entities; labor's role is adversarial, restricted to negotiating wages and benefits; and the state's role is strictly regulatory. The conditions that might support a corporatist approach to the problem—such as those in Germany where the telco is state-owned, labor participates in its management, and there is minimal competition—simply did not exist and probably could not be developed in the British context.

---

22. See the discussion in Commission of the European Communities, *Towards a Dynamic European Economy—Green Paper on the Development of the Common Market for Telecommunications Services and Equipment* (Brussels: Commission of the European Communities, 1987).

Britain's decision to privatize British Telecom precluded a statist approach to the reorganization of the community's telecommunications service sector. It is certainly possible in most European countries for the state-owned telcos to serve as a vehicle for the commission's telecommunications priorities. Europe-wide services and equipment standards could have been imposed by government-owned monopolies, restricting the opportunities for private entities. This option was essentially foreclosed because of early privatization and liberalization in the United Kingdom. The commission could not very well have established different policies for "private" and "public" markets in Europe. Such a policy would have been ineffective and undermined efforts by the commission to harmonize the community's market.

Most importantly though, the pluralist/private policy approach was adopted because it fit the institution-building agenda of Brussels. The commission wanted to reduce the myriad, different national regulations, standards, and other intra-European entry barriers to the industry. Brussels also hoped to reduce the power of national telcos and ministries, and increase its own authority over the telecommunications sector. For the most part, these goals could not be accomplished through cooperative negotiations with the government ministries, national telcos, and labor representatives. Any type of consensus on reducing their influence over policy-making was unlikely.

To accomplish its goals, the commission has adopted almost unilateral initiatives designed to empower the forces of change and undermine the status quo. First, the commission has set out to enhance the role of private entities in service provision at the expense of public telcos. Second, it adopted policies built on broad-based, pluralist norms of participation and eschewed approaches that required extensive consensual negotiation among established forces in the telecommunications industry (i.e., government-owned telcos and their labor forces). By promoting broad-based participation in the setting of standards and the regulating of the industry, it hoped to undercut the power of national telcos, thereby providing Brussels with an opportunity to increase its authority. The participation of a wide range of interested parties would also provide a check on efforts to impose intra-European barriers to the homogenization of the community's telecommunications service and equipment industries.

Pluralist policies promote high degrees of transparency in their application, as opposed to the relative ambiguity that characterized regulations under the statist (French) and corporatist (German) administrations examined earlier. Their formulation and application is not a matter of negotiation among major interested parties. Rather, they provide very open and easily accessible means for challenging the rules themselves or their application. The establishment of the European Telecommunications Standards Institute (ETSI) by the EC represents an important step in this direction. This body is charged with the responsibility of developing standards for new telecommunications services and equipment. Voting members in ETSI are the representatives of national standards bodies, but their deliberations will include representation of interested parties and the national representatives are specifically charged with eliciting the input of consumers who have often been ignored in these deliberations. One of the main goals of the commission's "Green Paper on Telecommunications" is the separation of regulatory responsibilities from operational functions in an effort to make the process more unbiased and accessible to interested parties. Finally, the Commission has taken positions on the harmonization of standards for ISDN and Open Network Provision (ONP) that will minimize the possibility that telcos could use their monopoly positions to arbitrarily erect entry barriers to potential service or equipment suppliers.

Commission policy initiatives will have the effect of significantly increasing the presence of private, as opposed to public, providers of service and equipment. Since the publication of the Green Paper, the Commission has taken steps to force member nations to liberalize the sales of terminal equipment and the provision of value-added services. Both these initiatives will have the effect of significantly increasing the share of European telecommunication markets accounted for by private firms, at the expense of government-owned telcos. Commission efforts will also ensure that these private providers are not excessively burdened with governmental oversight.[23]

The tactics employed by the commission in its efforts to transform European telecommunications further illustrate the proposition that pluralist, as opposed to corporatist, institutions are more conducive to change. Commission officials adopted a distinctively adversarial, rather than cooperative, strategy to promote the liberalization of the European telecommunications market in equipment and services. They recognized that member governments would be reluctant to see their significant telco revenues threatened by increased competition, that state-owned telcos would not cooperate in the dismantling of their monopoly powers, and that labor would not support any efforts that might reduce their job security. In 1988, the commission decided to circumvent the established interests and employ the seldom-used but powerful article 90 of the Treaty of Rome.[24] The article allows the commission to issue laws forcing public monopolies to comply with the treaty's competition

---

23. For example, the efforts of the French to impose registration and licensing requirements on providers of value-added service have been rejected by the commission.

24. "European Telecommunications: O What a Tangled Web We Weave," *Economist*, 28 October 1989, 77.

rules. Moreover, it can issue these laws without the approval of the Council of Ministers or the European parliament.

A formidable weapon indeed. This tactic has antagonized a number of the community members, including France and Germany, who challenged the commission's action in the European Court of Justice. They see this initiative as an inappropriate usurpation of the law-making authority of the Council of Ministers. But the underlying antagonism concerns the pluralist nature of the initiative—it is an attack on the statist and corporatist institutions in France and Germany. The French have been particularly vocal in their opposition because the directives seriously challenge the norm of continued state control that has guided liberalization in France. In the case of Germany, the directives are alien to the norms of stability and consensus that have characterized telecommunications policy-making in the last century.

The overwhelming challenge of the twentieth century is change. Global economic pressures have forced corporations to adapt to a quicker pace of change than they have been accustomed to in the recent past. The evidence presented in this book suggests that firms will best meet this challenge in an environment where political constraints are low and pluralist institutions predominate. Underlying the efforts to accelerate the political and economic integration of Europe is an effort to enable European industry to better meet the global economic challenges of the next decade. The commission is proposing a set of fundamental, radical changes in the community's political and economic institutions. I have argued in this book that such political and economic change is greatly facilitated by pluralist structures and inhibited by corporatist and, to a somewhat lesser degree, statist institutions. The commission's success in engineering these dramatic changes will, therefore, be contingent upon its ability to impose pluralist norms that facilitate change onto corporatist and statist institutions that are inherently conservative and inhibit change.

Index

Act of 1863, 219
Act of 1868, 219
Aérospatiale, 32, 55
Africa, 58, 60
Agency costs, 24–26
Agritel, 176
Aharoni, Yair, 39–40, 46, 62
Airbus venture, 16, 55
Air Canada, 29, 43
Air France, 22
Airline industry, 6, 18, 19, 116; and consumers, 23; and contestable markets, 89; deregulation of, 91
Alcatel, 184, 187, 190, 199
Alfa Romeo, 32
Amtrak, 29, 34–35
Argentina, 4
Arrow, K., 16
ASEAN countries, 265
Association des Ingénieurs des Télécommunications, 190
AT&T (American Telephone & Telegraph), 14, 42, 44; divestiture of, 98, 233, 240; and MCI, competition between, 189; and France Télécom, 201
Australia, 36, 66, 68; classification of telcos in, 45, 46; value of the Private dummy variable for, 77–78
Austria, 43, 45, 46, 126, 267; data terminals per 1,000 inhabitants in, 71–72; value of the Private dummy variable for, 78; economic decision making in, 109
Automatic exchanges, 131

Bangeman, Horst, 161
Banking, 71, 116, 118–19; "universal," 119–20; in Germany, 135, 136, 137; in the United Kingdom, 228–30, 235. *See also specific banks*
Bank of America, 147
Bank of England, 118
Banque de France, 119
Banque nationale de Paris, 206
BASF, 33
BAT (British-Electoral-Technical Approvals Board), 232
BAT Industries, 33
Bayer, 33
BBC (British Broadcasting Corporation), 117, 222
BC Tel, 44
Becker, Gary, 101, 102, 214
Beer, Samuel, 112
Belgium, 4, 45, 46, 68, 70; data terminals per 1,000 inhabitants in, 71–72; value of the Private dummy variable for, 78; and the telecommunications equipment market, 92–94; 1887 telephone developmental levels for, 126; GNP per capita in, in 1960, 130; telephone penetration levels in, 134; telephone density in, 172
Bell Canada, 44
Bell Holding Companies, 44
Bell system, 98; divestiture of, 19, 44, 233, 239; and scale elasticity, 87
Benn, Anthony, 227
Bildshirmtext, 149–50